Rome

W E N

Mediterranean

S e a

Milano

Po

Marseille

Geneva

Rhône

Belfort

Lyon

ims

Orléans

Bordeaux

Paris

Loire

Chartres

Rouen

Le Havre

Nantes

Caen

St Lô

Avranches

Cherbourg

ish

Channel

Portsmouth

Southampton

Brest

N

Bristol

Plymouth

Appledore

Falmouth

Richard Edes Harrison 1945

TOP SECRET

TOP SECRET

RALPH INGERSOLL

NEW YORK
HARCOURT, BRACE AND COMPANY

TO MY WIFE

Acknowledgment

I COULD never unscramble my sources of information for this book. None of it is based on information of which I am the exclusive possessor—or got exclusively from one source.

To the best of my knowledge, what I used in this book does not violate the security of information permanently "classified" —in fact, I have denied myself the use of a considerable amount of material on the grounds that it might possibly be of value to some future enemies of the United States. The source material I *have* used was of value to our enemies only while we were at war against them.

Of the innumerable fellow officers to whom I am indebted for help in trying to solve the mysteries of how the campaign in Europe was fought, I shall name none—and they will understand. I have given my own evaluation to events—and called the shots as I saw them—and my associates and superiors may well disagree with some of my interpretations.

This book has been written after I left the Army, and my viewpoint is that of a civilian looking back on the experience of having lived for two years with a single problem—the defeat of the Wehrmacht on the continent of Europe. I have, therefore, *not* written as a member of any staff, nor as the representative of any organization. None of the commanding generals under whom I served has been burdened with seeing the manuscript before publication—not even the Field Marshal.

Until the end of the campaign in Europe, I had no interest whatever in collecting material for a book; from the day I landed in England, however, it was part of my job, as a member of a planning group, to keep myself informed as best I could of what was going on. In the course of this work, I got to know hundreds of officers in various headquarters, and the numbers with whom I worked in close association run into scores. All these contributed to the sum of my knowledge, and their contributions deserve to be acknowledged—if they only could be, accurately. But even if there were no other reasons, it would be a literal impossibility to segregate and evaluate what I got, when and from whom.

I also regret that the necessities of writing a narrative made it impossible for me to identify more than a handful of the sixty-some divisions and the hundreds and hundreds of independent units and commands that fought the war on the Continent. I started to put in as many names as I could, only to find that the book was turning into an encyclopaedia—and that the only way I could get the story told was to do without the interruptions inherent in identifying all the units concerned. The men who served in the units involved will also, I hope, forgive me for concentrating on The Big Picture when they are quite right in believing that it was in the foxhole, not the office trailer, that the war was won. I will be recompensed, however, if I have given them some understanding of phases of the war with which they may not be familiar.

R. I.

Contents

Maps

Maps by Richard Edes Harrison

PART ONE

FOOTPRINTS ON THE SANDS
OF GROSVENOR SQUARE

1 The Johnnies-Come-Lately

In May of 1943, an American general named Andrews and his chief of staff were flying through a fog over the southern tip of Iceland when a mountain rose up in front of them. Their plane crashed and they were both killed. In this plane died the command of the European Theater of Operations of the United States Army, just eight days before Churchill and Roosevelt, meeting with the Anglo-American Combined Chiefs of Staff in Washington, made the final decision that northwestern Europe should be invaded from the British Isles—and thereupon directed the British and American armed forces to proceed at once to plan and prepare for an assault to be made during the spring of 1944.

The first of the men who succeeded Andrews and his staff sat in the Pentagon in Washington and read their inheritance. It came to them in the form of mimeographed "appreciations" and directives. They drew shiny new helmets, .45 automatics, and gas masks. They whispered to each other about the secret they now shared and drove out through the spring dawns to the planes that were to fly them off to the Big Adventure. Their boss was the new Commander of the European Theater of Operations, Lieutenant General Jacob L. Devers, and when they got to London on their historic mission they were to be called the Johnnies-Come-Lately. It was interesting that the nickname should have been given them by a man who was an American officer himself.

The officer who called Jakey Devers and his staff the Johnnies-Come-Lately was a major general named Barker whose extraordinary title was "Deputy Chief of Staff to the Supreme Allied Commander (Designate)." To the initiated, these long words testified to the following inventory of facts:

1. That Churchill and Roosevelt had agreed that there would one day be a single Supreme Allied Commander over both British and American forces in the European Theater of Operations.

2. That this Commander had not yet been named. (That is what the qualification "Designate" stood for.)

3. That pending this momentous choice, a headquarters had been created for the Supreme One—and put under the command of a chief of staff who could speak for him, even though he did not yet exist.

4. That this interim headquarters—this organizational scaffolding—would be a combined Anglo-American headquarters, employing the device of "opposite numbers" to see that both countries were equally represented. In British military parlance "opposite numbers," employed in this connection, meant that there would be two individuals for every job, one British, one American. One of these two individuals, of course, would have to be the senior, but the principle of equality would be served by alternating (on successive levels) a "British senior with an American deputy" with an "American senior with a British deputy."

The way General Barker's title read made all these things plain to the initiated and, since the American Barker was referred to as "Deputy," his superior, the "Chief of Staff to the Supreme Allied Commander (Designate)" himself, would surely be a British officer. This was true. His name was Lieutenant General Frederick E. Morgan.

Lieutenant General Morgan's office had been created in March and because of its initials was known as C.O.S. (to the) S.A.C.— or simply COSSAC.

In May the original plan for the invasion of northwest Europe was being written by COSSAC and it had already been given the name of OVERLORD by Winston Churchill himself. Throughout the war the Prime Minister took a very personal interest in the selection of code words describing future operations. You could almost always read his attitude in the word he chose. When the prospect of Germany's using long-range rockets first emerged from the Intelligence reports, Churchill chose the word CROSS-BOW to describe the undertaking, suggesting an obsolete, clumsy and inaccurate weapon. When rockets became a somewhat more real menace the code word was changed to BODYLINE, which students of cricket will recognize as carrying an overtone of international unfairness. "Bodyline bowling" (in American: "beanball pitching") shook the British Empire when Australian stars first employed it to terrify English batters in international matches.

COSSAC Headquarters were in Norfolk House on St. James' Square, just off Piccadilly and around the corner from St. James's Palace. A mile or so away, the Johnnies-Come-Lately moved into Grosvenor (pronounced *Grove*nor) Square in the heart of Mayfair. Grosvenor is a pleasant square, rather larger than most in London—big enough to hold the American Embassy, several large blocks of very expensive flats, a number of private houses and a barrage balloon named Romeo flown by WAAFS in gray pants. On gusty days Romeo gyrated about the Square on its trips up and down and leered into the windows of 48 Grosvenor Square where the American Commanding General and his principal staff officers made their headquarters.

The Americans on COSSAC staff were anything but Johnnies-Come-Lately. They seemed to us Johnnies-Come-Much-Too-Long-Ago. They were bedded down in London and each seemed to come complete, equipped with an American uniform of British cloth, cut for him by a London tailor, a working vocabulary of British military initials, a pretty British girl driver, cards to night clubs, a favorite pub and a well-developed feeling of inferiority towards his British opposite number.

The American at COSSAC felt inferior to his British opposite number, not simply because he was an alien in an alien land, but also because he had come to London originally representing an army that had never fought a battle. He had come to work in—to be absorbed into—a headquarters of veterans, working in the capital of their own country, in their own language. If he kept his individuality and remained American, he was a failure; it was his job to be absorbed, to learn new ways, new British ways. If he cultivated his better born cousins—and those who survived had had to—he simply perfected himself in the role of poor relation.

This process, of the selection and assimilation of such American officers as were qualified for the role, had been going on in COSSAC for a long time. We wondered about them when we called to pay our respects.

I flew into London, well down on the tail of Jakey Devers' kite, a week after the big conference in Washington. A score or more of us came together and scattered out through the offices of 48 Grosvenor Square. My job was in a planning section, presumably because in America I had been trained in what little was then known about amphibian assault landings—and because of my expressed desire to learn a military trade rather than to attempt to convert my civilian experience into Army Public Relations work.

In my section at least, I was one of a minority of Reserve or ex-civilian officers. With the decision to invade, the European Theater got some priority on officer personnel and almost all my associates were Academy graduates or at least Regulars. But they were almost as green as I, as they came off the planes in twos and threes and sat nervously through their first briefings on what was up. This was curious because the American Army at the time had a sizeable group of field grade and general officers who had helped to plan and direct a successful invasion of Africa. But instead of bringing these men back to London for The Big Push, they were being left in Africa to plan and carry out the side show invasion of Sicily.

The first old friend I met in London was a journalist who had just arrived and he was congratulating himself on making it, because he expected the invasion to begin any minute. The day after I met him I made a trip into the field to see the American troops the world so confidently expected would be storming Fortress Europa that summer. They consisted of one corps headquarters, which had under its command a single infantry division of fifteen thousand men. These troops were spread out around Bristol, where Corps Headquarters were. They looked as neat—and as peaceful—as the fields through which they marched, suffering the rigors of an exceptionally mild English spring. Military exercises were few and far between because maneuvers involved trampling over farmers' land and the Ministry of Agriculture, not the War Ministry, had the say as to what the soil of England was to be used for in the spring of 1943.

The Mediterranean Theater had the experienced troops and officers; it also seemed to have priority on the attentions of higher echelons in the United States. All we had when we got right down to it, it appeared in Jakey Devers' headquarters, was a piece of paper that said we were to prepare to invade the Continent of Europe at the earliest possible moment, then presumed to be the following spring. At first we did not even have the invasion plan. They were putting the finishing touches on it in Norfolk House on St. James' Square. It simply wasn't available.

The piece of paper we *did* have was a directive from the Combined Chiefs of Staff, but it was brief and unspecific. It was at the first meeting at which we sought to bring it to earth—to agree upon an organizational chart which would define authority and responsibility—that we got ourselves labeled Johnnies-Come-Lately. To the gentlemen of COSSAC, we were Johnnies-Come-Too-Nosey, too, threatening to disturb the calm of settled relationships with our urgent questions, with impertinent whys and why nots—and with too many ideas on subjects about which they felt we knew too little. All in good time, we were told; everything was in hand. Plans were being made by qualified men who knew the English Channel, and the Channel beaches, and the enemy. When the time came, these plans would be implemented. We would be told when that time was, and what would be expected of us then.

It was all very reasonable—it was true; we *were* Johnnies-Come-Lately, ignorant and naive. Only it still didn't make sense. There was, on the one hand, the immense effort that would obviously be required to invade Europe and, on the other hand, the utter unpreparedness of the Allied armed forces in the United Kingdom for any effort at all. It was an unpreparedness that went far beyond the fact that we had but a single infantry division on hand, and that a division which had never even practiced getting in and out of landing craft because in all England there seemed to be no beaches that could be spared for it to play with. The unpreparedness began with the somnolent inertia of everyone concerned, from the British generals and their staffs to the civilian agencies

preoccupied with raising and rationing food, distributing manpower and requisitioning land and buildings. But when we turned
to the American officers who had spent the last year in London,
we found only apologists. Were we to cable Mother Washington
and say, "We can't bear it here, we're coming home"—a few weeks
after we had come, all scrubbed and shiny, to our new boarding
school? We felt without friends.

Battles in the field are easy to write about. The enemy is tangible, his strength and purpose are more or less understood. There
are one's own resources, which can be inventoried; there are clear-
cut intentions, a plan of action. There is terrain which can be
mapped and studied.

In London, as the summer of 1943 began, there seemed to the
Americans to be none of these things. There was no enemy, no
issue. There was only a world of interminable politeness in high
places—and inaction. And yet there developed a struggle and a
contest of wills which each month became more real and more
intense. The struggle was between the Americans under General
Devers and every Britisher with whom they had to do business.
The struggle was over the nature and the rate of preparations for
the invasion which had been ordered.

We had no trouble writing down a list of what we sought. We
were to mount an invasion from the southern coast of the British
Isles to the northern coast of France, a combined assault in which
British and American armies would prepare, set sail and fight,
side by side. We needed, then:

—To reach an agreement with our British allies regarding the
command and control of the forces which would actually do the
invading. (There was that purely theoretical agreement that there
would one day be a Supreme Commander over both forces—but
would this commander be a field commander actually responsible
for the invasion, or would he be a political generalissimo who
would delegate responsibility for command in the field—and, if
so, to whom and how?)

—To locate and secure ground suitable for giving our American
troops their final training for battle.

—To locate and secure a strip of beach suitable for practice in amphibian assault landings.

—To agree upon an amphibian assault procedure which could be developed and taught simultaneously to both British and American forces.

The writing of the tactical plan itself had been entrusted to General Morgan's headquarters; the Commanding General of the European Theater was not authorized to meddle. But there was no need to wait for the plan itself to get on with these businesses. And even before the finishing touches were on the plan, could we not—

—Agree upon whether our principal reliance would be on surprise or on our ability to deliver a bombardment so crushing that surprise would not be necessary? The whole problem of equipping and supplying the American assault forces depended on the answer.

—Agree upon the scale of the assault itself—how many and what troops would be involved? In round numbers? The answer to this question could not be disposed of simply by ordering more or fewer troops into the line. It involved the craft that would have to carry them, and the manufacture of these craft. The manufacture of craft took time, would have to be geared into American production.

Without agreement upon such elemental and fundamental points, nothing could be gotten on with.

The first trouble with getting something done about these things was that, as Americans, we were a house divided against ourselves—which was no fault of anyone's in London. Lieutenant General Jakey Devers had been sent to London as Commanding General of the European Theater of Operations with orders to get the American forces there ready for an invasion. But the Combined Chiefs of Staff, in their infinite wisdom, had already created the Combined Anglo-American Headquarters, COSSAC, which had an American major general as its Deputy Chief of Staff, and which also had orders to prepare for an invasion of Europe, by writing a plan for it. COSSAC was to make a plan, but it had no troops to carry it out and no authority—nor even a commander.

Yet, organization-wise, as the present symbol of a future Supreme Commander (Designate), it was the senior headquarters.

Thus two groups in London had the same mission. One had the plans but no means to carry them out; the other—Jakey Devers'—had the command of all American forces, and the authority of the United States War Department behind it, but lacked either the plan itself or the prestige of being the highest echelon. It was also required to mount a major military operation in a foreign country in which it had even less authority than the headless COSSAC—which at least had a personal friend of the Prime Minister's on its payroll, the British General Morgan. Thus, Jakey could issue orders to his troops, but there was no place to which he could order them without first negotiating the billets and the facilities from the country that was his host. He could not begin a stockpile until he had talked the site out of someone. In crowded England he could not fire a gun without moving someone out of the way of where the bullet might go.

Wherever Devers turned, there was not merely the problem of finding elbow room on this snug little isle; there was also a war to keep out of the way of. It was a war which was being fought with a most intricate set of coastal defense and air-raid defense regulations. And in the United Kingdom a whole cramped civilian economy was trying to feed itself and produce for war, more or less under fire.

So while on the higher echelons there was intangible mental confusion, on the lower there was a maze of the kind of wholly tangible problems which are commonly solved in wartime by the exercise of extraordinary powers created by the emergency. The Johnny-Come-Lately Americans were required to solve them without any authority at all. To get the simplest thing done, it was necessary first to persuade the British Government to exercise its authority in their behalf—to clear a field, to make a train available, to requisition a house for a headquarters.

In wrestling with these problems, the Johnnies-Come-Lately got no help from the man who had christened them that, the Deputy Chief of Staff to the non-existent, some-day-to-be Supreme Commander. Although he was also an officer of the United States Army, he was no longer an American. His national identity had been absorbed into his international identity as an officer of an Anglo-American body. Theoretically, COSSAC was responsible to neither government but only to the sum of them both.

Devers' problems in carrying out his orders would have been difficult enough to solve in any atmosphere. What bothered him, as he waited for the tactical plan of the operation to emerge from the toils of the COSSAC planners, was the suspicion that there was something wrong with the atmosphere itself. At first the self-evident difficulties seemed to account for all his troubles—for the fact that first days, and then weeks, slipped by without tangible accomplishment. The committees the British set up to help him in his business gave birth not to action or accomplishment but only to other committees. Committees, committees, committees—they grew like jungle weeds, they multiplied like rabbits, and finally they began subdividing like amoebas. And still, the more committees there were to do things, the less they got done. Yet it could not be that this was the best performance our allies could turn in. Only an Anglophobe could have said so.

There was too much evidence all around us that the British could get on with the job when they had a mind to. The officers with whom we dealt were intelligent and well informed. Man for man, and rank for rank, they were more experienced soldiers than we. They were more experienced, and this was their country.

Great Britain was a well-run country, even in wartime. For all their respect for tradition, the British were obviously able to adjust rapidly to a new situation. When the enemy had threatened, the air defense of Great Britain had been created overnight, with its circles of fighter fields on the alert, its intricate radar network. This was at once a scientific and an organizational feat of first magnitude. When London burned, its Fire Department grew from a few thousand to thirty thousand in a month, made fire engines of taxicabs, kept itself in business with wire and water mains out. England was making some of the world's finest aircraft and making them in plants newly dispersed and under fire. The Admiralty's anti-submarine organization was technically brilliant, alert and aggressive.

There was more recent testimony to the ability of the English to get what they wanted done. The Anglo-American invasion of

Africa had set out from the British Isles. The forces had had only a little while to prepare; yet that invasion had sailed on time.

But now we were embarked, in Britain and with the British, in an infinitely greater undertaking. The still undefeated German Army waited there across the Channel for us. The German industrial machine was still virtually unscratched—was still, in fact, growing more powerful as the German python slowly digested the industries of the nations it had first crushed and then swallowed. The huge Allied navies seemed barely able to keep the sea lanes open, the sea lanes through which whole American armies would have to pass before they could even begin to prepare to begin to fight. There was an historic urgency; the air was heavy with it; and yet to meet the urgency there seemed only interminable talk—and always talk of obstacles, never talk of how anything could be done. Striking out into its inertia was like driving your fist into a punching bag of wet manure: it gave a little, it swayed gently—but when your fist came away, its shape filled out again and it was as if it had not been touched. Only you felt soiled.

It was obvious that the British made sense when they wanted to. The corollary was just as obvious. When they made no sense it could only be because they didn't choose to. We had not been in England a month before we had bumped into enough trees to know that we were in a forest. The British forest-which-had-become-a-maze was clearly a disinclination to co-operate with us.

It was not long before it was possible even to inventory the techniques by which we were being frustrated. Roughly they included:

—The advancement of carefully prepared arguments against anything we proposed which would speed up preparations. The British set up their committee meetings with such thoroughness that the Americans always found themselves confronted by a long array of tangential arguments each of which had to be met if the principal decision was not to be lost on points.

—The use of exceptionally articulate officers who could present and debate their case better than the Americans. The American Regular Army officer is not as well trained in parliamentary procedure or presentation as his British counterpart.

—The pulling of rank. The ranks of officers available to us were, of course, limited by our table of organization—we could have only so many generals, colonels, lieutenant colonels, etc. The American representative in an Anglo-American committee characteristically found himself confronted by an officer at least one rank higher than he. If he found a British officer of like rank at the first meeting, the chances were that he would find the British officer promoted at the next—or a British officer of higher rank substituted.

—Fast work with the agenda for a committee meeting. This consisted of slipping in a crucial point, innocuously worded, well down in the agenda. The British relied on the Americans not having time to study or analyze the agenda before the meeting. Agenda were distributed only at the last minute. Sometimes the point to be made was slipped in during the meeting—after hours of tiring conversation. However presented, the idea was to skip quickly over the disputed point and then to record it in the minutes of the meeting as a firm and fast agreement, concurred in by all. This happened so many times that it could be recognized as what is known in American military language as "standard operating procedure."

It seemed also British standard operating procedure to seek first to win over each new American officer coming into the Theater by charm.

Perhaps the percentage is not scientifically known, but out of every hundred Americans there are so and so many to whom British traditions and British ways have peculiar appeal. This percentage can be counted on, just as the restaurateur may count on such and such a percentage of his customers liking such and such a dish on his menu. The British always first tried being charming. If successful, they Anglicized the individual to a point where in any Anglo-American argument he would, at worst, be neutral and, at best—and more frequently—an active exponent of the British point of view.

At the opposite end of the spectrum, there is also a percentage of Americans who experience a sharp, emotional revulsion against the British and their way of living. The British technique for handling these individuals laid the foundation for one of their

most ingenious ways of removing an opponent of the Home
Team's point of view. To begin with, the British appeared to
face the problem of the Anglophobe frankly. They said, in effect:
"Let us be realistic: there are certain Americans who just can't
abide the British and, unhappily, there are certain British who just
can't abide the Americans. But we have got to work together to
defeat the enemy. Therefore, let us agree that a basic policy of
our working together shall be that however able the Anglophobe
or the Americanophobe, we will get rid of him."

Everyone agrees, and Jim Brown and Sir Cecil are both
thrown off the Anglo-American staff team for the good and obvious reason that each is unreasonably nasty about the other's country. All well and good. The process, however, has only begun.
What has been established is a principle of which the British now
make very effective use. Colonel James Brown is gone, but the
British still have the problem of General Whosis.

General Whosis is *not* an Anglophobe. He is an amateur stu-
dent of English history, his wife loves Elizabethan furniture and
used to entertain British authors. He greatly admires many British
institutions, and the courage, character and charm of most of the
British officers with whom he has come in contact. But on a purely
military issue he differs fundamentally with his British opposite
number. It is extremely difficult to beat him in argument because
he has the courage of his convictions and he is a stubborn fellow.
How shall General Whosis be handled?

The answer is easy. Go back up to the highest echelon and say,
in strictest personal confidence: "Whosis is a marvelous fellow.
He couldn't be more able—as a soldier. We all admire him—we
are rather fond of him, good old bear. We don't know what we
have done to him or how it happened, but somehow he's just one
of those people who doesn't seem to like us. Like Sir Cecil, you
know—the chap we had to send out to India because *he* didn't like
you. It's really quite a problem and what would you suggest?" In
the early days of the war, the chances were ten-to-one that the
American War Department would remove General Whosis to a
theater of war where he didn't have to come in contact with the
British—and he would never know why.

If there was not enough evidence against Whosis, it could always be manufactured. Whosis could be gotten into a series of arguments with a conveniently unpleasant Englishman until, his temper rubbed thin, there would presently be good authentic quotes on the Whosis record to prove him biased on the subject of the British in general. One of the ablest divisional, and later corps, commanders of the American Army was thus removed from the Combined Staff in Sicily, the final added argument being that he was "too strong a personality to make a good staff officer." Actually, what caused this general's removal was his advocacy of the very tactics later used by the American forces in the field—without authorization. When they were first proposed the British felt they would give the Americans too prominent a role.

Almost the reverse of this technique for removing opposition is one which involved a still more subtle approach. In almost every Anglo-American working committee one was apt to find at least one British officer who was aggressively *pro*-American. His position, which he stated articulately and with grace, was that Americans and American ways were the hope of the world. His own countrymen had everything to learn from us. He listened attentively, absorbed American arguments and agreed with them. Firmly planting himself in the American camp, he criticized his fellow-British officers freely and with vigor. In the committee meetings he attended, differences of opinion between British and Americans were most often argued with this individual skillfully representing the *American* point of view. And he always appeared to win and yet somehow, someway, finally, he seemed to be so worn down by the weight of logic on the other side that he could only shrug his shoulders and say, "Well, for once the blighters seem to be right."

In the beginning the Americans went away from such sessions with a warm feeling that they had been championed by an honest and sympathetic fellow. They couldn't understand how their side had come to lose the argument.

These American-lovers among the British usually affected some item of American uniform—for sentimental reasons. Lieutenant General Morgan, who headed the original Anglo-American planning staff, always wore an American field jacket in his headquarters. It was a curious sight to see him furious at one of his fellow-

British generals in a committee and then to catch a glimpse of them some hours later arm-in-arm chatting gaily together.

When the British found an American who would argue their point of view for them, they had a more genuine article. The ultimate of the "taking-into-camp process" was when they were able to place a sympathetic American in a position where they could reward him by backing his promotion or giving him the command he sought. They would then have a friend who would go down fighting for them.

The British weapon which was at once the most intangible and the most effective, however, was something which was not a trick at all. It was what might be called the Party-Line Approach. The British are a highly individual people. In their traditions and in their common law they have probably done more to establish the importance of the individual vis-à-vis the importance of the masses than any other people. It is this disarming fact that makes it so effective when, in combat, they submerge their personal differences to present a common front to their opponents. When the British State is for or against anything, then—with extraordinary consistency—every individual representing the British State, each in accordance with his character and to the best of his ability, falls in line and argues or conducts himself in the best interests of the policy—entirely regardless of what his personal feelings or plans were before the policy was set. This is true in large things and it is true in small things too.

I recall a British officer who was once my opposite number. Over a period of months we had sweated out a military policy in perfect harmony. I lived with him in the field. He was smart, and an amusing fellow to work with. I liked him very much and I believe he liked me. And we really trusted and respected one another—at least I did him. At five o'clock one evening this officer and I planned the arguments we would submit in favor of our common policy at a meeting with Supreme Headquarters which was to be held the next morning. My friend was to represent us; I was to go along as sort of assistant counsel. I didn't see my friend again that evening or before the meeting in the morning. Then the meeting began and I could hardly believe my ears when I heard him concede the very point that meant so much to us, the point we believed would be of vital importance to success in the impending battle.

I had no official right to speak at the meeting, but I spoke anyway. And I was slapped down. By the time the meeting adjourned, I was boiling mad, not at losing the argument—that's too everyday an affair in military life—but at what I felt was a betrayal in a personal relationship. So I took my opposite number for a walk and I asked him what the hell. He told me quite calmly that the argument which our opposition had advanced on the floor of the meeting had convinced him. That was *too* much! You must remember that he was a good friend of mine and that I felt I knew his ideas as well as I knew my own. I told him that this just wasn't so, that he was lying to me and that I proposed to know why.

It was a very painful session. Presently he broke down and confessed that he had been ordered the night before to make the concession he did. This seemed so anticlimactic that I said to him, "But look here, this is silly, our having gotten into a misunderstanding over such nonsense. All you had to have done was to tell me before the meeting that you had orders and I would have understood. Everybody gets overruled by orders. But why did you have to pretend you'd changed your mind?"

At this my friend became even more embarrassed and told me that there was no way out of it for him now but to explain something he had no business telling me—because it involved his code as a British officer. He said his code required that when he had been overruled by his superior he had not merely to accept the order but had also *to conduct himself in such a way that no one realized an order had been given*. He *had* to make it appear that he had changed his mind.

A general I knew in Africa, who got along famously with his British opposite number, told me that his associate's mind was changed so often by orders which he would not admit having received that it got to be a standard joke. Everyone knew when the arguments the British officer advanced were no longer his; but he himself would never own to it.

In London it took time for us to understand these things and the first effect was simply confusion—and resentment. The sour ones told horror stories of the duplicity, stupidity and inefficiency of individual Englishmen (the Scotch were understood to be a slightly better breed). But to the average American officer, as I have said, these horror stories didn't make sense. Obviously the English were not a people set off from all the rest of mankind by uniquely unpleasant characteristics. And life in London was far from unpleasant and most individuals, although never absorbed into English life, made sensible compromises with it, found friends and enjoyed a casual unmilitary life. Even battered and scarred, and covered with the dust of a hundred bombing raids, London had charm. I had a great many English friends, some made before the war, many of them when I visited London in 1940 during the Big Blitz when I had seen, felt and been inspired by the reaction of the British when faced with the hourly threat of annihilation.

They had been truly heroic then, the British, in the most literal sense of the word. A year later when I visited England on my way home from a trip around the world through China and Russia, I had found them let down after the stimulation of the bombings had passed, surly, bad tempered and tired. Now, on my third stay in England during the war, the people seemed in yet another frame of mind. They were quieter, less argumentative, more resigned and so visibly tired as to seem close to total exhaustion. Their war effort was as thorough as ever; it had simply slowed down to a pace that seemed almost lethargic to one recently arrived from a country that was only just beginning to take on the load. In this atmosphere, it was easy for the British Government to stage its slow-down strike on the Americans.

The average Britisher's attitude towards the American troops was in general friendly—with reservations. As far as the troops went, it was policed so scrupulously by both sides—with educational campaigns spearheaded by pamphlets and moving pictures, and by large numbers of carefully thought out prohibitions and regulations—that it was hard to tell what relations might have been had both parties been left to their own devices. To make them welcome in a hungry country, for instance, Americans were given extra food to bring with them when asked out to a meal. Clergy and gentry hovered anxiously over the manners of the British host. There seemed the usual component of unpleasant rumors flavoring the conversation on the other side of the tea table but I believe that the consensus was that the American boys, if bumptious, were harmless and, in general, gentle and well behaved. Among our troops it was agreed that the British household was as hospitable as it was able to be with its ration-limited resources. A friendly old lady I used to call on in a nearby farmhouse when I was in camp in southern England summed her side of it up for me by saying, "Well, they grumble about this and that that your boys do, but I won't have any of it. Better to have them here than the Germans any time, I always say."

The real combination was between our young soldiers and the young English girls, particularly among farm and factory workers. This was almost a case of spontaneous social combustion, so satisfactory did each seem to the other. The English girl is brought up to respect her men folk and to consider their pleasure her law. The American boys were bowled over to meet girls who were instinctively polite and obedient, inexpensive to entertain and anxious to please. On her side, the English girl was initiated into the charm of being with boys who, however rough or ignorant, had been brought up to put a woman's wishes before their own— whether it was in a matter of choosing which movie to go to or who would carry the heavy bundles home. The American was also characteristically generous—he could afford to be with many times the pay of his British counterpart. British girls and American boys were instant successes with each other.

It was lovely in London in the early summer of 1943. There were no raids from across the Channel, no rockets yet. There were theaters to see and girls to dance with. There was beer in the pubs and Scotch from Harrod's if you had a receipt from the last bottle you had bought. There were billets with soft beds and clean sheets. There was the sweet countryside of England close by. There was everything a soldier might like except action. Not just action in the field but any kind of action.

At least soon now we would get The Plan itself, the secret plan for what we were going to do—COSSAC's plan for the transchannel Operation OVERLORD. Perhaps all our suspicions would dissolve in it.

2   The Tape Is Dyed Red

In July, when OVERLORD came from Norfolk House to Grosvenor Square there was great excitement. The masterwork the COSSAC planners had been preparing came printed and bound in cardboard covers, fastened with tape tied in a bow-knot to keep the book from falling open. The tape was dyed red. It came, one copy, numbered and certified, to the Commanding General of the European Theater of Operations of the United States Army. We got it late in the afternoon and we sat up through the night in an inside room with the doors locked and a sentry outside, an inside room with fluorescent lights and maps of the Channel and of Europe shrouded in drawn curtains so that if an uninitiated visitor were to come they would be hidden from even his casual glance. They were beautiful maps—of the southern coast of England and the beaches of northern France and of the whole of Europe. And they could have been set up in Trafalgar Square for all the use they might have been to the enemy then, for there were no symbols at all on them; they were just maps of where we were *going* to put our troops and where they were *going* to fight—when anyone would tell us what to do in something more specific than a world directive. Well, now Plan OVERLORD had come and we would know.

First we would put the plan up on the maps, sketching it in little red and blue symbols * drawn with grease pencils on sheets

* In the American Army, blue for friendly forces, red for enemy. In the British Army, the reverse—which did not make co-ordination any

of acetate tacked flat against the maps themselves. Thus we would show who would go where and do what, when. This was the way Europe would be pried open. This was where we would kill and get killed and where we would meet the enemy and break him.

First it would all be set down on this secret map in this secret room. Then orders would be issued on the basis of it, secret, fragmentary orders. So little would be divulged in each written order that no one but those authorized would understand the whole. The troops would come in ships, and they would be moved here, and here, and here. And this equipment would be gathered for them, and this training given to them, and it would all work out so that, on such and such a day, these forces would come down to the shore and these little boats would meet them. And then they would go across the Channel to land—secret of all secrets—HERE! First thousands, then hundreds of thousands, and finally millions of men would be involved.

In this great effort which was to rise like a genie from the words within the covers of the book with the red tape wrapped around it, our microscopic part in headquarters would be to aid in the release of its energy—by thought and analysis, by the translation of its reasoning and its directives into specific orders to specific individuals. It would be our group responsibility to request from America what we needed to carry it out, to foresee the obstacles to its execution before they arose, and to overcome them—and, doing all these things, as staff officers, simply to advise a commanding general who would then make up his own mind how to execute the orders issued to him by his superior.

We were replaceable cells in a military brain, as the riflemen who would carry out the plans we analyzed would be replaceable cells in the military fist that struck the enemy. But at least, with the plan there in front of us, we felt that at last we were *that;* we were real again, after the unreality of the weeks that had followed our arrival in England. What we sought, civilian and professional soldier alike, was the destruction of the armed forces of the enemy that had made war on our country. Now our purpose

easier. The American Army ended by using blue for its own troops, black for the British and red for the German.

had an instrument and we were a living part of the body that would use it.

We untied the ribbons of dyed tape and we opened the covers of OVERLORD, the plan for the invasion of northwest Europe by an Anglo-American striking force.

The moment of sentiment passed quickly.

The question that Plan OVERLORD had to answer, when it arrived in Grosvenor Square from St. James' Place, was: Did it solve General Jacob L. Devers' problem of how to carry out his orders to invade Europe, or didn't it? Presumably, with the completion of the plan, the COSSAC Headquarters that had created it would cease to exist as a factor until and unless it were to serve as the headquarters of the still unnamed Supreme Allied Commander. COSSAC was not an operational headquarters; it was simply a kind of brain trust.

Armed with COSSAC's plan, the British War Office would proceed to prepare the British Army for battle; the Commanding General of the European Theater of Operations already had his orders to get the American armed forces ready. Technically, the British War Office, the Admiralty and the Air Ministry each would take OVERLORD and prepare the forces of their respective commands. On the American side, following the American principle of unity of command, all American forces in Europe were under General Devers. He would direct the preparation not only of the ground force but also, through appropriate generals and admirals responsible to him in the European Theater, the preparations of the American air force and such of the American Navy as would participate.

The strategic Eighth Air Force was an exception to this, since all strategic bombing in whatever theater was centrally directed by the Combined Chiefs of Staff. However, Ira Eaker, who commanded the Eighth Air Force, was a good friend of Jakey Devers' and for practical purposes all purely American efforts in Europe were integrated under Devers that summer. Now that Devers had the plan he should be able, with even the most elementary co-operation from the British, to proceed directly with his preparations. But before the plan had come, the suspicion had grown that there was more to the problem of preparing for the invasion of Europe than met the eye. In the light of this suspicion, what had OVERLORD itself to contribute?

OVERLORD was a beautiful thing to look at. It was a volume of one hundred and thirteen legal-size pages with ten accompanying maps. Although the staff that produced it was presumably as much American as British, OVERLORD was written exclusively in British military parlance and required a glossary to translate the terms it used. For instance, the key verb "to maintain" meant "to keep in repair" to Americans, but to the British it meant "to supply." Hence "beach maintenance" did not mean maintaining the equipment used on the beach but stood for "supply across the beach." "Lift" did not meant "raise"—nor did it refer, as in London, to an elevator; it stood for the fleet of landing craft and ships required to ferry forces and supplies to France. "Hard" was not an adjective but a noun; a "hard" is a beach paved to facilitate the loading and unloading of landing craft.

But it was not the language in which OVERLORD was written that bothered those who read it first: it was the wall of conditions with which the planners had surrounded the project. An invasion of Europe, said COSSAC, could be mounted *only*—

—If the wind were not too strong.

—If the tide were just right.

—If the moon were just right.

—If the weather forecast at the particular time that the moon and tide were just right, were also just right;

> —if these conditions were not met, the invasion would automatically be postponed the month it would take the moon to get just right again; and

> —of the twelve months in the four seasons, only the months of one season were practical at all;

—If the German defenses in the meantime—between the writing of the plan and its execution—had not been improved.

—If the Germans happened at the moment to have no more than twelve mobile divisions in reserve in northwest Europe—and providing Germany were unable to transfer from the Russian front more than fifteen first-quality divisions during the first sixty days.

—AND IF, at the same time, the German Air Force (very much

alive and kicking when the plan was written) were materially reduced in fighter strength.

If all these conditions could be met simultaneously, the OVERLORD planners conceded that it *might* be done. (*Minor* qualifications—such as completion of a landing craft building program, the gathering of sufficient forces and supplies—had to be taken for granted as having been met.)

Reading these qualifications, the Johnnies-Come-Lately were appalled. If this plan were approved as written, it would be easy to bring about a situation in which it *could not* be executed—in fact overt sabotage actually seemed unnecessary. The Germans could hardly be expected *not* to improve their defenses during the coming year and, with plenty of troops available and the shadow of invasion falling on them, who could believe that Hitler would not reinforce his armies in France? Yet under either of these circumstances, the invasion would automatically be postponed indefinitely!

Even if everything went right, the sailing of the invasion fleet still hung on the slim thread of that uniquely favorable weather prediction—not "any time during a season of good weather" but precisely and specifically on a certain date, when moon and tide were such and such, and when there was a wind of no more than nine knots blowing! The whole thing was demonstrably absurd if anyone chose to make it so—or even to insist that the plan be followed literally.

These jokers one side, the plan itself seemed to us a masterpiece of cautious, unimaginative, but extremely thorough, painstaking and logical reasoning. It lacked style or dash and there was nothing ingenious about it, but every step it took was documented. Plan OVERLORD stood stolidly, as hale and hearty and tangible as the figure of John Bull in a friendly political cartoon. Any attempt to camouflage it by orthodox means was once accurately described as like trying to put crinoline pants on an elephant to make it look like a southern belle. It was that kind of a plan.

Looking at the coast of Europe, the OVERLORD planners first eliminated all the places they were sure, for one reason or another, we could *not* invade. This narrowed the eligible coast down to a section from east of Calais to, and including, the

Channel coast of the Cherbourg peninsula. The planners then took a look at the Pas de Calais, where the Channel is narrowest, and painstakingly reasoned that out of bounds too. The cliffs of Dover are only eighteen miles from the Pas de Calais beaches, but for that very reason the Germans were observed to have erected their most formidable fortifications there, and to have concentrated their reserves behind these fortifications. So the Pas de Calais area was ruled out as simply too formidable.

The elimination of the convenient Calais beaches reduced the eligible coast to a semicircle from the Seine to the Cherbourg peninsula—and this area now got the nod, by default.

The selection of the actual landing beaches themselves made itself, as this reef and that cliff eliminated competition.

The most fundamental assumption of OVERLORD was that, once ashore, the invading armies would require a minimum of two major supply ports to keep themselves in the field. But early in their reasoning, the planners had talked themselves out of direct assault on a fortified port—once again, as too formidable a task. Having thus reasoned themselves onto isolated beaches for their landings, they now had to direct the capture of the vital ports from the land side.

Cherbourg was an automatic choice for at least one of these ports, since it is at the end of a peninsula jutting out into the Channel, a peninsula which might be cut by a drive overland from the original landing beaches. The OVERLORD planners, as we will see, left it for history and the field commander to decide whether the nearby Le Havre or the much further away Brest would be the second port to fall after the landing.

Cherbourg and Le Havre or Brest having been taken, the Continent was considered open to major forces for the battle of Europe. Following the amphibious assault phase, ninety days were set aside for the development of the captured area—for the opening of ports and the repair of railroads—to receive the follow-up force, elements of which would be continuously arriving direct from the United States.

The air and sea phases of the operation were gone into in great detail. In the air, fighter support over the assault beaches was a principal concern. This would naturally be limited by the length of time a fighter, taking off in England, could stay in the air over France and still get back to its base with enough gas in its tanks to maneuver for a landing. OVERLORD was a conservative plan. Its figures were based on the range of the British Spitfire, despite the fact that the American Air Force had already developed fighters with considerably greater range. The Norfolk House planners had not bothered to go into this with General Eaker, whose Eighth Air Force was already fighting over France at the time—so that the air support picture in OVERLORD was made to seem most precarious.

The scale of the entire operation was wholly dependent upon the lift available. This fact was noted. An inventory of world resources showed that there would only be enough landing craft available to put three divisions afloat in assault types. Four more might be floated in larger vessels, which could unload only after the beaches had been cleared. No attempt was made by the OVERLORD planners to break this bottleneck, or to recommend that steps be taken to break it. Although the earliest date at which the invasion was foreseen was almost a year away, it was simply accepted that nothing could be done about the landing craft situation, even though it so limited the assault forces as to endanger the success of the whole undertaking. To invade Sicily, planners in Africa had figured that six or seven assault divisions were essential; the assault on Fortress Europa, OVERLORD seemed to think, had to resign itself to an initial striking force of not more than three.

It was for all these reasons, but at the time particularly for the last two (the curious ignoring of the range of American fighter craft and the resignation to an inadequate fleet of landing craft for the assault), that the Johnnies-Come-Lately felt that Plan OVERLORD, far from ending their troubles, only began them. If they had unwilling partners (for whatever reason they could not yet perceive), then the fate of the invasion seemed to hang on a single paragraph. This paragraph was the paragraph which said who would be the boss of the invasion and which recommended an organization for the command and control of Operation OVERLORD.

It was still only July and the decision in Washington called for an invasion the following spring. There was plenty of time to take Plan OVERLORD in hand, to crack the landing craft bottleneck, to give the problem of support over the beaches to the long range American fighters, and generally to strengthen the plan so that the escape clauses would be superfluous. The job could be gotten on with—providing it were under the management of someone who wanted to get on with the job.

All this put a premium on that phase of the plan which concerned the command and control of the whole. We set to studying it.

The management chart which was recommended by the British General Morgan and his Anglo-American staff seemed to us cunningly contrived to obscure the issue of who would be the boss of the invasion. There was to be a Supreme Allied Commander, but great emphasis was laid on the fact that he was not to command. He was to be a semipolitical figure, presiding over a temporary Anglo-American military state and negotiating, as the head of this state, with the exiled governments in England, whose token forces would be under his nominal command, and whose countries his British and American armies would presently liberate. But by definition this individual would take orders from the Combined Chiefs, passing them on to his field commanders. He himself would not be a field soldier and he would be furnished a staff not of field soldiers, but of men qualified to operate in the rarefied air of international diplomacy. Thus, the Supreme Commander would be neither authorized nor equipped to handle operations in the field, and would *have* to delegate his authority over the physical preparations.

The real commander of the armed forces of the temporary military state thus created would be a committee—a committee of three Commanders-in-Chief, one for land, one for sea and one for the air force. This committee had such enormous powers that it would be in a position to nullify the Supreme Commander's policies easily, if it chose.

The Supreme Commander's would be an international headquarters. But each of the three Commanders-in-Chief would be authorized to run his show any way he pleased. In addition, each Commander-in-Chief had authority to integrate the Anglo-

American force under his command to suit himself—with a single limiting proviso that, on the ground, no force smaller than a corps of two 15,000-men divisions of one nationality could be placed under the command of another nationality. Thus, the entities of the two navies and two air forces could be completely merged operationally, and the entity of the two armies could also be merged providing neither was chipped into pieces smaller than the size of a single corps.

All this meant to us, in the light of our experience in London, that if the three Commanders-in-Chief—or even if two of them—were British they would be in a position to interpret Plan OVERLORD any way they pleased—to postpone the invasion at will or to make it seem impossible.

Other and more immediate considerations bothered us. The British command and control setup called for the creation of four huge headquarters—those of the Supreme Commander and his three Commanders-in-Chief—with what we felt was an inevitable duplication of effort and confusion of responsibility. The whole structure seemed ponderous and unnecessarily complicated—and as Americans, we had little faith in the efficiency of co-ordination by committees. We liked our command channels as clear of organizational obstructions as possible.

The whole concept of merged forces worried us. Setting national pride to one side, there remained the fact that the very concept of the merger involved monumental efforts in the education of individuals and the simplification of organizations before it could be even begun. Almost every phase of military procedure in the British is different from its counterpart in the American Army. Everything is gone about in a different way—the language is different, the doctrine is different, the traditions are different. The American Army, expanded around a minute corps of professional officers, knew little enough then about its own job—and yet, if the British plan were followed, it would now be required to master another and wholly foreign military organization almost overnight—with consequent loss in time and efficiency.

Moreover, even the British plan for control had to admit that the merger could only be a temporary one. Eventually the American force would be several times as large as the British and a separate American command would be required. Facing this, the British planners reversed themselves and agreed that at some future date British and American ground forces would each revert to their own Army Group commands. The Supreme Commander would then descend from his Olympian heights at least far enough to name successive strategic objectives to each of these Army Group Commanders.

When this change would take place, OVERLORD did not prophesy. The original committee of Commanders-in-Chief would remain in command through the assault—and until the issue of the initial campaign was beyond doubt. Presumably this would be after the defeat of the German armies on the Channel coast, or even after the fall of France.

The whole idea of defining the invasion command in terms of co-equal Commanders-in-Chief offended us. On the field command level, the plan ignored the first command principle established by the American President for American arms in World War II: the principle of unity of field command in any given theater under a single field commander chosen from any one of the three branches. The Anglo-American planners at COSSAC, it appeared, had not even considered the possibility that a force that one day would be four-fifths or five-sixths American should be given a command in accordance with American principle.

The net of our feeling was that the now-revealed plan for the command of the invasion, far from solving our problem of how to get action, simply made it even more complicated—or at least had the capacity for compounding difficulties.

There is always more to a paper than what is written on it. The COSSAC staff had power only to make recommendations, but it had also opinions beyond these recommendations. COSSAC's opinion—and its General Morgan made no secret of the fact— was that because of the scale of the American contribution, the Supreme Commander should, by grace, be American. The three Commanders-in-Chief, therefore, should be British. This, COSSAC felt, was particularly apropos because the British, having fought the war now for almost four years, and having come successfully through the bitter trials of early defeat, had—his clear implication argued—a monopoly on commanders qualified to lead so momentous a venture.

This was General Morgan's case: the authority of the British Navy in the Channel was unquestioned; in the air there were the victorious air marshals who had beaten the Luftwaffe and won the Battle of England; and, on the ground, there was Bernard Montgomery, victor at El Alamein, conqueror of Rommel and the Africa Corps, liberator of Tunisia, and his veteran officers who together had accomplished all of these things with the famous British Eighth Army (admitting the help of some "minor" pushing and pulling by American forces on Rommel's flanks towards the end).

Not only were the commanders available but—and this General Morgan was even more precise about—the invasion they were to lead would set sail from the United Kingdom, be supplied from there and be supported in the air from there for a considerable time. It was only sensible, then, that the offensive that was so dependent on the British Isles be commanded by Britons.

As to the status of the Commanding General of the American forces now or about to be in the United Kingdom, General Morgan reassured General Devers that his authority would be in no way curtailed by turning his troops over to General Montgomery to command. He, Devers, would retain administrative authority— authority to promote or remove officers—and court martial jurisdiction. If the American armies were to be impressed into British service, the right to try them for misbehavior there would still be exclusively an American prerogative. American control of sanitation facilities was also mentioned.

There remained no longer any mystery about COSSAC or what it would recommend, along with its tactical plan, to the next international conference.

If the OVERLORD paper were approved as written, there would be nothing the Americans could do about making the plan work—and its execution would be wholly at the mercy of men who seemed more interested in what *could not* be done than what *could*. True, there might be an American Supreme Commander, but he was defined to us as a diplomat and super-statesman. All the real authority for organizing and directing the invasion—and the later authority for commanding the forces on the far shore—would be in the hands of the British. If they chose not to like the year 1944, there was nothing to keep them from picking any other good year to cross the Channel—they could always show good and sufficient cause for the postponement.

The international conference which was to approve, disapprove, or alter Plan OVERLORD was already scheduled for the month of August in Quebec. With these thoughts in mind, General Devers prepared to convey his reservations to this conference. In the meantime the work of solving even the most elementary problems of getting ready for the great invasion was brought to an almost complete standstill, pending the ground rules that Quebec would establish.

The Johnnies-Come-Lately had now been in England for better than sixty days. They had the carefully prepared plan for the invasion, and they had the ideas of the British on how it should be commanded. They also had, not lessened but reinforced, their suspicion that something was still being left unsaid, that there remained some fundamental reservation in our Ally's attitude. The counter-plan that Devers felt would untangle all this was a plan for command and control as blunt and homely and American as the COSSAC plan was subtle and complicated and British.

OVERLORD had already divided American and British forces geographically, with the British on the left and the Americans on the right. Embarking for France from southwest England, the Americans had their back to the Irish Channel ports, through which ran their supply lines from America. Devers simply said: let each of these military areas be autonomous, each under the command of its nationality. Let the British run their preparations any way they liked; all forces in the American operation would be trained and be led by a single American commander—all air, ground and naval forces.

On the shores of France, OVERLORD also segregated the Allied forces into British beaches on the left and American beaches on the right. Therefore, said Devers: in France let the British run their show any way they liked; the Americans would simply fight by their side, under their own unified command. Both American supply and command channels would thus run without interruption from the battlefield back to the War Department. These supply and command channels would pass through southwestern England during the mounting of the invasion; after ports were opened in France, they would run directly across the Atlantic from America to France.

In Devers' plan, there would, of course, be a Supreme Allied Commander but, in addition to the functions assigned to him in the British plan, he would also be responsible (1) for naming the successive objectives of the two autonomous forces and (2) for co-ordinating their efforts where co-ordination was required. With command autonomy, however, the problem of co-ordination would shrink to small dimensions and would be principally concerned with matters of air support, where it might be necessary for a single commander to direct the concentration of the air forces of both nations in some particular or unusual action.

The Supreme Commander would maintain his headquarters in London where he could be close to the Governments with whom he dealt, but, in Devers' plan, he would also maintain an advance echelon to keep in touch with the field commanders.

With the command set-up so simplified, Devers believed that the invasion could be driven home in the early spring—in fact he felt that, given shipping priorities to get the troops, he could have mounted the assault in the fall of 1943.

Two principles underlay Devers' reasoning: first, the principle of American command of Americans, the principle that Pershing fought for in the last war; and second, the homely New England principle that good fences make good neighbors. He felt that it would require all of our respective energies, British and American, to prepare for and to win our own battles, without burdening both with the necessity of learning how to merge our forces and having to work through the intricate paraphernalia of a headquarters of combined nationalities.

Devers was hardly the most tactful of men. He made no secret of how he felt about either the command set-up or the British reluctance to cross the Channel. The one—and I think the only—time he was ever asked to dine with Winston Churchill, the Sicilian invasion was in the act of being mounted. The Prime Minister was in a very fine humor, and he figuratively slapped the

American commander on the back and said, "Now there's an operation for you, General Devers. It's going to be a cheap victory and the world is going to love it. That's what the world wants—cheap victories." It was when this conversation was reported to us later in the evening that some of us on General Devers' staff began betting he would never survive the Battle of London—for he admitted that he had answered the Prime Minister by saying, "If you will forgive me, Sir, I think that's bunk. I think one squad of soldiers on the Channel coast of France will mean more to the world than two armies ashore in Sicily."

As an organizer, Devers thought clearly. He had able general officers to advise him. By Quebec, his headquarters had begun to make sense. He had energy, drive, persistence and the courage of his own convictions. He was also naive, unsubtle and inexperienced in his high rank—he had gotten his promotions for his strictly intramural job of organizing an Armored Force in the American Army. He was ambitious, too. He wanted to fill the job he had defined for an American field commander himself—which was natural enough, but that fact compromised his arguments for the principles involved. And he suffered from a confusion of soul which was his undoing.

Devers' soul was confused before Quebec by the fact that he did not know where he stood with one man, General Marshall—who had created him, who had given him his job, of whom he was frightened and to whom he was intensely loyal, and whose confidence he was now suddenly afraid he had lost. He did not know whether he had lost it or whether he had not. As his dilemma had shaped itself in June and July, Devers must have written Marshall, and they must have been long letters, frank, worried and finally pleading. And to these letters he must have gotten no replies.

Long before Quebec, Devers' staff had advised him that the only possible solution to his untenable position was to get on a plane and fly back to Washington, there to lay the situation frankly before the President and his Chief of Staff—to lay it there and simply to ask, "Now what is expected of me?" But Devers could not bring himself to try this simple solution. He wrestled with the problem for days and satisfied himself that he had no right to go. To have gone would have meant leaving his post. MacArthur, he said, had not come home from Australia to whine. Neither had Eisenhower from the Mediterranean. Yet both had their problems. Marshall, thought Devers, might not think it right of him to come home—it would have been against the military doctrine both had been taught.

In vain, Devers' staff tried to point out that MacArthur and Eisenhower had shooting wars on their hands, while he, Devers, had a conference war on his. He simply could not face the idea of facing Marshall, in a dilemma and with his problem unsolved. His unanswered correspondence would have to carry the load— his unanswered correspondence and, at the last moment, a few individuals like Averell Harriman, whom he had known before the war. He left it to them to plead a case he considered of momentous seriousness to his country.

When the reports came back to us from the Quebec Conference, we learned that General Devers had lost on all points. Churchill had met with Roosevelt and Hopkins, and both sides had been advised by their Chiefs of Staff for all three services.

The Conference had:

1. Approved the outline Plan OVERLORD.

2. Approved the recommended organization for its command and control—in principle.

3. Directed General Morgan to start detailed planning and preparation.

Thus the defeatist planning staff at COSSAC was to continue in existence and the development of OVERLORD would continue to be under its direction.

Almost everyone at Quebec went on record as concerned with the landing craft bottleneck, and it was recommended that the situation should be improved by (1) sending more craft from the Mediterranean to the Channel and (2) upping the American manufacturing commitment by 25 per cent—Admiral King thereupon directing his procurement people to take immediate steps to explore expansion of production of landing ships and craft.

The British Prime Minister contributed a little rhetoric, stating that the attack should be strengthened and delivered "with violence and simultaneity." When his attention was pointedly called to the limitation imposed by the lack of sufficient landing craft, his reaction was "more landing craft must be procured."

The American Chiefs of Staff contented themselves with straightforward approval of Plan OVERLORD, but the British Chiefs took the occasion to go on record with three reservations of their own:

1. They felt the conditions necessary for success should be emphasized *even more strongly* than in OVERLORD.

2. They felt the Allies' margin of superiority was, in general, too slim.

3. They felt that the projected rate of advance was too optimistic.

COSSAC itself, to whom the project was now returned for translation into even greater detail, delivered itself of an opinion, extraordinary in view of the official approval of their own plan by the two Chiefs of State. They "called attention to the fact" that OVERLORD *might not be undertaken at all*—and that in this event there would be "political pressure" for an operation of some kind against the Continent. Facing this situation, COSSAC made an exception to its Mediterranean first rule and suggested that a small scale, headline-catching diversion against Norway be reconsidered—even though this had been twice before rejected.

Despite this, and still backing its approval of the plan, the Conference ordered the highest strategic priority be given the bomber offensive which was to precede OVERLORD and stated, as an unqualified directive, that OVERLORD should have preference over the Mediterranean Theater on resources. To spell out this last directive, the Conference specified the return of seven divisions from Africa to the United Kingdom, three of them British and four American, and it was left to General Devers to arrange with the Supreme Commander of the Mediterranean Theater, General Eisenhower, for this transfer of resources. The Mediterranean Theater was also to contribute a stated number of landing ships and craft.

Thus, despite the reservations of the British Chiefs of Staff and the warnings of the men who had written the plan itself, OVERLORD was approved as a military operation—and despite the quite different reservations of the American Commanding General in the European Theater, the set-up for its British-type command and control was confirmed. There is no record I know of that General Devers' arguments were ever even officially discussed. The only outside comment appears to have been Harry Hopkins'. In addition to echoing the concern of everyone about landing craft, he said he felt that the resistance groups in Europe should be made use of and ought to be incorporated in the operational plan.

The Conference in Quebec ended with the month of August. Our apprehensions seemed confirmed. The invasion of Europe, which was to be carried out with predominantly American forces, had slipped entirely out of American channels and it would now presumably be beyond American power to control or even to influence. But for some reason which was not clear in the papers we read, the Conference seemed scrupulously to have avoided the question of who the commanders of the invasion should be. Their titles were approved, and the definition of the relationships amongst them, but no individuals were named or even discussed. General Morgan would continue to head the "Supreme Headquarters" as its Chief of Staff, but still as its Chief of Staff only. General Devers would continue to be Commanding General of the American Forces in the European Theater, but still without clarification as to whom he should take orders from—the non-existent Supreme Commander (through his Chief of Staff), the American War Department to whom he reported, or the Combined Anglo-American Chiefs of Staff themselves.

In this ambiguity, this near vacuum in command, the Johnnies-Come-Lately stepped up for one last turn at bat. Until the *actual* Commanders-in-Chief and their *actual* Supreme Commander were named, Devers & Co. were still the senior *American* headquarters in Europe; they could still request men and supplies from America, and they could still issue orders—to their own officers and men—in England. They had one last chance at putting over the invasion of northwest Europe—a better chance than they had ever had before, for now the directives and the priorities were even clearer than they had been before. As for their own role, they had everything to gain for their country and nothing to lose for themselves. It was the last chance for the Johnnies-Come-Lately. They made the most of it.

3   Exit Without Music

It is still 1943, but September has come to England and the days are getting short again. The Johnnies-Come-in-May are almost veterans now—in the kind of warfare that is waged in London. The Committees are as numerous, the agenda as interminable, but the Americans know where they stand now—which is nowhere, except that they are still expected to prepare an American army to invade Europe.

The first problem on the Johnny-Come-Lately's list was that old one of finding a strip of seashore on which the troops could train—in all the United Kingdom there hadn't seemed a mile of coast we could use. When we finally got it, near a little village called Appledore, there was the training establishment itself to set up. It was called the Assault Training Center and there a young engineer colonel named Paul Thompson built a full-scale replica of a German strong-point area, a mile and a half square, studded with concrete bunkers six feet thick. Beyond it were four miles of beaches onto which the troops could ride in landing craft. From a long hesitant American Navy came a real live admiral in the flesh—and the landing craft crews themselves, for him to drill in carrying the troops. As the assault divisions arrived, they would go, a regiment at a time, to the Assault Training Center, there to renew their skill at arms or to learn it.

The only trouble was that after we had acquired the beaches and built the pillboxes and staffed the school, there was no curriculum for it to teach. OVERLORD had cautiously refrained from committing itself on how the actual attack itself should be made—using what weapons, with what formations, at what hour of day or night. It was COSSAC's business to say but now, confronted with the formal question, COSSAC could not make up its mind. So the American colonel and his thirty or forty officers were ordered by Devers not to wait but to proceed, by trial and error and experimentation, to make up their own minds and to be prepared to teach their conclusions to the American troops at least.

There are two ways to take any military objective: by surprise and by force. Surprise is best achieved in the confusion of darkness; force is best applied in the bright light of day. The first question that Thompson and his staff in the Assault Training Center had to decide was whether it was best to sneak ashore by night or to bull your way in in daylight. African experience in landing on an undefended coast was of no value. On the Channel, the British Commandos, with their blackened faces, had always struck by night. In the book, there was no question: everything is against landing on a beach when the enemy can see you. His guns, firmly implanted on shore, can't be matched in volume or accuracy of fire by your guns, firing from the decks of ships. From the shore, he has observation—coming in, you are on a flat plain and he is on a slope, looking down at you. He has cover and concealment—he is hidden and his positions are camouflaged; you are a fly on a baby's naked belly. He has what are known as "fields of fire"—he has studied his terrain and has placed his guns where they command all approaches; from the sea, you have a free field of fire only from your boats to as far as the beach itself.

The enemy also has maneuverability—he can shift his troops at will behind the dunes, on the road net just over the hill. You have no maneuverability whatever. Your assault waves must come in through a path cleared in the underwater mine field. Your boats must follow one another in line, as if running on rails. At the time when you need your maximum strength—when you come onto the beach itself, with its wire and its mines and its crossed fields of fire—you are at your weakest. Here your men are still half sick from their voyage; they have no heavy weapons with them; they have only the ammunition they can carry on foot.

They are confused and unco-ordinated, without adequate communications.

But if we sent our troops in by night, the confusion would be worse and the darkness, which should shield us, could be partially dispelled by the enemy's flares. The enemy would not even need his eyes to use his crossed fields of fire—his guns would already be sighted to rake the beach, and his soldiers would merely pull the triggers. His mine fields and his wire would be even more effective at night.

They were still debating these things in Norfolk House while Thompson and the single regiment of engineers that had been given him to play with were trying them out at Appledore. In the beginning, Thompson said, all he found out was that night was impossible. Commandos were specially selected and trained individuals. They built scale models of the harbors they were to raid, and practiced against them for months, each man learning his role as if it were a ballet dancer's. Surprise by night could be managed by such methods, but only on a small scale. Thompson convinced himself that the same technique would not work for large bodies of troops, whole divisions and corps. The climax argument was that while Commando technique might get past shoreline fortifications with fewer casualties, these fortifications would remain to fire on succeeding waves when dawn finally broke and the follow-up forces arrived.

If night were impossible, then it had to be day. But by day the enemy would blow you out of the water. But by day it's got to be—and the enemy can't be allowed to blow you out of the water. So, Thompson reasoned, we'll start with what we've got by way of power to bombard from ships and aircraft, and we'll add, and add, and add fire power—using every kind of weapon, from every kind of craft—until we *know* there are enough guns to break down anything on shore. We'll use battleships' guns, cruisers' guns, gunboats' guns, destroyers' guns—and then we'll use field cannon mounted for the first time in landing craft, and landing craft with batteries of rockets, and the tanks themselves firing while still in the landing craft. We'll use gun piled on gun, battery on battery, everything that will shoot. What if some of the fire is inaccurate? It's all going ashore. And the bombs will be coming down from the air. If there's enough of all this, presently there'll be nothing left on shore to fire back.

This is a gross simplification of a highly complicated and technical problem in bombardment and in naval and artillery fire power. It's fundamentally sound, though, and it's exactly the way the American officers at the Assault Training Center came to their decision to rely not on the tactics by which the Commandos had been successful but on naked fire power delivered in the naked light of dawn—from the air and from the sea, with only the uncertain cover of a will-o'-the-wisp smoke screen to hide the craft with troops in them and the ships with the guns. And on the basis of their own unauthorized decision, at the Assault Training Center they began their still unauthorized teaching of their unauthorized assault doctrine.* On the very highest levels, the argument about whether the invasion would be by day or night continued—long after it had been settled by the Assault Training Center and the training was proceeding accordingly.

Meanwhile, in London, the American headquarters had picked up a new weapon—the only new secret weapon on the invasion— to play with. It was the amphibian DD tank—which is an ordinary tank floated by means of great canvas hoopskirts fastened around it, with a propeller of its own drilled into its behind. It came from an inventive British source. It was the invention of an English officer who had been unable to sell it to the War Office and came peddling it to Jakey Devers. Devers gave the plans to his Operations officer, who ordered a demonstration. The DD was to waddle out of the mouth of a landing craft, splash into the water and proceed on its own.

When the test came, the skipper of the landing craft did everything wrong but still the DD floated. The secret weapon which put tanks ashore in the first wave to land in France was forged. Hitherto, the defending enemy had nothing to worry about from tanks until the landing infantry had fought clear of the beach and thus made it safe for the attackers to put their heavy armor through the surf.

* First reports of the American landing on Tarawa came while landing doctrine was being written at the Assault Training Center. On Tarawa, tanks had been landed by daylight and had proved to be of enormous value.

Actually, the forging of the weapon itself was typical of the problems with which the American headquarters wrestled. Conversion of an ordinary tank into an amphibious DD is not difficult, as such things go, and when the demonstration proved successful the British War Office agreed to convert such and such a number—for their own forces as well as the Americans. It was hardly a big enough problem to send back to disturb the production lines in America. It was a secret small-scale operation, which simply required the right orders being given and the production followed through. Yet between the agreement to convert the tanks and the time the first were due—and the Americans began politely to ask when their delivery might be expected—the War Office managed wonderfully to forget about the whole order. Barely in time to do something about it, it was discovered that nothing whatever had been done about the matter—which might be normal snafu in any army except that the DD tank was a top priority secret weapon which was to change an important aspect of the whole assault formation and its development shouldn't have been left to the mercy of routine snafu.

The Johnnies-Come-Lately had no friends before, during, or after the Quebec Conference. In the Mediterranean Theater, Allied forces had landed in Sicily early in July, but the Quebec Conference had reaffirmed the fact that this assault was a diversion with a maximum objective of completing the collapse of Italy by shock. Under no circumstances were the Allies to venture up the boot of Italy. Now, in the first week in September, the Sicilian invasion had accomplished its mission; the government of Italy had capitulated and Italy was officially out of the war. But instead of this victory releasing American troops and craft for us, it now suddenly appeared that the demand for them in the Mediterranean was to be even greater than ever. Now the Mediterranean Theater wanted to pursue the enemy, by land and by sea. Even the forces we had been promised from the Mediterranean had to be pried loose.

Despite this, preparations in England continued. There was a whole area in which we had at least begun to be effective, and that was in supply. Perhaps we did have friends after all—for if the highest echelon in Washington seemed unconcerned, the working echelons of the War Department were turning in a spectacular performance. What we asked for we got, as fast as convoy space to carry it could be obtained.

That now became the rub—convoy space. Again it was Mediterranean trouble. Not only was that theater now giving grudgingly but also it appeared, when we sat down with the naval officers who had moved in next door to us on Grosvenor Square, that the Mediterranean's call for supplies and still more supplies for Italy had tied up the very bottoms we needed to bring our supplies to England. Priority in the European Theater we had, on paper—but for future operations only. In the Mediterranean they were fighting present battles, and these battles had to be supplied as long as they went on. And they went on, and on.

The British Army Commander in Sicily and Italy was General Bernard Montgomery. Now *his* shadow commenced to fall on the British Isles. With an army group headquarters, he would one day lead at least British field forces. In Devers' headquarters, we began, a little forlornly, to set up an American counterpart—an American army group headquarters to command two or more armies—even though, according to OVERLORD, this headquarters would not take command until long after the invasion was established, perhaps after the war was virtually won. We were directed to set it up and set it up we did, just in case. In Devers' mind there may have been a lingering hope that somehow, someway, it was still to be his own headquarters.

After Sicily, confidential cables told us that Omar Bradley would command an American field army in the invasion. In late September he came to England himself and learned for the first time of the plan to invade Europe. He was briefed on the plan and flew back to Washington to confer with Marshall about his responsibility.

The army Bradley was to lead would be made up largely of the divisions he had commanded in the Mediterranean, the divisions that Quebec had called for and which were now finally being released. When Bradley and Devers conferred, neither knew more about the eventual American command than that Bradley would have *one* army of it.

All the time that these things were going on, the most important problem of all became even more important—and remained just as much of a problem. It was the procurement of landing craft to carry the troops across the Channel. At Quebec it had been assumed that there would be scarcely enough landing craft to float the OVERLORD assault, and everyone from the President and the Prime Minister down agreed that 25 per cent more should immediately be procured.* But fall followed summer and, instead of getting better, the figures got worse.

At Quebec the COSSAC planners had commented that "the situation with regard to British landing craft is somewhat confused," admitting to a shortage of 870 bottoms or 13 per cent of the total lift. But when we started to take the British figures apart we found not 13 but almost 55 per cent missing. That is not strictly true—the missing bottoms were there all right—but they were laid up in repair yards from the Thames to Scapa Flow. They were not laid up in these yards for carburetor adjustments; they were laid up for want of essential parts, or whole engines, or hulls that required complete rebuilding. Not only were they laid up in these yards for these complaints, but now there seemed in all England no stockpiles from which the parts to repair them could be drawn and no maintenance yards with facilities and trained men to machine new parts. And when you asked the Royal Navy, the civilian authorities had the personnel; and when you asked the civilian authorities, the Royal Navy had it—or the Air Force, or the Army.

At first we had not believed the figures—had not believed that the situation *could* have been that bad. So we went to the yards and saw the craft and we talked with the skippers and the idle crews, with the admirals and the captains and foremen in charge of the yards. It was true. Yet there was nothing that we in the

---

* British Commandos evolved the first landing craft, developed the ramp gate in the bow—which the Japanese also used on the other side of the world. Americans contributed the "Higgins' bottom"—scooped out so that a landing craft's own propellers can wash water under it and float it sternward off the sand. This ingenious construction was originally developed to solve the Caribbean bootleggers' problem of how to land a heavy cargo on a secret and hostile shore, and back away off the beach after the delivery was made. It made an important contribution, but the standardization and mass production of landing craft of all types were America's greatest gifts to the mechanics of getting ashore where you're not wanted.

American headquarters could do about it—for these were British craft under the command of the Royal Navy.

This was the situation with the British craft which were scheduled to carry three-fifths of both forces. And where were the 25 per cent that the American Navy was going "to take immediate steps to explore the expansion of production of . . ."? You could scour the horizon with cables and find no trace.

How a war is won? This one may have been won because Donald Nelson, the chairman of the War Production Board in America, needed a rest and thought it would be interesting to take it by making a tourist trip to England, and because, when he got to England, a group of young Regular Army officers conspired to give him so many figures, and got him so interested in the shortage of landing craft for the coming assault on Europe, that he telephoned back to the United States and played a trick on the production priorities. He ordered the already approved quotas of landing craft for 1944 put in the shipyards, not in the appropriate quotas of the coming year but immediately, as fast as the drive of his whole organization could get them in the works.

When Donald Nelson first heard the story of the landing craft crisis, he had exploded, "But that's crazy; I can give you all the landing craft you want." But when he heard the whole history of the futile attempts to do something about it, he made his telephone conversation off the record. It worked. His orders went through. As a result of this transatlantic telephone call in September of 1943, by early in 1944 landing craft production in America was a full three months ahead of itself.

After the Assault Training Center was opened, and after Bradley had paid his fleeting visit, and after Nelson's historic telephone call, I made one trip myself back to Washington. It was October. My mission had nothing to do with high level planning. But it took me to the Pentagon Building and, because I came from the European Theater, I was in touch with most of the officers who were concerned with it there. It was amazing how little they knew of what was going on in London.

The limitations of Plan OVERLORD stared them in the face—the bottleneck in the number of landing craft available was obviously catastrophic. But the officers who had studied these figures reported only frustration in their efforts to get something done about them. The Navy seemed to be fighting any re-allocation of steel from fighting vessels to build landing craft; nobody with more rank than a colonel's seemed to be taking landing craft trouble seriously anyway. The British had told them everything was all right.

I had a week's work to do and then I got a few days' leave. When I was on leave, I called up Harry Hopkins and went to see him in his office in the White House. I could talk to Harry Hopkins as a pre-war acquaintance; if I had tried to see the President, it might have embarrassed General Devers—for the War Department could have regarded it as an attempt on the General's part to go over Marshall's head and to use a staff officer's personal relationship to appeal to the Commander-in-Chief. Besides, while before the war I used to take political problems to discuss with the President, I had been an editor and publisher then, and now I didn't know quite what I was. I did not feel like burdening him with an exploratory conversation. I had no authorization from Devers or anyone else to see anybody outside the Pentagon. But I wanted to do something; the business was too important not to try to do something.

At least I wanted to lay what I knew on the table before someone who might make sense with it. Then I could leave without asking or even recommending anything. This was precisely what I did with Harry Hopkins. As far as I am aware, General Devers never knew of this conversation.

I put two situations before Hopkins. The first was the wholly tangible landing craft situation. Where were the vitally needed craft to come from? There was barely time enough to manufacture them now, even if the priorities were allocated immediately. Did Hopkins know of this situation?

He said he did not. He was extremely interested. We talked a long time about it. He seemed to be astonished—and a little skeptical. As long as he could remember, he said, landing craft had always been the bottleneck and he asked rhetorically why the problem had not been solved for once and for all? I left him with that one.

Next I asked him if he was aware that the coming invasion was still under no one's command. The Americans would obviously bear the major weight of it* but the American Theater Commander did not know whether he was working for the War Department, the non-existent Supreme Commander, the latter's chief of staff, General Morgan—or merely his own conscience. Under such circumstances, he was handicapped a thousand ways. From an organizational point of view—in elementary logic—this made no sense. There was too much to be done in too little time—if the show were really to come off. Such a colossal operation required the drive of a commander who knew where he stood and that his government was behind him.

Hopkins' first reaction was to ask how the Americans in the European Theater really felt about the chances of OVERLORD's success anyway. I said that the headquarters I was in felt that the difficulties were magnified by our allies, and overrated. Devers and his generals were sure the invasion would work. I said that to most Americans who had been studying the problem, it seemed as if our allies' looking for trouble was intentional—part, perhaps, of an organized effort to discredit or discourage the idea of invading. I explained that I said this as a reporter, that obviously I was not qualified to give an opinion as a military expert—or as a diplomat.

The turn of the conversation gave me a chance to pass on the prophecy that at the next international conference, the British offer would be to trade us the Supreme Allied Commander, American, in exchange for the three field commanders, British— and the opinion that these three would be the real bosses. I said that this trade would look most attractive but that there would be two catches to it. Catch one: the Supreme Commander, American, would be elevated (by the definition of his powers and responsibilities) to so high an altitude that he would have little effect on the strategy in the field. Catch two: the Commanders-in-Chief in the field, British, would insist on having all American

* By the end of the war there were sixty-one American divisions in the field, thirteen British. There were also five Canadian, one Polish and twelve new French divisions, making a total of ninety-two in the Allied force. Counting the vitally important service troops, there were 2,909,602 American soldiers in Europe.

forces involved under their command and, having gotten them there, would spare no efforts to merge them with the British forces—which didn't seem to make sense from any angle. I told him that I was hardly speculating about this because the senior British planning officer, General Morgan himself, had been quite frank, even before Quebec, about how *he* thought the command posts should be filled.

I said that it seemed to me that the American Army was good enough to fight under its own command and that since, in the end, it was plain that the American force would be many times the size of the British force, it was neither militarily nor politically reasonable that it should be asked to fight under foreign command, however brilliant.

I remember Hopkins as agreeing with all these points. *Of course* an American commander should be named—but the timing, he felt, was the important thing. In hindsight, it is obvious that Hopkins was thinking of the coming conference in Teheran—it must already have been agreed on. He felt that the appointment should wait until then, even though the preparations might suffer by the delay. He did not tell me about Teheran, however. Instead he said that Churchill was the problem—that Roosevelt had decided that we were entitled, and quite able, to run our own show but that the problem was to find a general who could "stand up to Churchill." He pictured Churchill as very strong minded on military matters and quite able to dominate his own generals.

Hopkins gave it as his personal opinion that Marshall was the only man qualified, but volunteered that although Roosevelt had gone as far as to tell Marshall that he could "have any job he liked," Marshall seemed reluctant to make any decision regarding his own future. Marshall was taking the position that the President should not ask him where he wanted to go but, instead, should simply tell him.

In general, on command and control problems, Harry Hopkins was both sympathetic and reassuring. Here he seemed aware of what was going on and assured me that while the British might well try to make the deal we foresaw, they would not succeed. The invasion itself, he said, would be under American command, and the commander would probably be General Marshall himself, because "he is the only general in the world whom Churchill is afraid of—when Churchill gets oratorical, Marshall just listens quietly and then brings the conversation back to earth with just the right facts and figures to destroy the P.M.'s case."

Hopkins gave me to understand that when General Marshall became the Supreme Allied Commander things would be quite different, that he would consider himself as *really* in command of the invasion, and not simply as the theoretical head who would turn over his responsibility to three commanders-in-chief in the field. After all, Marshall was a strong proponent of unified command—unified American command.

I went back to England reassured. I did not know Marshall or any more about him, really, than that he was the American Army's boss and that that army's first campaign in Africa had ended successfully. But I was sure that Devers would be glad to see Marshall made Supreme Allied Commander and obviously Marshall enjoyed the confidence of President Roosevelt. If Marshall were appointed, the Americans in the European Theater, serving under him, would no longer be exiles and expatriates.

Six weeks later, in December, at Teheran, it was not Marshall but Eisenhower who was made Supreme Allied Commander (American)—and all forces in the United Kingdom necessary for the assault, British and American (excepting only the strategic air forces), were placed under a committee of three Commanders-in-Chief (British).

In London all that we knew about the Teheran Conference was the gossip traveling officers brought back to us. Almost gleefully, we heard that the Russians, reading OVERLORD, had pounced on the same escape clauses which had bothered us—and had put a line in the history book about one of them. When Joseph Stalin had read that the whole show was dependent on the Germans having no more than twelve reserve divisions in northwest Europe, he was described as putting the paper down and saying solemnly, "So—what if there are thirteen?"

We also heard that the Soviet Staff had insisted that an actual date be named, that they had asked for the first of April and settled for the first of May—which was now a firm commitment.

It was clear that Roosevelt had had an effective ally in bringing pressure on the British to "firm up" the proposition.

So far, Stalin had been our friend. Now he inadvertently undid us. Apparently still seeking to bring the invasion to earth on the shores of Normandy, Stalin gave it as another Soviet demand that. Roosevelt and Churchill name the men who would be responsible for the invasion, and make public their appointments. He felt that until the commanders were named, the "world" (in Russia, substitute "The Soviet Republics") would not believe that the Western Allies' intentions to invade were sincere. It was pointed out to him that if the world were told, so would be the Germans. Stalin replied that he was not interested in what the Germans learned —and the appointment of the commanders became an issue. Evidently Roosevelt and Churchill had not yet reached a final agreement. When Stalin remained obdurate, Churchill and Roosevelt's concession was that they would meet immediately *after* the conference had closed, pick their commanders and announce them within forty-eight hours. They wanted to do the picking all by themselves.

Stalin was satisfied, but his insistence forced the discussion of the appointments in an atmosphere of haste. Perhaps it had been predetermined, but it seemed to us in London that it was because of this atmosphere that we lost our last chance to get a unified American command for the invasion of Europe. The British set-up prevailed.

The trading at Teheran was not yet done. A deputy supreme commander was named for Eisenhower and a British officer put in this post. He was Air Chief Marshal Sir Arthur Tedder, who had commanded the British air forces in Africa and had several times saved the British ground forces when Rommel threatened to run them out of Egypt. Tedder was one of the ablest officers in the British Army. Young for an air chief marshal, charming, and energetic, he was already experienced in handling and working with Americans.

The British also managed to persuade the Americans to remove Devers' friend General Eaker from command of the Eighth Air Force, switching him with the Mediterranean strategic air force commander, General Doolittle—in order to make a clean sweep of the old American commanders in England.

General Dwight D. Eisenhower, who, as the Supreme Commander in the Mediterranean, had spent the summer and fall competing with the European Theater, now found himself the Supreme Commander of it.

At last, the Johnnies-Come-Lately were really through. They were sold down the river to serve in the same Mediterranean Theater that Eisenhower had left—under Field Marshal Sir Harold R. L. G. Alexander.

4   High Level Horsefeathers

By December of 1943, when the Johnnies-Come-Lately were banished from England for their pains, it was time to take stock of what the Anglo-American war effort was all about. On the surface many things still did not make sense but there was enough on the record now to suggest the pattern into which history was being pressed.

Based on international decisions made shortly after Pearl Harbor, the Anglo-American war against Germany was run by Roosevelt and Churchill, meeting personally in a series of "historic conferences." At these conferences, Roosevelt and Churchill together decided what to do next, and between these conferences the conduct of the war in the West was governed by these decisions.

Continuity in the management of the war was provided by a group of senior officers of each of the three services of both countries, these gentlemen together being known as the Combined Chiefs of Staff.* This august body was split between Washington and London, but its existence was continuous and it had world jurisdiction. British members always had representatives in Washington to speak for them. All members traveled wherever the international conferences were held.

* For the United States of America: General George C. Marshall, Chief of Staff of the United States Army; Admiral Ernest J. King, Commander-in-Chief of the United States Navy; General Henry H. Arnold, Commanding United States Army Air Forces, and Admiral William D. Leahy, Chief of Staff to the President.

The first function of the Combined Chiefs of Staff was to advise their respective Chiefs of State at these conferences—that is, they gathered and prepared all the necessary information and presented it to the Chiefs of State in such a way that decisions might be arrived at. Each "historic conference" lasted a week or two, and here is a table of when and where they met, and the principal actions taken at each:

1. December, 1941—*Washington:* Decided to give the defeat of Germany priority over the defeat of Japan; decided to prepare and launch a trans-Channel invasion sometime in 1942. (Subsequently the invasion of Africa was substituted and the trans-Channel invasion of France was postponed. This decision, however, made in July of 1942, was negotiated in London without benefit of an "historic conference" complete with Chiefs of State.)

2. January, 1943—*Casablanca:* Decided to invade Sicily—pending further preparations for the again postponed trans-Channel invasion.

3. May, 1943—*Washington:* Decided to invade northwest France in the spring of 1944, preparations to begin at once.

4. August, 1943—*Quebec:* Approved plans for the invasion of northwest France in the spring of 1944, and the command set-up, "in principle."

5. November-December, 1943—*Cairo-Teheran:* Set a definite date (May 1) for the invasion of northwest Europe and named the commanders of the invasion force.

6. September, 1944—*Quebec:* Planned for the defeat of Japan, following the apparently imminent collapse of Germany.

7. January-February, 1945—*Malta-Yalta* (the conference at the latter place was also known as the Crimean Conference): Continued to plan for the defeat of Japan, following the again apparently imminent collapse of Germany. Directed the strategy of the final assault on Germany and agreed on the postwar partition of Germany into "occupation zones."

The Combined Chiefs of Staff, as we have seen, was composed of senior members of each of the three services of both the United States and the British Empire. Each of these individuals, then, served in two capacities—one, as a member of the Combined Chiefs of Staff and the other, as a member of the senior military council of his own country. These latter bodies had, of course, separate identities, each being responsible to its own Government. The Americans were known as the Joint Chiefs of Staff; the British simply as the Chiefs of Staff. In international military parlance "Combined" always meant a combination of American and British; to Americans "Joint" meant a combination of all three services—land, sea and air. Technically, of course, the Combined Chiefs of Staff should have been called "The Combined *Joint* Chiefs of Staff," but the body was usually referred to simply as the Combined Chiefs.

Since the individual Chiefs of Staff of each nation doubled in brass, when they set out to implement an international decision as the Combined Chiefs they simply told themselves what to do in their other, or national, capacities. Co-ordination was automatic and there should never have been any friction except for the fact that between international meetings the two groups of Chiefs of Staff acquired individual personalities of their own and represented, on occasion, opposed schools of military thought. You then had the Chiefs of one nation attempting to influence the conduct of the commanders in the field without clearing through their alter ego, the international Combined Chiefs organization.

In Europe, the most frequent offenders were the British Chiefs of Staff, whose headquarters, of course, were in London. Forty-eight hours before the American Seventh Army set sail from Italy and Corsica for the invasion of southern France, for instance, the British Chiefs communicated directly with the British Theater Commander in the Mediterranean, instructing him to consider abandoning the whole invasion of southern France in favor of sailing the army concerned all the way to Brest, which they understood had just been captured by General Patton. The British Chiefs were, of course, out of bounds—because the Supreme Allied Commander in the Mediterranean was theoretically responsible not to them but to the Combined Chiefs of Staff as a whole—and they should have been bound anyway by the decision of the previous Chiefs of State conference which had directed that the invasion of southern France should be made. The British Chiefs did send an information copy of their cable to their American opposite numbers in Washington—and the reaction revealed some very strong ideas on the subject of short-circuiting agreed-upon channels. It also caused some very sharp words, and the notion of abandoning the invasion of southern France was itself hastily abandoned. It was at best a curious idea, because there existed at the time no shipping in the Mediterranean capable of transporting the American army concerned over the long sea route to Brest. The incident passed simply as an outward and visible manifestation of an inner and invisible conflict in policy which characterized the whole conduct of the war and which we will come to presently.

By and large, however, the management of the war by a combination of the Chiefs of Staffs of both states, under the executive direction of the two Chiefs of State meeting personally when historic decisions were called for, was spectacularly efficient. There is no doubt whatever that it represents the most effective example of management of allied armed forces in the history of warfare. Its simplicity was its brilliance—its simplicity and its reliance on direct personal contact, on man-to-man negotiation, to avoid misunderstanding. But what is significant, in understanding the war, is not how smoothly the International-Meeting-Combined-Chiefs mechanism worked but the revelation, in its decisions, of the conflict in objectives that existed between the two allies—the conflicts which the mechanism itself arbitrated, smoothed over and served to camouflage. The conflict itself remained very real and involved these considerations:

Both the British Empire and the United States of America sought the complete destruction of the armed forces of the German, Japanese and Italian Empires.

The United States of America sought this practically without qualification—that is, sought to destroy the armed forces of the enemy in the shortest possible time, by the most direct route, with only reasonable regard for risk to life and limb and no regard whatever for the expenditure of material resources. In seeking to win the war, the United States of America had no regard, either, for political considerations—it was as willing to trade with a Darlan to secure an advantage in Africa as it was to allow Stalin an advantage in the Balkans, both acts having only to pass the single test that they speeded final victory over the armed forces of the Axis. You might sum up the American objective as: "To destroy the armed forces of the Axis PERIOD."

The British Empire also sought to destroy the armed forces of the Axis—but only by the employment of such strategy as would best further the highly complex economic and political interests of the British Empire. In the chemical sense of the word, there is simply no such thing as a "pure" British military objective—or at least there is no such thing in any military action larger than a skirmish. The British *always* mix political with military motives.

I am not here debating the relative merits of the two approaches. I am seeking simply to report factually—to stay within the limits of what seemed incontrovertible to us in England (by December, 1943) on the basis of our experience.

For six months we had been studying the strategy of the war as a whole, and following the actions that resulted from the Big Time international decisions. It was our job to understand the military nature of the war and, in conjunction with our allies, we were engaged in mounting the greatest invasion in history. By December, 1943, the American Army had had the experience of two years of war, including the successful campaigns in Africa and Sicily and the beginning of the Italian campaign. That this fundamental conflict between American and British policy existed, was now beyond dispute. It was simply a fact of nature—a military obstacle, if you like, which as military planners we had to take into consideration.

As the focus narrowed to the European sphere, the conflict between British and American objectives was seen to be primarily a conflict over whether the principal road into Europe should be via the Mediterranean or across the English Channel.

The history of this conflict is a history of almost monotonous repetition. In an "historic conference" it is agreed to strike at the heart of the German Empire across the British Channel. The conference breaks up but instead of the forces of both nations proceeding, without let or hindrance, to the accomplishment of this objective, something quite different happens. The conferees meet again and a second time it is decided to put the trans-Channel invasion first. The conferees lock their brief cases and depart, and again events mysteriously conspire to postpone preparations for the trans-Channel adventure. And *again* the Chiefs of State and Staff meet, and *again* there is enthusiasm for coming to grips with the enemy at once—and *again*, the meeting ended, somehow, someway, something happens to discourage action.

The monotony does not end here. In every case, the substitution for the trans-Channel effort turns out to be another effort in the Mediterranean area. Specifically:

Early in 1942, the Chiefs of State agreed that a trans-Channel invasion should be mounted that fall. When the American Navy said it was not ready to take on the commitment of ferrying the forces across, the American Army stepped into the breach and General Somervell set up the Engineer Amphibian Command at Cape Cod to gather, man, and maintain the necessary fleets of landing craft. But the build-up of troops and landing craft in England had no more than begun in the summer of 1942, when the Channel invasion was judged unfeasible. But England was now filling with troops, British as well as American, and the world was crying for action. So the troops that it was not practical to transport twenty miles across the Channel were loaded in transports and taken one thousand miles across the open sea to land in Africa.

A few weeks after Pearl Harbor the President of the United States had said that the Mediterranean was a British problem, that we should concentrate on the main chance: the Continent of Europe itself. But now a whole American army turns up on the African side of the Mediterranean, embarked on a campaign that is absorbing all our resources.

When the President and the Prime Minister met again at Casablanca, the world presumed it was not to map the next step of the campaign but to determine the step *after* the next step. Actually, the armies in the field had already outrun all agreed-upon objectives. There were no orders for what to do next, or even any agreed-upon plan.

American production and mobilization were only just getting into their stride; the campaign in Africa had used everything we had ready. The campaign had originally been simply to provide useful employment for the troops we had sent to England for the abandoned trans-Channel invasion. Now it was eating us out of house and home.

The campaign in Africa would soon be over, it's true—and the troops that fought it would soon be available. But they would still be in Africa, and where was the shipping to bring them back to England for the trans-Channel invasion they had originally planned to make? There had been shipping to bring them from England to Africa but now there seemed no shipping at all to send them back from Africa to England!

So the Casablanca Conference decided to begin again at the beginning—to wait until more troops had been trained for the trans-Channel invasion and more supplies produced in America. But in the meantime the world was still clamoring for action. There was not merely the Russian demand for a second front, which had not been satisfied by the African invasion; there were also the people in America and England who were expecting a quick capitalization on the impending victory in Tunisia. And there was also the effect of the Allies' conduct of the war on the now shaky satellites of the Axis—and on such important neutrals as Sweden, Spain and Turkey, to say nothing of the morale of the occupied countries, and the people and the leaders of the uncounted millions in Asia. So when Churchill proposed *another* interim step—still "pending the Channel invasion"—Roosevelt agreed. The mountain of headlines that Casablanca had become labored mightily and six months later brought forth the Sicilian mouse.

In the conflict of military opinion over whether to take the Channel road to Germany or the long way around through the Mediterranean and the Balkans, the decision to put the northern route first was unchanged—but we had now already gone *two* steps along the southern route. When Churchill and Roosevelt met again in Washington in May, the Sicilian invasion was still in preparation. It now occupied not only all British and American forces already in Africa but (since it was an impending operation) it had priority on such additional military strength as we were able to create and, as we've seen, on convoy space to carry it to the scene of the battle.

This last is a particularly important consideration because the convoy route from America to Africa is so very much longer than the route from America to Great Britain. A prime consideration in the Americans' original enthusiasm for the Channel invasion, of course, was the fact that the shores of France represented the nearest point at which we could strike the Axis forces directly. In mounting a trans-Channel invasion, American shipping was more than twice as effective as in mounting an invasion in the Mediterranean; the same ship could carry twice as much to England as to Africa, make twice as many round trips in the same length of time. Moreover a *British* army in England requires no shipping at all to equip itself with what is built in England; in Africa it has to live entirely on what the convoys bring.

So when, for a third time, an "historic conference" reaffirmed its unshakable determination to put the trans-Channel invasion first, it had to face the fact that its "concession invasion" of Sicily was draining all the resources England and America could produce and transport *—so that in May the conferees had no choice, if they were to name a D-day at all, but to name it a full year away. By then American production of men, machines and ships might reach such fantastic dimensions that it could support *two* efforts—one in the far away Mediterranean and the other in northwest Europe. Poor old Pacific—the Mediterranean was fixing it for that theater, too!

To follow the story further, you have now to leave the "historic conferences" and consider the kind of thing that goes on between them. The invasion of Sicily was specifically defined as an invasion with a limited objective—as pointed out, it was hoped that with Sicily in our hands, the Italians would give up the ghost. This would be nice politically and provide us with air bases. But no sooner has the invasion been auspiciously begun than the cry is on to let it inch a few miles up the toe of the Italian boot. This is agreed to by the Combined Chiefs of Staff, with the specific proviso that the Mediterranean armies are to go just far enough to clear the gunfire from the Straits of Messina—and no, *no*, NO farther. But at this moment in history, the Italian Government does indeed capitulate and the Sicilian invasion—which was known

* Over a thousand ocean-going vessels were required for the assault phase of the Sicilian invasion alone.

by the code name of HUSKY—fulfills the mission assigned to it at the "historic conference."

This, then, should be a happy ending not only to HUSKY but to the whole Mediterranean diversion. With Sicily taken and Italy out of the war, the victorious Allied armies and air forces—and fleets of assault landing craft—should be immediately available for the trans-Channel invasion to which everyone is committed. No one thinks seriously that the Germans, with defeated Italy on their hands, are in any position to strike a counterblow in the Mediterranean—a counterblow which would have to be an amphibian adventure against Sicily or the faraway coast of Africa. The Italian fleet is now in Allied hands, and the British have airtight control of the inland sea. So, leaving a small defensive garrison in the Sicilian hills, whole armies and air forces may proceed to England, followed by their landing craft—and in England they will all be vastly enriched by the shipping that is released when the lifeline to America is thus shortened.

But none of these things happen.

Why?

It is September 8, 1943, and the conferees at Quebec have just dispersed. There will not be another international conference until November in Cairo. So the Chiefs of Staff of the two nations, each on its own, and acting together as the Combined Chiefs of Staff, and all three bodies appealing to both Chiefs of State, somehow between them manage to authorize the Mediterranean Theater to continue its advance into Italy. This time it is to go as far as Naples and no further, the Germans having inconsiderately moved into Rome in some force and chased our advance negotiators out. Naples requires another amphibious operation, which is made at Salerno—with appropriate loss of landing craft due to enemy action and wear and tear—and a commensurate increase in the amount of supplies which must now be diverted to the Mediterranean to run out the hit.

The Johnnies-Come-Lately proved they had come lately, all right, when they failed to understand what was happening to them that summer in England, following the firm decision to let nothing bar our way to the invasion of Europe. It is curious that Mr. Harry Hopkins, who at the August meeting commented on world shortage of landing craft, should still have been surprised in October when I reported to him that landing craft were in short supply in the Channel!

The deciding factor in September's decision to continue into Italy—the decision which was made without benefit of an "historic conference"—was the weight of the British Prime Minister and the British Chiefs of Staff. Long after the war was all over Marshall was still reflecting his misgivings when he wrote in his famous report that ". . . it was our purpose to avoid the creation in Italy of a vacuum into which the resources of the cross-Channel operation would be dissipated as the Germans had bled themselves in the North African campaign." Marshall gave the statement prominence by making it the final conclusion of his paper on the strategic concept of the whole war.

The sand is now running out of the Italian glass and, in narrative, I am now past December of 1943 and into the historic year of 1944. Naples has fallen, after bloody fighting. Again "just one more" objective is named in Italy—this time Rome itself. With Rome, the Mediterranean Theater says, we will be content.

It is now late January. The first of May, the date set for the trans-Channel invasion, is hardly more than three months away. The landing craft that will have to carry it are not built yet. No one even knows whether they will be completed in time. Yet one more amphibious operation is mounted and launched in the Mediterranean! It sails up the coast and lands at Anzio. This one is Winston Churchill's own personal undertaking. He has thought of it while recovering from pneumonia at Marrakech, in Africa, and it has been put together in a scant three weeks. The plan is that the landing force is to be joined by a column striking overland through Cassino and the hills. Within a week after the landing at Anzio on January 22, the Supreme Commander in the Mediterranean, the field Commanders-in-Chief in the Mediterranean, the Chiefs of Staff of the two nations and their respective governments all know that the Allied offensive in Italy has been stopped cold. The land column has been halted in the ruins at Cassino; the amphibious operation has been contained at Anzio. In the name of prestige, now, we will hang on at Anzio; and we will battle on through the pass at Cassino—until, many terrible months and many thousands of dead later, the link-up is finally made.

The campaign never made military sense. In the end there was not even any politico-military sense left to it. When in June we broke through into the port of Cherbourg, we found the streets plastered with a highly decorative German propaganda poster which showed a snail crawling up the toe of the Italian boot. From the snail's horns flew a British and an American flag, and the caption explained that in Italy a real snail could indeed have traveled faster than the Allied armies.

What seems to have happened, historically, is that the British quarterback, bent on lugging the ball over the goal line of the Balkans, was tackled first by Roosevelt who hung on, successfully slowing down the runner but being himself carried almost to the five-yard line. There, in December at Teheran, Stalin too jumped aboard the flying runner and brought him almost, but not quite, to his knees—by making the Channel invasion a put-up-or-shut-up proposition. But with Stalin and Roosevelt both on his back, Churchill was still able to continue a yard or two further. Ironically it took Hitler himself, on the one-yard line at Anzio, to bring the British ball carrier to earth—and to seal his own doom in the ruins of Berlin a little over a year later. If Hitler had let the landing at Anzio succeed, he might have caused the final abandonment of the Channel invasion—and postponed the end of the war a year.

Just to show that the British are a great people and may be down but are never, never out, the British Chiefs and their commanders still managed to scrape together enough troops and supplies to put on one final offensive in Italy in the very last days of the war. "Scraped together" is the accurate way of putting it, for Field Marshal Alexander used Poles, French, Brazilians, Canadians and, of course, Americans as well as British, to inch his way up the Apennine Mountains. There in late April of 1945 he was able to cross the Po and get within striking distance of Trieste before the whistle blew. Trieste is the doorstep to the Balkans.

What was back of the Britons' passionate preoccupation over the Balkan route into Germany, I leave for later conclusions. The coming campaign in western Europe was to throw light on it. For the present, it is sufficient to say that by the end of 1943, this preoccupation was established beyond dispute. The Balkan route was a positive magnet towards which, however you jiggled it, the needle of British strategy swung.

This preoccupation was in the beginning, and remained until the end, a constant force, always in conflict with American military strategy in the European Theater. It carried the British State to such lengths that the Prime Minister himself even coined a deceptive phrase to popularize it—putting in circulation the notion that the most ornery and easily defended mountain barriers on the Continent constituted "the soft underbelly of Europe."

Churchill's desires were so intense that they often carried him over the boundary lines of truth—as when, to get American aid at the beginning of the war, he diverted history with a single phrase—spoken to a confused America: "Give us the tools and we'll finish the job." Churchill, and everyone else concerned, knew quite well that, short of the then undiscovered atom bomb, there were no tools in the world which would have enabled England to finish the job alone. And there was no reason why England should have been asked to.

The British had a positive desire to throw the combined weight of Anglo-American forces against the Balkans. At the same time, by the end of 1943, it was equally clear that they also had strong negative reasons for not wanting to cross the Channel.

Here at least they were not without friends on the American side of the conference table. The Channel invasion, per se, had powerful enemies in high places, in America as well as in England.

The first were the higher-ups in the American Air Forces. General Arnold, who headed the American air arm and was also a member of the Combined Chiefs of Staff, still believed that air power could bomb Germany into surrender—if only he could talk enough men, matériel and priorities out of the rest of the war effort. He and his generals, and his public relations officers, fought the invasion—subtly but definitely—by pressing for ever greater expansion of the air arm. They stood constantly for delay and postponement, to give themselves time to get the fleets that were building and training into the air and over Germany. Their motives seemed a mixture of sincere enthusiasm for their weapon (in the Billy Mitchell tradition) and intense personal ambitions. Playing military politics, they felt that if they could subdue Germany by air alone, the air arm would automatically become the senior service.

In fairness, no man yet knows whether they could have done it—whether the Germans could have continued to wage war with, say, five thousand heavy bombers a day over Germany. Even by the time of the invasion, the largest fleets were hardly more than a thousand four-engined aircraft strong. The Air Force people never got more than a percentage of what they asked, but a year before Normandy they were already far and away the strongest American military force in England and they continued to ask to be allowed to carry the ball at the expense of the other services—which indeed would have been unnecessary if they had been able to prove they were right.

The American Navy was even less friendly to the invasion than the American Air Force. The Navy is the most highly integrated and, in any catch-as-catch-can argument, the ablest debater of the American services. It knows its own mind and its representatives speak with one voice. The Pacific was its war. It had no real interest in the invasion of Europe, which meant the Atlantic. The Atlantic was a British party—a party to which the American Navy was not invited and to which it contributed grudgingly and critically. Because the Pacific was the Navy's war, its heart was not in its approval of the world strategy of defeating Germany first.

This reluctance to give to the European Theater was greatly aggravated by the intense personal and professional distaste of the American Navy for the British Navy, which the Americans considered stupid, obsolete and vastly overrated.

There isn't the faintest suggestion intended in these remarks that the United States Navy intentionally sabotaged the invasion of Europe. They went along with Roosevelt's decision to put the defeat of Germany first. They were "good soldiers"—and good sports. Eventually they even made major contributions. But they never really got into the fight for American interests in the European Theater at the conference tables and, vis-à-vis the British, Admiral King and the other top American admirals were the strongest, smartest and surest fighters we had. The British were scared of them; they never licked the United States Navy.

The Navy's heart not being in the European invasion also meant that the American Army had actually to fight the American Navy to get, first, the landing craft and, finally, the naval fire power for the invasion itself.

For reasons involving prestige, the Navy had conducted a successful campaign, just before the decision to invade Europe had been made, to keep the Army out of the landing craft business—the Army, as we've seen, had been planning to carry troops across the Channel in its own bottoms in 1942. In 1943, therefore, the Army was at practically the complete mercy of the British Navy in the matter of getting its troops ferried from England to France. This put the British in a position positively and finally to control the scale of the assault—by naming the number of craft they could make available for it. The only way to break this bottleneck was to get assistance from the United States Navy—and the shipbuilding facilities in the United States, which the Navy officially controlled. This bottleneck was broken at the last moment. But the Navy's negative attitude constituted a major obstruction for many months.

The other American services were not the only opponents in Washington with whom the Army had to contend. Certain individuals who advised or influenced Roosevelt could also be counted on to throw their weight against the invasion. I cannot put my finger on them by name or motive, but I do know from indirect evidence that they existed. The American headquarters in England presumed at the time that hesitant counsel in Washington was a carom shot from the British cue. I doubt that; there is always plenty of hesitancy and confusion in Washington. But whatever their motives, there were important people at home who contributed a note of sharp indecision and timidity which was still sounding as late as sixty days before the invasion took off. Only Roosevelt's own great will stilled them.

What is easy to forget, now that it's all over, is that there was plenty of highly responsible *military* advice around during 1943 to the effect that the successful invasion of Fortress Europa was demonstrably impossible. In their struggle to make it happen, the

Johnnies-Come-Lately were not only naive and unsophisticated; they were also brash or brave, depending on your point of view.

This real worry about whether a trans-Channel invasion was militarily either practical or advisable supported the British in their special pleading against it.

Like all good cases, the British military case against invading Europe could be argued from many points of view and each argument led to the same conclusions. One argument was that the British wanted to win the war with a minimum of casualties and, quite sincerely, they felt that they could not storm the shores of France, and battle the German Army into defeat without suffering calamitous losses. Now, every nation would like to win its war with as few casualties as possible. The British desire to save bloodshed, however, was something special and peculiar to their problem. This was the line of reasoning that put a special premium on the avoidance of bloodshed:

The British dwell very realistically on their political and economic failures during the 1920's and 1930's. Enough of the most thoughtful of the British to make a kind of intellectual power bloc believe that these failures were the direct result of losses incurred on the field of battle in World War I. It is a real and vital part of the British leadership principle that the aristocracy risks its life in battle and maintains its leadership in crises by the display of personal courage. Moreover, the leadership in England is drawn from a very narrow class base—considering the size and resources of the Empire, from a fantastically small number of chosen individuals, specially educated in England for their task. The concept of rising from the ranks to the peerage in England is a real and important compromise but even with such talent as filters up from the lower and middle classes to the top, the group that makes the crucial decisions affecting the lives of 550 million inhabitants of the British Empire is almost infinitesimal.

The British are therefore in a very real dilemma if they have to fight too much of a war themselves. Their principle of personal leadership by the upper classes gets too many of these tiny few killed. Until another generation grows up, they have not enough trained and qualified leaders in little Britain to run their world show—or so they feel. British losses in France in 1914-18 really were calamitous among the young aristocrats—and as the British aristocrats were killed off and their places were taken by the ablest members of the middle class, these in turn suffered high losses.

The British, then, laid their mistakes of the 1920's and 1930's in important part to the fact that they let too many Britons get killed in World War I. They felt there had literally been a generation lost. They acquired, for this reason, a deep conviction that the leadership of the British Empire by a small group of residents of the British Isles could not stand another decimation. The losses in air and sea warfare were bad enough for them but prolonged and bloody ground warfare was something else again. The Government of England dreaded it as an individual dreads the impending effect of a fatal disease.

Another equally cogent way of putting the British case against the invasion ran this way:

In the fall of 1940, the Empire had had the narrowest squeak in its entire history. It had survived against seemingly impossible odds—and miraculously. In surviving, it had found its soul. Its inner insecurity—which was the cause (or the result) of its failure in allowing World War II to materialize—was gone and it was really united under Churchill's personal leadership.

The comeback from the awful days that followed Dunkirk had been spectacular. In the summer of 1940, the Germans were an odds-on bet to conquer England and to destroy the Empire as such; by the summer of 1943, with the Russians on their way back from Stalingrad and America in the war at last, those who had historical perspective felt that England had pulled through. Under these circumstances, why take a chance? What did it matter whether the war took one year more or five—or even ten? In the long race of history, the British horse was in.

This case can also be—and often was—put more cynically by Americans and Europeans. The cynics felt that from 1942 on, the British were spending Russian lives and American dollars and getting a profitable banker's percentage on both. So what's the hurry? The profitable percentage on Russian lives lay in the fact that the longer the Russians fought, the weaker the Russians would be at the end of the war and the better chance the British had, vis-à-vis the Russians, in the postwar struggle for the domination of Europe. The percentage on the American dollars was even simpler, for the whole British war economy was drawing heavily on lend-lease which the British Government, despite its later "surprise" at the termination of lend-lease, knew very well was purely a military arrangement. Never in the history of two nations has one borrowed from another on such terms.

There is always the danger of becoming too subtle in appraising, or of over-analyzing, an individual's—let alone a nation's—motives. There is still another way of arranging the Briton's military argument which, while completely consistent with all of the above, has a larger content of what Americans would call simple horse sense.

The net of the *experienced* military advice during the summer of 1943 was certainly against hasty invasion of northwest Europe. The betting odds on a successful landing—and this is as important as it is inescapable—were on the Germans. German armies had yet to be beaten on the field of battle except at the end of outrageously extended supply lines—as at Stalingrad and in Africa. Up until World War II, *no* amphibian invasion in modern war had *ever* been successful.* *In* World War II, prior to the assault

---

* In the month of August, in 1942, a Commando-type force, largely of Canadians, under the command of Admiral Lord Louis Mountbatten, crossed the English Channel and forced the heavily fortified harbor of Dieppe. They landed tanks, fought their way some miles inland and stayed on the Continent of Europe for approximately twenty-four hours. Presently, what was left of the raiders fought their way back to their boats and returned to England. They suffered extremely heavy casualties—and began a military controversy which raged with varying intensity from that date until the successful invasion of Normandy in June of 1944.

Was Dieppe a success or a failure?

The British were proud of the heroism displayed at Dieppe, but often, during the planning of the later invasion, took the position that Dieppe had demonstrated how difficult it was to establish a beachhead on the far shore of the Channel. When the Americans became too optimistic, wounded veterans from Dieppe were frequently introduced into conferences to remind us of the hazards we talked so glibly of overcoming. The Dieppe experience was quoted so frequently to prove that things could *not* be done that some Americans came to believe that the purpose of the raid had been to furnish arguments against any further attempts at landing in France.

General Devers' planners, however, studying the record of Dieppe, always used the same facts to prove that the landing had been not a failure but a

on Europe, the amphibian invasions of Africa and Sicily had been helped by lucky breaks—and had met only inferior enemies (politically undecided French and tired Italians) or had landed on undefended coasts (in Africa), or had been favored by the calm water of the Mediterranean. The German defenses on the Atlantic coast were thought to be even better prepared than they were. The enemy had the labor and material of a continent available to improve them. They were defended by land-based aircraft; whole German armies were unemployed and available to throw against any breach.

Therefore, with the Allies winning the war—with the tide running our way—what reasonable man would advise such a hazardous adventure as a trans-Channel invasion? Failure would certainly turn the whole tide of the war back against us, depriving Europe of its last vestige of hope. It would cause us to start our vast military preparations again from the very beginning—and once our invasion had been defeated, the huge German armies in western Europe would be released for employment against the beginning-to-tire Russians.

It is obvious that there were just as strong arguments *for* the invasion—the American arguments which moved Roosevelt and his American advisers.

The gist of these arguments was that the Germans could be had —by strength and boldness—and that it was not safe to leave them to their own devices with a continent to play with and the worst of intentions. This was a sound argument, even without the humanitarian consideration of ending the suffering of untold millions on the Continent. It was also backed by the supply considerations already noted: France was the nearest territory the enemy held to America; if we could open a front there, we had only the short Atlantic crossing to make to supply it—and our other war in the Pacific was languishing for want of shipping. Moreover, the whole American war effort, stemming from and based on our national character, was dependent on quick success—on rising rapidly to

success. They pointed out a lodgment had been secured by a relatively weak task force, and argued that the excessive casualties were the result of the assault not being followed up—as, of course, it would be in an invasion planned to stick.

deliver mortal blows to our enemies. And after the European war, we had the war in the Orient still to finish.

This was the American case that eventually prevailed. It was also the American case to which the British never completely resigned themselves. Repeatedly they agreed to it on the record—and immediately began arranging things so that it should not prevail at all. By December, 1943, it was clear that this was not an opinion but a simple statement of fact. The returns were all in; it was that kind of a war we were fighting.

The logical question an American officer in London had then to ask himself was why the British were so effective at it. By every physical yardstick—men, money, and matériel—we were the senior partner. And we always won the decision in the international conference. Why did we, as a nation, have so much trouble making these decisions stick?

In general terms, the answer is that in a struggle between the strength, vitality and ignorance of youth and the wit, experience and stubbornness of age, the latter are often effective. We were paying the price for our youth. Our problem involved intimate co-operation with a foreign power and we were wholly inexperienced in how to deal with it. Not just we, the Johnnies-Come-Lately, but we the Americans at home and abroad.

Our military men were better educated than their British opposite numbers in science—and were not educated at all in diplomacy, parliamentary procedure, or presentation. They were without background in dealing with the British—many of them had never even met an Englishman—and the British are a different people from ours and go about things differently. The British, on the other hand, had a large body of internationally educated, politically informed soldiers and civilians to draw from in putting together a team to deal with us. They were used to dealing with foreigners, and to getting their way with them—foreigners in their own Empire, such as Canadians and Australians, and foreigners of other nationalities. They had a hundred years of experience behind them. We had almost literally none at all.

But the British had even more tangible assets with which to offset our strength. The greatest of these always seemed to me their control of the information on which military decisions had to be made.

Decisions at "historic conferences" are no better than the information on which they are based. The British had an enormous edge on us in this respect, first in presentation, but more impor tantly in basic research and source material.

There are two kinds of information which are important in making war. The first is information about the enemy and the second is information about one's own resources. In matters touching the European Theater, the British had a 100 per cent airtight, hermetically sealed monopoly on Intelligence about the enemy—and this monopoly was made official in an early International-Conference-Combined-Chiefs-of-Staff decision giving the British sole responsibility for enemy Intelligence in Europe. How many divisions did the Germans have, what was their strength, what was their capability in any given situation? What was Germany's tank production, how many aircraft a month was she building, on what fields were they stationed? What was Germany's supply of oil? How good a general was Von Kluge? What did the German defenses on the Atlantic coast consist of? The British were the sole authority on these matters. They were sole and *unquestioned* authority, first, because we had no military Intelligence on the Continent worthy of the name and, second, because the British had—and an excellent one, too.

There were also certain areas of British Intelligence to which we had no access at all. This was not generally known, and if asked directly the British would deny it, but—and I state this as a positive fact—the British circulated documents amongst themselves labeled with a code word known only to them. This code word meant for "eyes of British officers only." British Intelligence operates on the sound and ingenious principle that the best way to keep a secret is to reveal 90 per cent of it in such a way that your opponents believe they have the whole story. When your opponents believe they have the whole story, they are persuaded to relax, to be content with what they have and to pry no further. This principle they applied in their dealings with us. They made a clean breast of everything—apparently. Actually, they always kept a vital residue to themselves, circulating it for eyes of qualified British officers only.

Intelligence was always the Empire's ace in the hole. When British fortunes were at the lowest ebb, it was their Intelligence organization which saved them. After Dunkirk, they lived literally by their wits—disguising their weakness from the Germans, bluffing skillfully with inferior forces. These were achievements of British Intelligence, which knew its business and was far and away the ablest of the principal British staff sections.

With a monopoly on Intelligence, the British could, in the beginning, arrange to get almost any answer they wanted to a military equation—by the weight they chose to put on the equation's most important variable: the enemy's capabilities and intentions. For instance, throughout the war, British Intelligence consistently, and without exception, underestimated German ability to produce, and thus (with an assist from the American Air Forces) encouraged the notion that an invasion was unnecessary because the bombing of Germany would "soon" bring the Reich to its knees.

One of the COSSAC planners' greatest contributions to military archives was a monster plan known as RANKIN. RANKIN was a plan for movement into Germany in the event of sudden collapse. One month after the "final decision to cross the Channel" had been made in Washington, COSSAC planners put on paper the statement—based, of course, exclusively on British Intelligence—that so near was Germany's collapse that RANKIN should have priority over OVERLORD for their attention.

At the same time that British Intelligence *under*estimated German capacity to wage war, it further discouraged the invasion idea by *over*estimating the strength of German fortifications on the Channel coast. German generals captured at the end of the war referred to our pre-invasion estimates of their strength on the coast as victories for German propaganda.

It was not until the American Army had fought in France for many months that it had the beginnings of an organization capable of keeping its commanders informed of the enemy situation on the basis of its own source material. Thus not only every international conference but also every decision concerning

Europe made between conferences was dependent on British Intelligence.

In the field of information concerning our own joint resources —Allied resources—the British had a similar airtight monopoly on information about *their* contribution to the whole, *their* resources and capabilities. The rule they established was that *their* appraisals of *their* capabilities were not debatable. That is to say, if the British set down that they could put twelve divisions and no more in the field at such and such a time—that was that. We might be of the opinion that, if the British rearranged their resources, they could strengthen their army in England at the expense of their garrison troops in distant parts of the Empire; we got short shrift if we advanced the idea. *That* was British business. So also it was none of our business if early in the war they chose to concentrate fighter planes in England at the expense of the Mediterranean Theater—or abandon daylight bombing in favor of night, accommodating their whole national training and production programs to the decision.

These considerations gave them absolute control over *three-quarters* of all information on which international strategic decisions were based. That is, control over *all* enemy information plus control over *half* of the Allied information.

They went one step further: while British appraisals of their own capability could not be questioned, the British reserved the right to argue *our* appraisals of *our* capabilities. They claimed this right on the basis of their greater experience—and got it, at least in appraisals of ground force and air capabilities. The American Navy was more inclined to consider its business its own.

This is not to say that in conference the British told us what we had or had not, or were or were not able to do. What they did was to use their accepted right to express themselves, to argue, to attempt to persuade. In the issue of day versus night bombing, they went even further. They first tried to persuade us to come along with their night program, then argued for our splitting our policy and, finally, when Arnold remained firm in his conviction that day bombing of Germany *would* work, they tried to cut him down by sending an officer with specially prepared exhibits of photographs to work on President Roosevelt's

Cabinet—as well as to persuade his wife and any possibly influential friends—in an attempt to get the President to overrule his Chief of Staff for Air.

It was the fashion among a number of senior American officers to feel, when we did not get our way, that we must have been sold out by the President himself. The conservative bias of many in high ranks made them mistrust the New Dealer in Roosevelt and the consensus amongst these was that the President was a sucker for Churchill. All the evidence is to the contrary.

With the superior position the British had through their control of the factual material on which decisions were based, and with the terrific moral and psychological superiority with which they entered the partnership—based on the sacrifices they had made, and their status as veterans, as the ones who had learned the right answers in the hard school of experience—the extraordinary thing seems to me not how little weight Roosevelt exerted but how much.

The whole question descends rapidly to personalities. Even before accepting the concept of combining the British-American Chiefs of Staff into a single body, Roosevelt had made his personal decision of how he would run the war that history had forced on him. His decision was to select his military advisers at once and to stick to them. He chose his commanders before any of them had fought a battle in World War II. He gave them *carte blanche*. Lincoln fumbled for his generals in the Civil War; Wilson's commanders never got in the Big Time for the British and French had fought the war too long before our entry and Pershing's army was both too green and too poorly equipped (it had to borrow artillery and had no air force of its own). But Roosevelt chose Marshall, Arnold and King and stuck by them through thick and thin, refusing to tolerate criticism of them either abroad or at home.

Admiral King is said to have opened the first meeting of the Combined Chiefs of Staff by announcing flatly that he had served under the British in the last war and now wanted it understood that he would never serve under them again, or permit any of his ships to serve under them "if he could help it." The British sought for several years to find some way to discredit King or to persuade

Roosevelt to replace him with a more co-operative Navy Chief of Staff. Roosevelt never wavered in his loyalty or confidence.

General Arnold came to grips with the Royal Air Force soon after we entered the war on the question I have already touched on—the question of whether precision bombing by day was feasible in Germany. The British tried every trick and argument they knew to persuade Roosevelt to overrule him and to build and train the American heavy bomber arm for night bombing—so that it could be integrated with the RAF which had converted to night bombing when its daylight raids on Germany had become too expensive. Arnold persisted, and developed a long-range fighter to go with the Forts on their missions. He also preserved the autonomy of the American air arm in England. He did this with Roosevelt backing him all the way.

Marshall is more of an enigma. There is no question but that, as Hopkins held, Marshall debated ground force problems with the Prime Minister as an equal, which no other general in either army succeeded in doing. But for some reason he was not as alert or as aggressive in backing the American ground forces' point of view as Arnold and King were in air and sea matters. Perhaps it was because, as the prototype of the sound American professional officer, he was honest, hard-headed, sincerely patriotic, but also literal minded, a little naive, and inclined to disbelieve that anyone whom he knew personally would really try to get his way with him by devious means. But whatever the reason, Marshall was nowhere near as alert as King and Arnold to the opportunities presented by the combined undertaking for one partner to get the better of the other by means other than a straightforward man-to-man argument across the table. The blunt fact is that Marshall often got pushed around.

Whatever the reason for this, there is no record that Marshall was anything but mildly confused and irritated as the succession of events through 1942 and 1943 continued to end periodically with the main effort of the Allied forces in Europe directed towards the Mediterranean again, and always shortly after Roosevelt had secured an agreement that the main effort should be expended across the Channel.

If, as Harry Hopkins prophesied he would, Marshall himself had taken the post of Supreme Allied Commander the subsequent chapters in the conquest of Europe might have been considerably different. In direct contact with opponents of his point of view, Marshall was no push-over. The man who did get the job is another story and to tell it you have to go back again—for one quick last look at the campaign which began our shooting war on the other side of the Atlantic.

Eisenhower's story starts with the invasion of Africa and the defeat of the Germans in Tunisia—and in the beginnings of the institution of the Combined Staff.

The Combined Chiefs of Staff, made up of the chiefs of the three great branches of both countries, in intimate touch with the Chiefs of State, was one thing. The Combined Staff in the field was another. Early in the game, the Combined Anglo-American field headquarters was recognized by the British as an especially effective device by which to control the situation and to offset, or to make up for, the about-to-be-overpowering resources of their ally. It was clear that if British generals were to run the battle—and the British saw no reason why they shouldn't —concessions would have to be made to American public opinion. After all, the Americans were putting up men and matériel and were even paying their allies' bills. The most effective concession then—the concession which would give them the best press for the least price in real control—would be to give the Americans the head man and, as they say in business when they make a Chairman of the Board out of a President they don't need—kick him upstairs. Besides, there was work for the Chairman of the Board to do—handling (and, if he slipped, taking the rap for) the more delicate of the political situations.

The advantages of having a front man were first demonstrated in North Africa, where the victorious Generals Alexander and Montgomery ran the military show and the American Supreme Allied Commander, Eisenhower, handled the hot political pokers and took the bows. At this stage of the game it didn't matter much to the Empire which American general got the spotlight. At the time, the British must have thought of themselves as still looking over American candidates for the larger responsibilities yet to come.

In the topsy-turvy command schmozzle which was Africa then
—while the Americans were still changing troop commanders
weekly, and the troops themselves were green and uncertain—
Eisenhower left Alexander in charge and defended his actions to
ambitious American generals in the field and to the War Department at home. He also saw to it that the press was handled so that
it came out all right in the papers.

Throughout the campaign, Eisenhower's preoccupation was
handling the French. De Gaulle, Giraud and Darlan were successive nightmares which the British graciously left him to deal
with on his own. When he succeeded without fatal scandal, he
was made.

The British, who had been standoffish, now began to back
Eisenhower in earnest, and to build him up, in the field and in
meetings of the Combined Chiefs, and in the kind of confidential
Capital talk that can either make or break a public figure. They
had a good man. As a diplomat, he was willing to take responsibility and able to get away with it; as a soldier he minded his
own business. He was tough enough to bat down a Patton for
being too aggressive about seeking autonomy for the American
command. He could be very abrupt with his subordinates. He was
also willing to fight for the institution of the merged Anglo-
American staff, despite unanimous opposition to it from American
commanders who had led troops under a combined command and
thought it clumsy and ineffective. And he stood well enough with
Marshall so that he was effective and won his fight. Marshall, three
thousand miles away, believed in him. But in the field Eisenhower
drifted gradually apart from his associates in the American Army,
keeping his own small staff of officers under his own Chief of
Staff Bedell Smith. He had become a political general.

All this is said without prejudice to later history. This was the
way things were in Africa, when the British were very definitely
in the military saddle, with a tight hold on the reins—and Eisenhower, like all the other American generals in the field, was
confused and inexperienced. Like every other American commander, he was groping to find his true position in relationship to
the whole undertaking, trying to find out what was expected of

him by Marshall and how he could adjust himself to the alien world he lived in and become effective in it.

Among the American generals, Eisenhower was immediately characterized by his shrewdness and his cold disinterest in any-thing but his job of serving both General Marshall and these strange new British characters who were molding his future. Other American generals were excited by the battle, were swayed by prejudices and personal loyalties. Eisenhower could take the battles that others were fighting in his stride, had no warm feelings to disturb him and could keep his eye always on the main chance.

So, in Eisenhower, the British found the man they needed to handle hot political situations—and to stand off the more aggres-sive American field commanders for them.

For nothing, the British also got a reasonably good administrator —no man born of woman is a good enough administrator to make a combined staff run efficiently—and a man who was more than amenable to argument. Eisenhower was by nature a conciliator and an arbitrator. At the time he even described himself as "not a general, really, but by nature a businessman."

Having accepted the title of Supreme Commander in the Medi-terranean, Eisenhower let Field Marshal Alexander—Alex—run the strictly military show throughout the Tunisian campaign. When the invasion of Sicily came, Eisenhower again fought the Ameri-can Joint Chiefs of Staff—for the resources to help the British to keep going up the rocky road to the Balkans, even though the decision had again been made to move the main effort back to the Channel. And again he was successful for them.

Thus tested in battle (high level conference type), when Te-heran came along, Eisenhower was the Empire's logical candidate —and the British popped him into the job of Supreme Com-mander in England. It was confidently expected by London that he would repeat his Mediterranean performance, stick to politics and leave the management of the war in the field to those with more experience while reaping the appropriate rewards and ele-vations in the public's eyes.

Omar Bradley's story likewise begins in Africa. Bradley's story begins with the American defeat at Kasserine Pass.

The landings in Africa had been militarily uncertain victories over uncertain opponents. The operation had been a real triumph, but a naval and a logistical triumph, a triumph in organizing and conveying so large a force so many thousands of miles.

Africa was also a triumph for military sleight of hand, the whole movement having been successfully disguised, and its intentions distorted.* In the confusion of surprise, the invaders came within a few miles of taking the port of Bizerte the first week—they reached a hillcrest within sight of the city but by that time were out of ammunition and gas. If they had taken the port of Bizerte, Rommel's supply column would have been lopped clean in two with a single stroke.

* There were actually two reasons why an American had been named Supreme Commander in this British theater. The first was the courtesy it accorded to American public opinion. The second, and perhaps the more important, was the mask it provided to disguise the campaign against the French in Africa as an American show. This was a wholly legitimate, politico-military maneuver aimed at confusing our enemies, saving casualties and insuring success. Before the invasion of Africa, it was accepted as an axiom that the French would fight the British but would hesitate to take on the Americans.

There was nothing secret about this and nothing really hypocritical—since it had all been agreed on in advance—nothing hypocritical except to the Vichy French, who were after all our enemies. Through Pétain, the Germans had made great capital of the British shelling of the French fleet at Oran and, to repeat, it was assumed in the high level planning of the African invasion that the French troops would be more reluctant to shoot Americans than to shoot British soldiers. It was for this reason that even the British assault waves were to include token forces of Americans carrying American flags—the whole enterprise in fact was decked in red, white and blue bunting as part of the "cover plan."

Similarly, on the diplomatic front, it was important to the British to have someone else do the talking for them with the French. A deal with the local Vichy government was always intended, and it was better that the Americans supply the fall guy if it backfired. Churchill had not only world opinion to contend with but also an uncompromising minority in his own government which was against appeasement in any form, for whatever practical purpose. When Clark and Eisenhower overdid it, Churchill simply called up Roosevelt and the latter made it clear that the understanding was only a temporary expedient.

All this façade was, as I say, thoroughly understood as such by everyone except the enemy. No one ever seriously contemplated that Americans should really be in command in the Mediterranean Theater, which was clearly a British sphere. Our War Department had no ambition to contest their military leadership there.

When the Germans came to and began to fight for their retreat corridor—Rommel was backing away from Montgomery around the curve of the Mediterranean—they caught the furthest American columns overextended and these green troops fell back sixty miles in a panicky retreat, with hardly a shot fired at them after the opening engagement. Later the Americans regained the field at Kasserine Pass, and kept the Germans from coming through and doing a real job of destruction on the new American dumps.

Finally, the Americans in Africa, growing in strength as well as in experience, were first to hold the flank while Montgomery drove up the coast of Tunisia and later, in an especially well-organized maneuver, to pivot from their old position and strike through the mountains to collapse the Tunisian pocket itself. There they played a major part in capturing 150,000 Germans.

Bradley's story begins with the defeat at Kasserine Pass, although at the time he was not even there and had no command. It was in Africa that the American Army began the search for field commanders who could win battles. The American Army had not fought a continental battle for over twenty years and had no idea which of its generals to trust. Fredendall was the first man at bat and he struck out at Kasserine Pass. A pinch-hitter named Harmon, who is a miniature Patton and also an armored force commander, went in and got a clean base hit in the second battle at Kasserine Pass. The next batter-up was Patton, and, in effect, the Germans walked him. Patton had done well enough in the landing and his II Corps had taken El Guettar and stood off a German Panzer counterattack there. But he had been ordered by his British commander not to capitalize on the victory. He was stopped from driving on to the coast, which was only some thirty desert miles away, to let Montgomery come through. The net of it all was that Patton's box-score in Africa was still no runs, no hits, no errors.

The American Army now tried a rookie named Bradley who had been a schoolteacher and seemed like a smart fellow. In his management of the final break-through, Bradley knocked the ball over the fence.

When Rookie Bradley knocked the ball over the fence he was junior to Patton, Clark. Devers and half a dozen other candidates to the top American field job. But he had done so well—and done it so quietly and unobtrusively—that Marshall and Eisenhower put him in again in the Sicilian invasion. And again he won the ball game. He had now earned a try-out in the Big League and was the unopposed choice to command one army in France, even before the Great Appointments of Teheran.*

Bradley's successes in the Mediterranean are interesting because they gave the first indication of the kind of commander he was going to be in France. In Africa, his first success was the result of his rebuilding the morale of some very shaky troops by purposely putting them in small inconsequential actions in which he was sure they would secure easy victories. With the doughboys' morale improved by these tactics, he put his infantry through famed 609 and the other hills that made the headlines and let Harmon do the rest with his armor. Harmon went through into the German pocket so fast that he didn't even bother to stop to pick up the German headquarters he passed. When the Nazi commanders finally caught up with him to surrender, Harmon's classic remark was, "Hell, unconditional surrender ain't nearly enough."

All this Bradley had planned and directed—but it was all over so quickly, and Alex and Eisenhower gave Montgomery and his Eighth Army such a lion's share of the credit, that it passed almost unnoticed. The world knew only one fighting army at the time and that was the famed British Eighth, which had turned the tide of the war at El Alamein and chased Rommel all the way from Egypt. Without detracting from the Eighth Army's accomplishments, it was Bradley's doughs who broke through the hills for Bradley's armor to go in to make the kill.

In Sicily, Bradley executed basically British plans. It was a combined operation under a combined headquarters, directed by Alex with Monty at his elbow. Bradley landed on the left and Montgomery on the right. Montgomery was to drive up the short side, forcing his way directly to the Straits of Messina across from

---

* Patton, Bradley's senior in rank, was already an automatic choice to command another army in France. The War Department's confidence in him never wavered even after Eisenhower's clumsy attempt to hush up the soldier-slapping business ended by getting Patton a very bad press.

which lay Italy. Bradley was to swing wide, clearing the whole center of the island. Bradley's troops executed his share of the plan with such dash that there now remained no question of their or Bradley's ability—even though Bradley was still nominally only a corps commander under Patton.

Bradley had met Montgomery on the battlefield of Tunisia but they had fought on opposite sides of the German pocket. In Sicily, they were separated only by the international army boundary which divided the two armies. Their first working encounters were not fortunate. Montgomery was hung up on his flank but the Americans got away, and one of Bradley's columns was about to enter a key road-center near the middle of the island when it was halted at Montgomery's request on orders from Alex—the town in question had been earmarked for Monty.

The local American commander waited for two days outside the town and was then encouraged by Bradley to go in anyway. British generals have very strong feelings about proprietary rights to military objectives on the battlefield and unpleasant things were said. The final collapse of Sicily, however, followed shortly after when American armor, traveling the long way round, reached the Straits of Messina almost in a dead-heat with the Eighth Army coming up by the shorter coast route. Already ordered to prepare to take a command in France, Bradley left immediately thereafter and Mark Clark was dusted off to take his place in the subsequent campaign.

On Bradley's left, Patton commanded the armor that cut across Sicily to take Palermo. After a day's tough going on the beach, his columns got underway, knifed ninety miles through enemy-held territory. Patton took the German and Italian garrisons completely by surprise and his Sicilian break-away still stands as one of the most successful single actions of the war. Now the battle returns were also in on Patton—and *his* job in the field in Europe was also secure—if the Channel invasion were ever to come off.

The shifts and changes in the American field command in Africa were more than a phenomenon of the early days of the war. They revealed a policy which the American Army followed through the whole campaign in Europe. It was an insistence that a field commander deliver the goods or else. Throughout the entire war, right up to and including such spectacular victories as the Remagen Bridge, the commanders of battalions, regiments, divisions and corps were bounced summarily, not simply for losing a battle but sometimes for failing to win it fast enough or thoroughly enough. The policy was unpublicized because the army likes to take its goats into its own backyard and shear them privately.

The policy of ruthless insistence on superior performance seems to peter out above the corps level. With army commanders and higher, the War Department is much more gentle—presumably on the principle that when a man gets an army to command he has proven himself—with ten cents on the side for the adverse effect on morale (or the boss' reputation) of admitting that a mistake has been made in such an important appointment.

I think I know personally a half dozen division and corps commanders who, on their records, are qualified to lead armies. It sometimes seems unfair to soldiers in the field that more of such men don't have a chance. But we didn't have a great many armies in Europe to command and the extraordinary thing seems to me the speed and decisiveness with which the War Department, out of the fumbling that characterized the early days in Africa, selected the men who won their battles for them in Tunisia and Sicily.

Before the meeting at Teheran, the Americans had picked two candidates for commands in the field in Europe. And after Teheran, under pressure from the Russians to make up their minds, Churchill and Roosevelt agreed upon Eisenhower as the Supreme Allied Commander, and appointed three British Commanders-in-Chief, one each for land, sea and air. Thus the command slipped neatly into the groove that had been carved for that purpose in the OVERLORD plan, rolled smoothly through channels and dropped into the laps of General (and presently Sir) Bernard Montgomery, Air Chief Marshal Sir Trafford Leigh-Mallory, and Admiral of the Fleet Sir Bertram Ramsay. The invasion in the North was now theoretically on again, and it was to be, as planned, under all-British management.

5 Bigot

BACK in England, as the Teheran Conference drew to a close, the Johnnies-Come-Lately were putting the finishing touches on their work. It would soon be over for them now. Late in December, The Great Montgomery flew in and did not even bother to call up the American headquarters. Instead he went directly into the field in southern England, ordered the American troops there into assembly areas and announced to them over loudspeakers that he was now their commander.

They looked curiously at the little man. He is very small and has the soles of his shoes built up to make him seem taller. They had not realized how short he was because he usually had his picture taken standing on uneven ground so that he would look bigger and more fearsome. He wore his famous black beret and looked very fit and neat, and his high-pitched, almost shrill voice carried well over the amplifiers. He promised that he would give the Boche a bloody nose and the boys on whom the blood was to splatter applauded politely.

When January came, Jakey Devers packed his kit and flew away to Africa followed by his Chief of Staff, David Barr, and his Assistant Chief of Staff, G-3, Daniel Noce. A score or more of officers, aides and assistants followed.

Meanwhile Montgomery moved into his headquarters which was called 21st Army Group. It was in a school on the edge of London, St. Paul's, where Montgomery had once been a pupil. The lecture halls now echoed to the shuffle of boots as the con-

ferees came and went. General Bradley had set up his army headquarters on the coast at Bristol—in Clifton College, the same
quarters to which I had gone so long ago to visit the lonely corps
that had then been the American Army in the United Kingdom.
He had to send a special detachment of his officers in London to
attend Montgomery's conferences, there were so many of them.
They were now called "syndicates" because that's the way the
British do their planning. For a simple discussion, it's a committee
meeting; to work against an actual operation, it becomes a syndicate. Syndicates are just as prolific, and in London multiply just as
rapidly as committee meetings.

The other British Commanders-in-Chief, Air Chief Marshal Sir
Trafford Leigh-Mallory and Admiral of the Fleet Sir Bertram
Ramsay, were just as busy as Monty, studying the inheritances
they had received when the will was read at Teheran.

Presently Eisenhower himself arrived and the new Supreme
Allied Headquarters—this time no "Designate" about it—established itself in what had once been Ira Eaker's Eighth Air Force
Headquarters on the outskirts of London. There, the officers of
many nations gathered under a camouflage net as big as Barnum
& Bailey's main tent. It was quite a circus. The Air Corps does
well by itself, but SHAEF (Supreme Headquarters, Allied Expe-
ditionary Forces) felt it was entitled by its position to even better.
In the old Eighth Air Force Headquarters, messes, cafeterias and
snack bars expanded briskly. The first decisions made by the
Anglo-American Headquarters included an agreement that they
would draw American rather than British rations, and turn their
housekeeping over to American engineers.

Eisenhower's Chief of Staff, Bedell Smith (whose name the
British papers like to hyphenate because they think it looks better
that way), came to rule over this empire. Lady Tedder preceded
her husband from the Mediterranean Theater and was cross when
she found that Ike's sergeants had already moved into the most
suitable residence in the neighborhood of the Headquarters but
she soon found the Deputy Supreme Allied Commander adequate
accommodations. She was glad to be back in London because, she
said, the Italians were abominable people and had caused her no
end of difficulties in her housekeeping for the Air Chief Marshal.

Having opened up their establishment, Eisenhower, Tedder, Bedell Smith & Co. soon disappeared into the rarefied atmosphere of high level international doings. After all, there were resident in London a large assortment of governments-in-exile, with whose rights and privileges Eisenhower had now to concern himself. Many of them even had token battalions trained and equipped by the British. Each now wanted a role to play in the liberation of its homeland.

The problem of finding enough interpreters for SHAEF was itself no mean one. As the COSSAC planners had foreseen, it was almost a full-time job for a Supreme Headquarters just to learn the protocol for dealing with so many fancy folk. With the command set-up what it was, it now made sense that the Supreme Commander delegate responsibility for the invasion itself to his three Commanders-in-Chief. These Commanders-in-Chief now issued their own orders—sometimes over the signatures of all three or, if the matter concerned only one branch, over the signature of the particular Commander-in-Chief in charge.

The Americans' headquarters were now scattered and "the Americans" as such—as an entity, with a common point of view and policy—ceased to exist. The American supporting air forces, gathered into the presently to be famous Ninth Air Force, came under Air Chief Marshal Sir Trafford Leigh-Mallory. His staff lived on a lovely country estate at Sunningdale, about an hour from London, and reported regularly to the Air Chief Marshal. Bradley and his First Army, as we've seen, remained in Bristol with a detachment of their planners in attendance at 21st Army Group's Headquarters. Grosvenor Square now belonged to General John C. H. Lee of the Services of Supply. Lee's headquarters continued to function to get what Monty needed from America, and to co-ordinate supply problems with the appropriate representatives of the War Office and Montgomery's headquarters. The American strategic air force, which before had been integrated, policy-wise, was now off on its own under its new commander, General Doolittle. The American forces seemed indeed as dispersed and scattered as any beaten army.

Loneliest of the American headquarters was poor forgotten FUSAG—F.U.S.A.G. standing for First United States Army

Group. This was the headquarters Devers set up for the command of an American group of armies when, as, and if there should ever be one. Having then no commanding officer, it had been run by a chief of staff, whose name was Allen. After Teheran, Bradley himself was given command of it—in addition to his other duties as Commander of the First Army. At the time, the First United States Army was also known by its initials, FUSA, a fact which did nothing to dispel the confusion that arose between FUSA and FUSAG, particularly after both acquired the same commander. It was partially to avoid this confusion and partially as a security measure that when Bradley took command of the Army Group in France it came to be known as 12th Army Group—and reference to it by its initials alone was forbidden.

The odds are that when Bradley was named Commander of FUSAG, the War Department had its fingers crossed about whether he should retain the command when—and still "as and if" —FUSAG took command. It is probable that in the rush, Marshall simply put Bradley's name down for both jobs with the idea that a general of appropriate rank could take over the group when the time came. There was a backlog of eligible rank in Washington— McNair who had trained the Army, Lear, and half a dozen others —and Bradley was junior even to Patton. Bradley's juniority is a point to remember, for it was to have its effect on subsequent history. At all events, when Bradley paid his first call on FUSAG, it seemed more as a tourist than as a commander. From Bristol to past the beachhead at Normandy, he concerned himself principally with his role of Army Commander.

In the winter of 1944, the Army Group Headquarters that Bradley would one day use to command four armies in France, languished forlorn and unnoticed in little Bryanston Square, on the wrong side of the railroad track, across Marble Arch from Mayfair's Grosvenor. "Forlorn" is correct, but "unnoticed" is too strong an adjective. FUSAG was hardly in existence a month before the mention of its name in London was as good for a laugh as a mention of the Brooklyn Dodgers in a Manhattan revue—for FUSAG had no troops, no mission and, as far as anyone could see, no future.

Since most of the jokes came from British headquarters that had an interest in discouraging the establishment of an American rival, this was understandable. But the officers in FUSAG certainly did their best to give them material. In London the principal contribution they made to the war effort was an excellent mess. The headquarters was a curious institution, a mixture of veteran planners brought belatedly from Africa and fresh recruits just in from America. The latter set the atmosphere. They fussed over thousands of unnecessary details and the high point in their career came when they met the problem of how to toughen themselves for their coming life in the field. No one seemed interested in renting them any English real estate on which to camp out so, after prolonged conferences, they made their big decision. There is a strip of earth that runs the length of Bryanston Square, flanked by tall, pleasant trees. Solemnly, one day, FUSAG moved out of the converted residences along one side of Bryanston Square, set up tents under the trees and served itself lunch there. After lunch everyone moved back into his office and billets.

Poor FUSAG. The unkindest cut of all was to come in March when the Luftwaffe made its last attempt to burn London down. Where would they have to unload their fire bombs, one night, but smack on FUSAG's roof. On all the neighboring roofs there were the fire watchers of London's famed air warden service—who promptly put out *their* incendiaries. But those that lit on FUSAG's attics found no watchers. The British had, of course, withdrawn their civilians and FUSAG had not gotten around to taking its own air raid precautions. So the incendiaries burned down the headquarters' post office, some of the personnel records and the office of the headquarters' commandant and some other odds and ends. This made a beautiful bonfire and silhouetted the lovely trees in Bryanston Square; and fighting the fires no doubt helped to round out the field experience FUSAG gained on its picnic.

The raid that burned down FUSAG was of some interest to me because at the time I was living in a miniature flat in an alley just off Bryanston Square. Being an old hand at air raids—and a proper veteran of the Big Blitz of 1940—I used to like to watch air raids and usually stuck my head out of the window when the first guns went off, just to see what was cooking. Now the day before this particular raid I just happened to have spent half an hour reading a paper on the interrogation of German pilots captured in the last air raid. From these one gathered that the Luftwaffe was trying a new bombing technique against London, an imitation of the RAF's pathfinder system. I thought, that night, I'd look it over.

The first German planes to arrive, the paper had told me, would drop markers in a pattern—one row of them, at right angles to the course, to indicate the start line; then another straight line, to mark the bomb run itself; and, finally, directly over the target, the pathfinder plane would let go a very bright red flare. This would mark the spot at which the succeeding waves of planes were to aim their bombs, the target for that night.

The night of the FUSAG raid, I no sooner had my head out the window than, sure enough, everything I had read that afternoon was spectacularly demonstrated right before my eyes. Those lights would be the start line. There come the bomb run markers! I could not have been more fascinated; it was like seeing a play one had just finished reading.

It was at that moment that I did my double-take and observed that the beautiful red parachute flare, which I had recognized as the target marker itself, was absolutely and precisely over my head. Two seconds later the air all around me was full of the swoosh and swish of light magnesium fire bombs, pattering into roofs and pavements like heavy raindrops. It was when I gave up the academic study of German bombing technique for the more active business of getting the hell out of my little alley that I found that FUSAG itself was burning.

One reason I had been reading prisoner of war interrogations that winter was that we had been alerted to the Germans' intentions to use secret weapons against England. We knew they were preparing both flying bombs and stratosphere rockets, and among our plans were plans for the evacuation of London. The evacuation was to have been of civilians only—the Government and our various headquarters were to have gone a minimum of sixty feet underground and there to have stayed, for morale reasons, and so that the Germans could not claim they had destroyed London as the functioning capital of the British Empire.

The first appraisal of V-weapons that was given me, I remember, was the equivalent of one boxcar of high explosives dropping on London every *two minutes*, for twenty-four hours every day. This was the estimated maximum capability of the flying bombs alone, launched as they were to have been from around the whole of the coast from Holland to Cherbourg.

Soon the ski-shaped launching sites were discernible on the aerial photographs that our reconnaissance planes brought back. I remember this well because, in what was left of Devers' headquarters, on the basis of it, we made one more effort to revive interest in speeding up the invasion. It was our suggestion that the best way to save London from "taking it" again might be to get on over the Channel and take the sites themselves away from the Germans.

It still seems significant testimony to the courage and character of the British that the very live threat of national disaster by pilotless planes and rockets did not appear to sway a single British officer's determination to let nothing hurry or distract him in his politics or his planning. It is not as if the capability of the V-weapons were underestimated or taken lightly. The whole priority of the Allied strategic bombing effort was presently to be changed in an attempt to cut down the enemy's launching capabilities. British scientists worked literally night and day but would guarantee the Government no certain counter-measure.

But the British remained unhurried.

As I remember it, I was half on and half off FUSAG's staff myself at the time. Devers had left a few of us behind, for one reason or another, and what remained of American planning activities straddled his old headquarters and the newer Army Group Headquarters. When the absurdity (of making plans when one had no armies under command to plan for) became too patent, FUSAG set up an advance detachment and sent it on temporary duty with the British Commander-in-Chief's Headquarters. The logical mission of this group was to familiarize itself with Montgomery's operations so that whenever the change in command came—whenever the American ground forces might revert from Montgomery's to their own command—there would be at least a handful of American officers who had a working familiarity with operations on the Army Group level to smooth over the transfer, and to keep a continuity to the strategic and tactical plans. About the middle of March, I became a member of this group and when Montgomery took his staff from St. Paul's into the fields just outside Portsmouth I went with them. We moved in and set up our tents on the lawns and under the trees of a lovely country estate called Southwick Park.

Thus it was that yet another American group was set up. In Portsmouth, we had intimate knowledge of Montgomery's plans but unless we journeyed back to London or took an eight hour drive to Bristol, we had no other Americans to discuss them with. We were what used to be called in some civilian conferences "observers not empowered to speak"—and with no one to speak to anyway.

The way we were received in Montgomery's headquarters, however, had been a distinct relief to all of us—after months of working with the British in an ambiguous relationship, at least we were now to learn where we stood. Monty's Chief of Staff, Freddie de Guingand, called twenty or thirty of us together in a big conference tent and made a speech to this effect:

"General Montgomery has asked me to tell you that he is very glad you are here. He would like you to understand that this is *not* an *Anglo-American* headquarters. This is a *British* headquarters. You will have no authority here—and no responsibilities. It is our intention, however, to tell you everything we know and to make you as comfortable as possible. As I understand it, your job is to keep yourselves informed on General Montgomery's operations—to know what he intends to do and how he intends to do it. We will help you in every way possible to get this information. It is simply that this is our show and we think things will run more smoothly if everyone understands that."

This was plain talk and we liked it. It was a refreshing sip of lemon juice to cut the sweet sticky taste of "hands-across-the-sea, Old Man, and really we think you chaps are wonderful—but don't you think . . ." It was also satisfying, in a wry way, because it sounded as if Montgomery meant business with the invasion and we were all way beyond worrying about who should be responsible for getting on with the job, as long as someone was. Moreover, we were relieved of an inner conflict over whether we had been right to oppose the veteran British with our novice ideas anyway.

The Johnnies-Come-Lately would have had their souls tried enough in 1943 if they had had only to worry about how to carry out their orders—their orders to prepare for a military operation which their allies did not seem to want. But what really frustrated them, what confused them most deeply, was what right they had to their convictions anyway. They believed that the operation could be mounted, and that if it were, it *would* be successful. But had they any real right to this conviction? They had, by and large, only book knowledge. The most experienced of them had no more than skirmished with the Germans in Africa. They had never crossed the Channel in landing craft, to beach amid mines and barbed wire under the guns of concrete emplacements—as the British Commandos had. And in backing their raw opinion, they knew they were gambling with hundreds of thousands of lives, and history itself. There was no certainty in their souls, no firm foundation of sure knowledge and experience on which to rest their arguments. In the pinches, they had only their faith in themselves and their countrymen, their native American confidence and optimism. Sometimes it was easy for their veteran allies to make them feel foolish.

If we were wrong, we knew that other men's blood would have had to pay for our naïveté. Now that the great Montgomery was in command, I think we all experienced a kind of relief; at least we no longer carried our dreadful burden of responsibility.

We got along well with our new British friends in Portsmouth, living and eating with them in tents spread under the big oaks. For the first time we were working with a group of British whom we respected for their accomplishments as soldiers and in whose organization our position was clear and unequivocal. Good fences were indeed making good neighbors in this small backyard.

Sometimes in the evening we talked about these things with our opposite numbers—about how they and we felt about the command of the armies that were about to take the field. Some of Montgomery's colonels had served with American troops and in American headquarters in Africa. They were half apologetic when they said, "But you chaps simply haven't the commanders.

Look how long it took us to find Montgomery—and you have only just begun your war." They called Montgomery "The Master" in his own headquarters and there was no question about their confidence in him. They told us to wait until we saw him in action in the field. Translated into American, the gist of their argument was that while we had good material—they liked Bradley and Harmon, for instance—we were about to play in the World Series, and the British had the only pitchers that could win for us. They really believed this.

We had only the slim records of our commanders in Africa and Sicily to answer them with so we replied by asking them if it was their position that because The Master had made a reputation at El Alamein, the American forces had no need to develop field commanders? Would The Master now supply the Allies with whatever command was necessary to win? And if they would admit there might still be a need, in the Allied cause, for senior American field commanders—with the American forces one day to be five times larger than the British—then how would that need ever be filled if their philosophy were to prevail and no American commanders were ever given large enough commands for them to gain the experience and prove themselves? Should all the Allied eggs be carried to market in Monty's basket?

The British saw no reason why not—Monty's and Alexander's. They confidently expected that once the OVERLORD assault had carved out enough of France for The Master to maneuver in, the enemy would have had it. Had not Rommel now been put in command of the German forces in northwest France? The Master knew what to do with Rommel.

We marveled at their confidence but we were reasonably respectful of it; after all, they had delivered the goods in Africa.

The commencement of Montgomery's command, however, was not as reassuring as we hoped it would be. He was hardly settled in England before he moved to postpone the D-day that had been agreed upon at Teheran. He made it a month later. This sent a cold shiver up our backs, because one more postponement beyond June and the show would automatically be off for another year. Plan OVERLORD's position was unequivocal on the fact that the invasion itself had to come early enough in the year to be followed by a whole season of summer weather. Everyone in England had a mortal fear of the fall storms in the Channel.

Nor was the way in which Montgomery made the postponement any comfort to us either. He did not postpone the invasion from the first eligible tide in May to the first eligible tide in June. He simply ordered it set back to May 31, a date which was obviously a phony, for it fell a full week before the tide and moon would be right. Clearly this move had been made to obey the letter and to hell with the spirit of the British agreement with the Americans and Russians at Teheran. The Russians had first argued for April 1, and had conceded the month of April in exchange for making sure of the beginning of May. When we asked the British whether the Russians had been informed of the postponement, we were astonished to learn that they had not. A special mission was later sent to break the news to Moscow, but it did not go until it was pointedly too late to reopen discussion of the date.

But the score on Montgomery remained a draw, for at the same time that he postponed the date he backed the enlargement of the assault—the strengthening of the attack for which so many Americans had fought so long and so vainly. Way back in Devers' day, the American Theater Commander had given his planners the problem of how best to enlarge the OVERLORD assault. They had selected a beach on the right flank of the original landing site—and the whole assault had been scaled up accordingly on paper. One of Bradley's first acts had been to call for these plans, so they had been polished up. The new beach lay on the American end of the line so it was quite in order for Bradley to do this, even though he had no power to translate the plans into reality. Now Montgomery backed this proposed addition, and got it—for his authority was unquestioned. Unlike Devers, he did not have to negotiate.

The Master was in command even over SHAEF—by reason of the powers delegated to him by the Teheran agreement. The winter of 1944 saw the strange command phenomenon of a junior headquarters summoning the general officers of a senior, and reading them a lecture on the subject of what to do next, and how. I was present at one such and watched Monty's Chief of Staff make SHAEF's generals eat humble pie. Montgomery's officers were authorized to sign orders in his name and even had the Foreign Office on the carpet once. They made history when they directed that diplomatic mail to neutral countries be suspended in the interests of security. But this came later.

In January there was first the postponement to discourage us, and then a fierce multiplication of syndicate meetings until we feared the whole operation might be strangled by them. The American Chief of Staff, Marshall, was to refer to the January schmozzle in London in his official report. He quoted Eisenhower as writing him at that time that:

"It is obvious that strong and positive action is needed here in several directions. The location of various headquarters, the exact pattern of command, the tactics of the assault, and the strength in units and equipment, are all questions that have not yet been definitely settled. The most important of all these questions is that of increasing the strength of the initial assault wave in OVERLORD."

Landing craft were still the key to the assault, particularly after the assault was finally enlarged—it was now that we learned that the British were getting away with that last piece of Mediterranean monkey business, Churchill's mounting of the "just one more" amphibian landing to take Rome. It was to use the craft, of course, which would have gone a long way towards solving all the difficulties in the Channel. The ever helpful Mediterranean Theater, now directly under British management, was at it again. In England we did not know then that this landing would be at Anzio, and that after the failure of the operation the race for the Balkans would be over.

After Anzio, there was no more hope for winning the war via the Mediterranean; the V-weapons were coming on, the war was not getting any younger and the British, now firmly in the command saddle, felt that if there must be a trans-Channel invasion, at least now they could run it their way. But all we were aware of in Portsmouth was that by the end of February—Anzio began on January 22—the outlook for the Channel operation was mysteriously improved.

The mounting of the Channel assault now began in deadly earnest, for everything was months late now—that is, everything that could be late was late. At long last, the Johnnies-Come-Lately were vindicated; the unwelcome preparations they had made now proved the pay-off. They had gotten just enough done, despite hell and high levels, so that the show could go on.

The Assault Training Center had solved the problem of how the actual assault should be made. Without authorization, the principle had been established, and the training of American troops was already begun. Montgomery had simply to legalize it.

The surplus landing craft in the Mediterranean were now stuck hard and fast on Anzio Beach, but Devers' staff, conniving with Donald Nelson, had other landing craft already being built in the shipyards in America. They would be ready in time.

The Johnnies-Come-Lately had also, before they left, won their long struggle to get the American Navy to take the problems of the invasion seriously. In the pinch, when more naval fire-power had to be had to cover the increased assault, the American Navy came through and was now prepared to furnish it.

The supply organization that had been hammered together under Devers, and which he had left behind, was functioning smoothly and the stockpiles were already better than begun. Equally important, there were, in the American supply set-up, a sufficient number of ex-Johnnies-Come-Lately who had by now thoroughly mastered the personalities and practices of supply and transportation in the United Kingdom. They had the indispensable know-how to finish the job.

All these tangible assets were the direct result of the work of Devers and Company, against opposition from their allies. They may not have known the score, but they had stepped up to bat and hit the ball. It was questionable, even, whether Devers and his staff would have been more effective had they been more sophisticated. It was their dogged insistence on taking British arguments literally that was their armor. On point after point they had simply worn their British counterparts down by the very elementary quality of their logic—"How can we train troops if we haven't a training ground? There are millions of acres in

England—all we want are a few hundred of them. Why can't we have them?" Their almost childlike persistence prevailed.

The mounting of the assault now began to be a reality—with troop concentrations and rehearsals. It began also with bloodshed and sudden death. The summer before, the strategic air forces had been given the mission of breaking the Luftwaffe by bombing its production of aircraft and by provoking battles in the air. The job was Eaker's Eighth Air Force's, now under Doolittle's command. It was their job—and not the RAF's—because the RAF bombers were still limited to night missions which could not pick out specific factories for targets or provoke dog fights in which enemy fighters were killed. Doolittle's precision bombers, with their long range fighter cover, now took on the Luftwaffe in earnest.

The real D-day for the Battle of Europe came unpublicized in the winter of 1944. It was unpublicized as such because it was hoped that the Germans would misinterpret it as an all-out attack on the V-weapon sites which the Germans knew we knew they were preparing.

At the beginning of January, the weight of the American strategic bombers in Italy—the Fifteenth Air Force—was added to the Eighth and welded into one striking force against the Continent, under General Spaatz. February saw the climax. General Marshall wrote: "The battle raged for a week. It was fought over Regensburg, Merseburg, Schweinfurt, and other critical industrial centers. The German fighter force was severely crippled, and our attacks continued with unabated fury."

Despite all these things, we still feared the joker clauses in OVERLORD—not realizing, to repeat, that after Anzio the British had no choice but to abandon their ambitions to keep the spotlight on the Balkan highway. But by April, OVERLORD's momentum was too great to be stopped. The show was really on and everybody knew it. Escape clauses or no escape clauses, high policies and pious hopes notwithstanding, the invasion of Europe was coming off. We knew this because the whole gigantic apparatus had acquired such size and momentum that the impossibility of stopping it was easy to demonstrate.

The forces that had gathered in England before—in 1942—were not so large but that their diversion to Africa was possible. OVERLORD was another thing. There were not hundreds of thousands, now, but millions queued up behind the embarkation points, queued up through England and Scotland and back over the convoy routes until they crowded the camps behind the Atlantic ports in the United States.

There were the supplies queued up over the same route, all the way back to the factories and the mines on the American continent.

All of this was ready, specially devised for the sole purpose of crossing the Channel to the continent of Europe. No individual, no group of individuals, no government could now have stopped it. The invasion had a life of its own. The show was far, far more important than any part of it, even the part which directed it, the part which had a piece of paper which said "you are in command."

By April of 1944, then, no one was in command of the invasion of Europe. It was too big for any man to command. Pieces of it were commanded—base sections, divisions, armies—but the whole was too large and too tightly interwoven to be commanded. By April it would have been almost literally impossible for Montgomery to have added even a thousand yards more of beach to the attack area. Eisenhower might order a jerky day or two's postponement but he could not have changed the timetable of the embarkation by a few hours without wrecking it. Too many millions of individual elements and items were involved. The whole could be grasped in no man's imagination.

Actually, the strange part about the historic invasion of Europe on June 6 was that, in a very real sense, no one man had *ever* commanded it. Two men, Roosevelt and Churchill, had finally agreed that it should take place; but no one man had ever commanded it. The Plan itself had been evolved over a period of years. It dated back to Commando experience. It was the product of no brilliant genius. It put itself together, as we've seen, by a process of elimination—by a selection of the least impossible places to go and things to do. It was laborious and pedestrian. And when it was finished, printed and bound into numbered copies, the men who had put it together were disbanded. None played more than a minor part in the translation of The Plan into reality. Yet already by the time Eisenhower and Montgomery came to take command in the European Theater, the Plan itself was such an enormous thing that they could make no material change in it.

The Plan, not Bernard Montgomery, was The Master. In January, the inevitable adding of weight to the assault made no fundamental alteration in a concept which selected the Normandy beaches simply because they had fewer disadvantages than the beaches to the north and south.

General Eisenhower, of course, had nothing whatever to do with leading the invasion. Faithfully fulfilling the bargain made at Teheran, he backed up the powers of attorney he had given his three British Commanders-in-Chief. As the British had predicted—and they saw to it that their prediction was fulfilled—Eisenhower was almost wholly occupied in England with the statesman's part of the role of Supreme Commander. He visited the field forces for official inspections only.

Not only was each of the land, sea and air forces commanded by its own Commander-in-Chief, but the co-ordination of the efforts of all three was effected by the three individual Commanders-in-Chief themselves, acting as their own super-syndicate. The sole purely military responsibility left to Eisenhower was as go-between between these three and the command of the strategic air force. Alone amongst the armed forces in Britain, the strategic air force was only indirectly part of Plan OVERLORD. It would be "diverted" from its main effort against Germany's production to help in the preliminary bombardment, but the invasion would rely for air support on the fighters and the medium bombers of its own air support commands. These were under Leigh-Mallory.

So although Eisenhower bore the public responsibility he could do little more about the invasion than pace the floor and listen to the weather prophets who told him that he might let it proceed. But the General and the Air Marshal and the Admiral, the three British Commanders-in-Chief, were little more effective than he, for all their enormous responsibility. They were foremen, not managers. They were sometimes desperately busy foremen, on whom the co-ordination of historic efforts rested, but they were without power to alter these efforts by guile, will or inspiration.

Such is the nature of an amphibious operation. On land, a general is in command. He can order his troops to advance or withdraw, to feint and maneuver. By his orders he can win or lose battles. But not so the man who is titularly the head of an amphibian invasion force. He cannot add troops because there are no more boats to carry them. He cannot even subtract, for so interlaced are all elements of The Plan that the alteration of a single part of it will throw all the rest askew. He cannot materially alter the action of his troops, in time or space. Like everyone else involved, he is simply a hired man, doing the will of The Plan without question.

Of all the senior commanders, Bradley was most nearly a free man. He was only the sub-foreman of the American effort, working under Chief Foreman Montgomery, but the very fact that he was not out in front gave him some little time and spiritual energy to plan what he would do with the forces for which he was responsible after they were ashore in France and he could do anything at all with them. It was in the months that immediately preceded the invasion that the outline of the strategy which Bradley was later to follow on the Continent began to take shape. Even before his forces set sail, Bradley had a clear picture in his mind of what might be the most effective way to employ them against the German Army.

Montgomery was candidly uninterested in Bradley's ideas because Bradley was simply one of his generals and no more to be treated as an equal than the general, say, of his Canadian Army or even the general of the British Army alongside it. It is in neither British military doctrine nor Montgomery's personality to be responsive to creative ideas on strategy or tactics from subordinate commanders.

Devers had had ideas about strategy on the Continent before Bradley. Devers had tried to sell those notions to the British. The difference between Bradley and Devers was that Bradley kept his ideas to himself. Bradley now thought ahead, past the consolidation of the initial bridgeheads, beyond the first mission that Plan OVERLORD had assigned him—the taking of the Cherbourg peninsula. He began studying the terrain to the south and southeast, speculating on what he might do in response to each of the enemy's possible reactions.

While all this was going on I was in camp in Portsmouth attending British staff meetings or traveling up and down the coast of southern England by jeep and liaison plane to visit the multiplying American units or to watch invasion exercises.

If the Americans and the British were more relaxed in dealing with each other, there was nevertheless a growing tension in everyone as the assault itself assumed reality. The cards were about to be laid on the table in one of the greatest military showdowns in history. It is hard to recreate the mood, looking back from the postwar world—like trying to remember how one felt just before dawn after the sun is high in the sky and there is no longer anything mysterious about the landscape.

In the winter of 1944, everything across the Channel was mysterious and, by and large, full of dread. What we were doing had no precedent. The veterans of Africa and Sicily—and even they were a small minority—had no comfort to offer. The more they knew, in fact, the less reassuring they were—for they seemed only to remember the confusion and the wreckage and the terrific dependence of the amphibious operation on chance, on the luck of weather and the enemy's mistakes after the landing.

The great rehearsals we staged only made this atmosphere worse. It was an integral part of the technique that a series of exercises should be held, each larger than the last, each involving more men and more ships. This was both for training and to confuse the Germans by crying wolf. The sailing of our big fleets would alert the enemy; then nothing would happen—and he would grow careless. And we should have grown more expert. But with each amphibious maneuver, through the winter and early spring, we seemed to get worse at it instead of better.

It seemed to take the total efforts of every man concerned, from the doughboy to the field commander, to get the troops down to the shore and into boats and back onto whatever beach we pretended was part of the enemy's coast line. When they arrived there, the troops always seemed hopelessly disorganized.

Vital equipment got lost, plans seemed forgotten and all sense of coherence disappeared.

It was an awful thing to stand on a cliff, imagining one was a German commander, and to watch the assault waves spew forth, tangle on the beach and make obvious targets of themselves. When their vehicles followed, these would grind into the sand and stall. They flooded out in shallow water, overturned in the dunes, sank in the swamps. Standing there, seeing the apparently hopeless confusion, one asked oneself, "How can such an effort ever be straightened out—squared away and brought into an orderly attack so strong that it will carry through the defenses on the most strongly fortified coast in the world?"

We knew too much about that coast too—from the big blown-up maps of the German defenses—for every pin-prick on the aerial photographs was enlarged and drawn in by careful draftsmen to represent wire, concrete, mines, guns, underwater obstacles, tank traps and batteries of artillery. It seemed impossible that an assault that came bobbing over the rough gray water of the Channel could even make a dent in such a formidable array.

The last of the three greatest of the Channel exercises was far and away the most confused and unreassuring of them all. After it we sat about dismally and wondered whether the pessimists had not been right. Demonstrably it could not be done. There was the evidence of one's own eyes, there were the reports of the unit commanders, there were the beautiful timetables all gone awry. And yet this rehearsal fleet had only sailed a few miles down the coast and turned back to land on a friendly beach. All we had to console ourselves with were the wry observations that an amphibious operation always looks like that, that the pessimism before we set sail for Africa was even greater, and that even after an unexpected storm had buffeted the invasion fleet, the Sicilian invasion had come off successfully.

There were other terrors. No one who had had a real dose of enemy air action against one of our ports in the Mediterranean could believe that the invasion fleet would ever put to sea intact. In the Mediterranean, the Luftwaffe had been unable to fling more than a handful of planes at any one time against any one place. And yet they often scattered troops and sank ships. Against the Channel ports, the full weight of the Luftwaffe would be directed from little over a hundred miles away. In a big show-down, it could afford to take its losses to cripple the invasion. In none of our exercises was more than a fraction of the full fleet assembled. Yet every time we watched one, we saw the tiny har-bors along the south coast—and the big sprawling mother harbor of Southampton—packed like miniature Pearl Harbors, with ships stacked gunwale to gunwale. They had to crowd so close to one another that it did not seem as if a bomber could drop a pea and miss one.

Finally there was the morning we woke up and heard that the E-Boats—the fast little German torpedo boats—had gotten into a convoy of our big LST's, sunk two and blown the stern off a third, not ten miles off Portland Bill. Five or six hundred Ameri-cans were casualties, wounded or drowned out there in the dark. Most of them were engineers, and the equipment that went down with them was vital equipment which would have been needed early in the attack—bulldozers to clear the obstacles and portable roads to keep the vehicles on top of the sand. If the Germans could do this—on our side of the Channel . . .

It seemed even worse than that. We asked ourselves why the Germans had chosen this moment to make their raid and the answer was obvious. It was to take prisoners who could tell them how we planned to attack. The exercise concerned was the first which involved a full rehearsal of the actual assault formation that would be employed. It was complete with such secret weapons as rocket boats and DD amphibian tanks. In Africa and Sicily, and at Salerno, the engineers and the infantry had had to go ashore first to make it practical and relatively safe to bring in the armor. But in Normandy we were about to try reversing the process, sending in the armor first, self-floated. These secret DD tanks were always kept covered under black shrouds, even in convoy. The complete pattern of our fire power in the assault—not only the rockets but also which types of guns were to open from what ranges—had been laid on in this exercise.

The $64 question: had the E-Boats taken any prisoners and, if so, what did these prisoners know? The secrets of a military operation are guarded according to the principle that no individual shall know more than it is necessary for him to know to accomplish his job. All information which might be of value to the enemy is divided into classifications and as you go up the ladder—from RESTRICTED to CONFIDENTIAL to SECRET and higher—fewer and fewer officers and men have access to or are indoctrinated in the knowledge which you want withheld from the enemy. In operations in Europe, the U. S. SECRET classification was the equivalent of the British MOST SECRET. After "U. S. SECRET equals British MOST SECRET" came TOP SECRET, which contained the precise plans of the invasion, including the organization of the assault waves and the arrangement of the supporting weapons—but neither the time nor the place where the actual invasion was to take place. This last information was reserved for still higher classification which was known as BIGOT. An officer who was entitled to, and did, know when and where the invasion would happen was known as a Bigoted individual.

Amongst the officers and men who took part in the exercises which had been raided by the Germans—it was called TIGER—there were a score or more—I forget the exact figure now—of Bigoted officers who knew the exact beaches on which we were to land, and at what moon and what tide of what month. By the end of exercise TIGER, there were thousands who had an enormous body of knowledge classified TOP SECRET—for they had just completed a real dress rehearsal.

The British Admiralty, which was on the precise center of the spot (because it was the Royal Navy's responsibility to protect the convoy from enemy action), established the fact that the convoy concerned had been attacked while on its way *to* the beaches. The troops aboard then would not have shared their officers' knowledge of what was to take place. Had the Germans happened on the convoy on its way back from the assault beaches, every GI on board would have been worth sending to Berlin for his interrogation—he would have been stuffed so full of TOP SECRET information.

But there remained the question of what had happened to the Bigoted officers. The Admiralty's representative on Montgomery's staff reported that investigation had proved that the E-Boats could have taken no prisoners. It was typical of Montgomery—or perhaps of any ground force officer—that he kept his fingers crossed and ordered his own investigation. I was a small cog in this investigation by the happen-chance that the American engineers involved were from an amphibian brigade, and my first year in the army had been spent as a member of the Engineer Amphibian Command. At eight o'clock in the morning I had orders to get into a command car and go see if I couldn't find a personal friend who could give me an eye-witness description.

Eight hours of driving later, I ran down two lieutenants who had watched the show from the deck of the LST whose stern had been blown off. Their story was considerably at variance with the Admiralty's account. The Admiralty had held that no prisoners could have been taken because the E-Boats had hit and run, under fire from the armed escort. The boys who were there told me that if the escort fired on the E-Boats, the action took place somewhere over the horizon. In the neighborhood of the vessels that were sunk, there wasn't an escort vessel in sight. The LST's that went down were the vessels immediately ahead and to the stern of their crippled LST. These sank in a blaze of exploding ammunition. The E-Boat that attacked my friends' vessel blew its stern off with the first torpedo, hove to in the dark waters a hundred yards away and then had the cheek to turn on its searchlight. This played over the bobbing heads of the survivors struggling in the water. The E-Boat cruised about through the survivors and finally slipped away into the darkness. Obviously there had been plenty of opportunity for it to pick up survivors.

When this and other news got back to Headquarters, the hunt was really on—for in the meantime a check-up had shown that there were something like ten Bigoted officers missing. There was a whole day in Montgomery's headquarters when it was seriously contemplated trying to alter the operation because of the knowledge which the enemy must now be presumed to have—the detailed knowledge of almost everything we planned. By one of those amazing miracles which characterize war, although the bodies of hundreds who went down were never recovered, the remains of every single one of the Bigoted officers were found. Each was recovered, its corpse floated by its Mae West, and properly identified. And, ironically, what prisoners the Germans could have gotten were under the erroneous impression that the assault would follow the pattern set in Sicily and at Salerno. The tactics we were to use were still a secret.

An interest in these tactics now characterized everyone concerned with the invasion—everyone from Montgomery and Bradley to the GI who sweated out his refresher courses in combat on the moors and stormed the full scale model of the German defenses. To hell with strategy now. The problem was how to get on the shores of Europe and stick there. To hell with high politics or who should command what—to hell with everything except getting on the beaches.

Everyone was now wound tight into the maze of The Embarkation. One could see this, flying over the sausages with the rows of tiny tents grouped into their eggs.

The sausages were the areas into which the component parts of the invasion force were marshaled or gathered. They were so called because they looked like sausages on the map. Each sausage enclosed four or five miles of road and field. In the fields were camps. The sausages hung, not end to end but in a row, parallel to each other. They hung down from the hills to just back of the beaches, all along the south coast of England.

The eggs were the camps which the sausages enclosed. Each sausage had a half dozen so-called "permanent" encampments of tents. Each of these encampments had a small staff of guards and its own kitchen and mess tents. Each was carefully camouflaged but it was recognized that the rows of tents could easily be picked out from the air so that the objective of the camouflage was simply to conceal from the enemy the knowledge of whether the camp was full or empty.

Through the spring, the eggs and sausages filled, bulged, emptied; and filled, bulged, and emptied again and again through successive maneuvers, so that even if the pattern were seen from the air, the final filling for the real thing would look exactly like the rehearsals. With permanent staffs in each sausage, the troops traveled through them without unpacking, their gear lashed down and waterproofed. They rested and were taken care of in these improvised field hotels.

Visiting civilian traffic along the whole south coast had long since been banned and the sausages themselves could not be entered, even by officers, without special credentials. When they were full, the vehicles of the assault columns jammed the roadsides. They were squeezed in together wherever there was the shade of a tree for cover, and crouched down under camouflage netting wherever there wasn't. When one looked at the vehicles closely one could see that their engines and moving parts were heavy with the wax of waterproofing. Out of each, rose the temporary stovepipe through which its engine was to breathe and exhale. The waterproofing would enable them to wade for short distances through water up to the drivers' waists. Wrapped in their heavy blankets of wax, they overheated easily and could be run for short distances only.

On the far shore, the waterproofing would have to come off just beyond the beach before they could go further. De-waterproofing an average vehicle required a half an hour, more or less, no matter how many skillful hands there were at work. That was one of the nice things to look forward to—de-waterproofing vehicles under fire on the dunes of France.

All the traffic in the embarkation areas was one-way traffic and there were special maps picking out the road nets in red and blue. The routing was to be circular. The convoys were to wind down through the sausages to the beaches on one net; the roads back from the beaches were woven into another.

During rehearsals, each vehicle made this passage round-trip; for the real thing it would be a one-way journey down the outbound net. Coming back, there would be only the ambulances returning with wounded. To meet the ambulances, the whole paraphernalia of field medicine now moved in around the sausages —the clearing stations, the ward tents, the operating rooms under canvas, the graves registration units. All day long the troops on maneuvers passed and repassed them, tidying up, laying out their scalpels and their bandages, getting ready, waiting for calamity.

Back of the hospitals there were the railhead companies bringing in supplies, the ordnance dumps, the repair pools, the sweet-smelling bakeries and the signal battalions with the big coils of copper wire that would one day unwind across France.

It was all there, the whole great army of invasion, packed in as tight as the little wheels and cogs in a Swiss watch. It was all there, crouched down in the soft green of the Devonshire hills, as neat and orderly and peaceful in preparation as it would be untidy, confused and violent when it was dashed against the hostile shore in combat.

, The memory, looking back, is of how clean it was, how neat and scrubbed everybody looked and how new the vehicles were. On the shore itself were the miles of little summer hotels and beach resorts in and out of which GI's in OD's and green fatigues bustled. They seemed to burst the seams of the hotels. Soldiers hung from every window to watch the show of which they were a part.

Some of the nicer hotels were Red Cross clubs and one could sit in a garden high on a promontory and look out along the beach with its rows of wire and metal obstacles, and watch little flotillas of the invasion fleet wind in and out of the inlets, practicing, rehearsing. The road along the shore was heavy with vehicles—not the vehicles of the assault convoys, for these would be safe inside their sausages, but just the excess of vehicles that had to be used in the normal business of shuffling the whole business together.

Out on the horizon, as you turned towards the sea, there would always be the little dots that were the destroyers on guard. Miniature barrage balloons floated up from most of the nearer vessels and on every rise of ground, looking landward again, there would be the cluster of guns that were part of the air defense, and the flash of the sun on the gunner's glasses as he swept them slowly across the sky and back, across and back. Way overhead, fighters circled slowly. Still farther up there were, now and then, the long white contrails of the bombers going over to the real thing while we still practiced.

The weeks went by and the rehearsals grew larger and no one had to be in on the secret to know that any day now it might happen.

By the middle of May, having been an American staff observer in a British headquarters for several months now, I felt I had learned my lessons as well as I could and I set to work to promote myself a job in the field.

I found a job with Colonel Edson Raff, whose military trade is parachuting but who was to command a task force of tanks, cavalry and glider infantrymen on D-day. Task Force Raff's mission was to land and run for it through the enemy lines, to connect up with the 82nd Airborne Division which was dropping inland, beyond the coastal defenses. On the first of June, I checked my kit under the trees in front of the tent where we lived with the 21st Army Group and wrapped it, gas-proof underwear and all, into a bedding roll small enough to tie onto the front of a jeep. Then I took off for Devonshire and Dartmouth where Raff's force was already gathered, waterproofed, fueled, rationed—and snuggled into its sausage.

The next stop would be France.

6   The Beachhead Is the Pay-off

WE stood on the deck which roofed the little cabin and all we could see through the black was the flicker of gun flashes along the shore and the twinkle of the shells bursting far up in the sky, soundlessly. The wind came across the water and slapped the waves up against the flat sides of the LCT and the air was full of the mist from them. The noise of the wind was constant. There was no room left in the air for any other noise; the noise of the wind and the water—and the low throbbing from the Diesels underneath us—filled it full.

The first Fort to catch fire carried a torch through the rippling sparkle of the shells breaking, drawing a long trailing line across the sky, flat and straight. Now it curved gently down, dropping, bending the line it drew; it turned down still more steeply until it balanced a trail of flame almost straight up and down.

In the light of the explosion the plane made when it struck the ground, we saw France for the first time. The explosion was a great orange and yellow thing, as symmetrical as the curve the plane made dropping out of heaven. It was shaped like a flat dome and the colors were dark at the base and lighter around the perimeter. It was very, very bright and must have come from a little way inland for it silhouetted an irregular contour of land and some craft further in shore, well ahead of us. It did not last long and after it was gone, there was again only the fitful flashing of the ack-ack batteries on the shore and the shells bursting on their evenly set fuzes, all at one altitude.

There were no lights on the 105-foot landing craft just ahead of us, or on the one whose nose wobbled and teetered only a few yards behind where we stood on the stern above the pilot house. We were hardly moving now, and it was 0430 hours on the morning of the sixth of June.

The second and third Forts came down, each flaming like the first. They arched down, dropped, exploded. When the bombs fell from the Forts still up there, they tore open great chunks of blackness and lit the horizon in a jagged pattern of angry bursts of color. But none were as beautiful or as awful as the explosions the Forts made when they hit.

We were very, very cold and I could not tell whether the cold came from within or without. We had been on the landing craft for three days and two nights and fear had come in so many different forms we were very bored with it and not even curious about its symptoms now. The first day when we thought we were really under way we talked about it and were interested in the fact that it made our throats dry and sometimes glazed over one's consciousness until one saw a man speaking and did not hear him. Moreover, I thought that fear—just fear all by itself—fear with nothing that could be done about it—made most of the men sleepy. They huddled in corners or stretched out under the tanks, and slept and slept as if to run away from the reality that everything that could be done had been done and there was now nothing to do but sit and be carried to where death was waiting.

A little lieutenant from Brooklyn, whose platoon of engineers was going overside to take out the underwater obstacles, had a waking fantasy. He used to lean on the rail next to me and say, "You don't suppose there has been an armistice and nobody has told us, do you? Gee, it would be funny if it were all over and we didn't know it, wouldn't it?" Every few hours you would see him kicking this idea around with someone. He liked it and his face lit up when he talked about it and it gave him comfort.

Most of the tankers didn't talk at all. They were very polite with each other about little things, like trying to find a place to rig a tarpaulin to keep off the spray and the intermittent rain. They gathered around one of the little aluminum stoves that tank crews are issued and helped someone make coffee in a big tin or heat up some of the ten-in-one rations.

There were enough ten-in-one rations aboard to feed three times our third of a medium tank company and the platoon of engineers that rode with us. We had six tanks aboard. The rest of our tank company were in the craft fore and aft of us. We had wound down out of the Devonshire hills on Saturday afternoon and loaded up in the inlet beyond Dartmouth. That night we spent moored a few hundred yards from where we loaded. As far as we could see from the highest point on the landing craft, the inlet was solid with other craft of all sizes and descriptions from little messenger skiffs up to the LCI's and LST's which looked as big as ocean-going liners to us.

On Sunday morning we were off. We wound down the narrow channel into the sea and along past the beach there were people on their holiday, swimming and picnicking on the sand. We passed only a stout hallo away, but they hardly bothered to look up and wave to us. They were local vacationists; the shore had long since been banned to visitors from the North. As local folk, they had seen convoys like ours steam past for months now, going and coming back, on maneuvers. Obviously they did not know these were troops going but not coming back.

All that Sunday we wallowed out into the Channel which grew first light gray and then dark as the sky closed over and blotted out the morning sun. The clouds piled up and dropped closer and closer to the sea. We could see neither the beginning nor the end of our line of ships and out on the horizon on each side of us we could barely make out the dots which were other lines of ships, without beginning or end.

The cabin of our LCT had two bunks and a table in it. It was the living quarters of the twenty-one-year-old British skipper and the twenty-year-old Australian first officer. They invited the Colonel and me to share the cabin and when one of the big raw-boned country boys who were their crew brought up a pot of tea from the galley, he brought cups for us too. We opened bacon and marmalade and sugar and Nescafé and condensed milk from the ten-in-one rations and amused ourselves cooking on a little gasoline stove I set up on the cabin table.

When the table was cleared off, Colonel Raff and I spread out our maps of the little section of Normandy which was to be our world, and played soldier. Solemnly, we decided which roads we would take and marked our march route knowing all the time and very well that after the beach we'd take whatever road or field lay in the direction we wanted to go. We had only one mission on D-day and that was to get our tanks over the beach and seven or eight miles inland to where the northernmost of the two American airborne divisions would be dropped. There was a hilly patch of country there, west of a town called Ste. Mère Eglise.

We were only reasonably frightened the first day, for we were still riding on the momentum of the preparations and our chaperoning of the tanks down to the beaches and the loading. It all seemed then as if it would be over very quickly. There would be just that day and that night at sea and the next morning we would go in. It was about three o'clock in the afternoon of the first day— the Sunday—when the young skipper came in and told us that we were turning around. He shrugged his shoulders. He did not know whether it was a temporary alteration of course, a movement to avoid some enemy action that might have taken place over the horizon, or a real change in plans. He had only the stern of the boat ahead to follow, and following it, he was now pointed back towards England.

The weather grew worse and the rain began to fall in thick squalls. By evening we knew the landing would not be the next day, for all afternoon we had wound north, first on one course and then on another. Just before dark, we came into a great assembly of ships all weaving and twisting and steering in tight circles. In the distance there was land. We saw a big battleship riding high among the little craft. It was at anchor. Our own craft drifted slowly to a stop and then we were at anchor too, for how long we did not know.

We had that night to ourselves to go all over it again, and I think that was what let the fear in. You could count on your fingers the things that could happen to you and nothing could be done about any of them. There were the E-Boats that had sunk our landing craft on maneuvers the month before, no further from the English shore than where we lay at anchor. There were the submarines we had our reasons for believing the Hun might risk in the Channel if he knew this was the real thing. There were the mines. Most of all, on a crossing like ours, there was the air. No cover could wholly seal the air over the Channel and the long lines of landing craft would be bobbing ducks in a shooting gallery. Six knots we made in convoy; if we ran for it, our craft could do eight.

On the far shore, there were the underwater obstacles and the shore batteries—I seemed to have memorized the pattern of them. But most of all, for us, there was that damn strip of beach with the flooded area just beyond. The closest beach to Ste. Mère Eglise was near a town called St. Martin de Varreville. This was the assault beach called UTAH.

The trick about landing on UTAH was that the beach itself was hardly more than a long narrow spit of sand beyond which the surface of the ground dropped a few feet. In normal times, the sand spit kept the sea away and there were fields beyond in which cattle grazed; now, these fields glittered bright with water in the aerial photographs. The Germans had flooded them, and they made a shallow lake two miles wide. On UTAH the first assault waves were to take the concrete pillboxes that were set in the dunes along the sea beach and then the amphibian tanks and the infantry—the infantry waist deep—were to cross this lake and fan out up the slopes beyond.

The slopes above UTAH looked down on the lake and the sand spit. There were whole batteries of guns there, and probably rockets, too. All the way from the sand spit, across the lake and up these slopes to several miles inland, there were also the fields of mines there would be no time to raise. But even so, the worst of UTAH was still that narrow sand spit. The vehicles of the invasion would have to pile up there in a single inevitable traffic jam—a foreseen and accepted traffic jam. The crews of each vehicle would have to halt there to tear the waterproofing wax from the motors and the moving parts. Then most of them would have to wait for the engineers to get the roads in across the lake, so that they could file across onto solid ground. In the planning, there had been no way around this traffic jam, for one could not get all the vehicles one *had* to have ashore to fight the battle without piling them up on the narrow reach of sands. One simply had to take the estimated losses in order to have enough vehicles ready when the lake could be crossed.

The amphibian tanks—if they worked; they had never been tried in battle before—the amphibian tanks could make it across the lake, and probably the infantrymen could, too. It was very hard from aerial photographs, or even from first hand accounts of friends on shore, to be absolutely certain whether the shallow water of the flooded area was three feet deep, or six. But those extra three feet would make all the difference to an infantryman.

UTAH was a wonderful beach to think about if you had ever been in action and seen artillery work. UTAH was just north of the elbow where the Cherbourg peninsula turns out into the Channel. To the south, high above the forearm of this elbow, bulging like biceps, there are cliff-like hills. On top of these hills— they were pretty to look at on an aerial photograph through a magnifying glass—you could see through the foliage the long row of barrels which were the guns that had been moved there from the Maginot Line. They were 10-inch guns, with a ridge behind them into which the gunners burrowed. In back of the ridge were the trees of an orchard. The guns were there to cover UTAH. They were lined up at right angles to rake UTAH from one end to the other.

On the sand strip where the traffic jam would be, below the 10-inch guns and under the slopes inland of the lake, there was no cover except the man-made cover of the concrete emplacements at irregular intervals, set tight into the dunes. The artillery experts had drawn little arcs on our maps to show how the fire of these guns interlocked. There were a few places along the beach where only two of the 88's could fire at you at the same time. There were 88's in close, with direct fire; 88's firing from the foothills, direct fire and indirect; there were mortars in the foothills—and the 10-inch Maginot guns up on the bluff. What was the use of counting the machine gun emplacements? Or guessing how the beach defenses might be reinforced by the men and guns of the German division that had been seen moving in the week before, unloading from trains all along the base of the peninsula?

It was somewhere along about here that one began to get bored thinking about what it would be like. It was a maze in the Sunday section of the newspaper when one was a child too young to cope with it. There was no way to draw a line through it and come out safely on the other side. Like a child with a problem too hard for it, one was bored and wanted to throw the paper and the thoughts away. There was no way through the maze and that was an end to it.

That was as far as the thinking went but after thinking there came an empty feeling and one didn't feel right. There would be talk and nothing said or heard. There would be hunger, and food to satisfy it, but the food didn't satisfy. And there was nothing whatever to do about it except to go out on deck and be curious and look at the great fleet gliding slowly southward. Or one could come in and curl in the corner and doze and maybe dream about something nice.

The second time we crossed the Channel, I read *High Wind in Jamaica*. The children became very real to me and I thought about them a lot. When night came the second time everyone seemed to have slept too much in the last two days, or France was too close, or it had gotten too cold, or we were too damp. We couldn't rest. We watched the steady progress of the convoys all night from the deck. There was some light in the sky behind the clouds most of the night and when the line of cruisers cut through the convoy at a right angle, crossing to the west, each one looked bigger than Gibraltar. They went through at fifteen or twenty knots, lightless, unswerving. The little landing craft bobbed and swirled and were swept aside by the great waves from their bows. They were brushed away by the rush of the water.

The cruisers were awful things in the dark and the price of sinking a few landing craft was an easy one for them to pay, with their great steel bows and the terrible urgency of their getting to where they had to be.

Edson Raff is a quiet fellow and nothing seemed to bother him until the stragglers from the airborne operation came back. We had, of course, the precise plans for the landing of the airborne division we were to join. The great fleet of aircraft that carried them was to fly over to the north of our course and, circling after the drop, should have come back directly overhead—or at least should have crossed our path flying low enough for us to feel the vibration of their flight. At three o'clock, I think it was, the first one passed us. One C-47 aircraft went by all alone, mast high and jerking through the air, trying to see down to where the water was and yet not strike the waves.

After the first plane, there came a flight of two more and then another—then nothing.

"They're gone," said Edson.

"Who's gone?" I said.

"I mean they're done for," he said. "Something's happened to them. There should have been hundreds—in formation—if they dropped right. Now they're scattered. It didn't come off."

We stood and looked into the night.

"What do we do now, Boss?" I said.

Edson grunted. "We can go on to where they were supposed to have dropped."

A dozen more planes came out of the night and sped over us in ragged formation, ducking and dodging like the others. Then no more at all came.

It was when the guns began to flicker on the coast that we knew we were near shore. It was four-thirty and the Forts had arrived. They bombed for a long time and there must have been many waves of them. The light from their bombs flared and faded like light from a prairie fire but the guns on the ground kept on firing and every so often one of the Forts itself came down. When the bombing stopped, there was no more fire on the ground and it wasn't burning there the way the communiqués said it burned after a Fort had bombed a city. There were no cities where the Forts had dropped their bomb loads but only sand dunes and fields and farmhouses—and the pillboxes so tiny they could hardly be seen from where the Forts had been, even in bright sunshine.

We did not ask ourselves how many of the pillboxes had been hit in the first barrage. It was over now and it had come and gone without sounds strong enough to break through the heavy hoarseness of the wind. When the battleships began, their broadsides were even more beautiful than the bursts the Forts made when they struck the ground throwing haloes of flaming gasoline. The battlewagons were nearer and their broadsides made a whiter light. There was one group off the starboard; another down near the elbow was on our port quarter. They fired and fired and made us feel better even though we could not connect the flickers on shore with their firing, for their shells did not seem to light up when they hit the way the bombs from the Forts had.

Edson Raff and I still stood on the roof of the cabin and looked down at the lashed tanks in the open hold below us. The little engineer from Brooklyn was checking his men's equipment, and they stood in groups of twos and threes with armfuls of nitro-glycerine in belts and sacks. All through the long voyage we had towed, twitching on the end of a heavy steel cable, a little forty-foot landing craft called an LCM. We were to reach the start line an hour before the first assault waves and put the Engineers over the sides into this LCM, and they were to go on in until they found the steel rails the Germans had sunk in the sand. They were to find them sticking up through the waves because it would be near low tide. They were to tie charges on them to dynamite a path for the craft with the assault infantrymen. Three or four times the cable towing the LCM had parted, and it had been ex-citing business getting it in tow again, waiting for it to start its own motors and then watching it maneuver alongside to take the light line with which to pull the heavy cable in. Other LCM's came across the Channel under their own power in big bobbing blobs of craft which looked like waterborne locusts swarming together. Our LCM was being towed to save its power, so that its tanks might be full for its early morning maneuvers. But hours before the engineers went off in it, the cable had parted for the last time and it had had to finish its trip under its own power.

Our tank crews watched the engineers getting ready in silence. They drew one side to make room for them. The engineers had been guests to the tankers—and not very welcome guests, with their load of high explosives that a single tracer could explode. Now for one little moment they owned the ship. They were the important ones. They were the men who went in before we did.

A patrol boat came alongside, the water a white snarl under its bows. Someone on its bridge was shouting profanity at us through a megaphone.

"Get that crew the hell out of there. Get 'em out, goddam it. Get 'em out."

The lieutenant looked up at me from the deck below and his eyes were sad and his hands went out in a hopeless gesture. He yelled up, "Get 'em out, he says. I lost my good sergeant the day before we sailed. How am I going to get 'em out any quicker than I'm getting 'em out?"

The substitute sergeant was shoving gear at his men by the armful and pushing them towards the rail. They climbed reluctantly and grabbed someone's hand on the LCM and leapt across as the two craft clanged together, shuddered and wallowed apart. The sergeant couldn't get the men to carry the nitroglycerine fast enough to suit him and now he began throwing it from one craft into the other. Then some of his men in the little craft decided they had forgotten things and one or two of them leapt back to the temporary safety of the LCT. The man with the megaphone on the patrol craft was still yelling "Get 'em out," but the current or the wind was carrying his boat away and he could hardly be heard now.

The lieutenant slapped the last of his men on the backside. He pushed them up to the rail, watched them leap, turned once and waved to us on the bridge, and then he too was in the LCM and the lines were cast off. A wave caught the little boat and it yawed away from us at right angles. Then its motors caught. A churn of white showed under the stern and the craft swung in towards shore. The engineers were gone.

The sky was a little gray now and the low coast line could be seen in silhouette against it. Against the gray, the flickering had begun again. It was not as bright as it had been, but there was more of it. There were no aircraft overhead now. The fire was coming out towards us or towards the battlewagons. But we neither heard nor saw a single shell. On the timetable three hundred minutes were to pass before it would be our turn in line. We had put the engineers over just two miles offshore. Now we circled slowly back to where the transports had come up behind us and were unloading.

The first assault waves passed us as we turned. They looked like any other of the craft with whom we had spent the week-end on the Channel. We did not pass close enough to see the men. They simply went by us, became smaller and smaller and then melted into the gray of the sea and the just a little deeper gray of the landfall. Look as hard as we liked and through glasses but we could not see what happened to them when they reached the beach. There was just that steady flicker of firing along the shoreline but nothing clear or indicative, and no sound yet penetrated the wind.

The engineers were gone, the first assault waves were gone and it was day. Far away the beach was white now and the land behind it black. Through the glasses you could see the shapes of trees and even a steeple.

We went down from the top deck into the little room where the wheel and binnacle were. In the corner of this miniature bridge there was a radio. The operator was listening on earphones. When he saw us come in he turned a switch and a voice came from an opening in the gray metal. It came very clearly and in good English with an Oxford accent. It was saying, "The confusion on the beach is terrific. The Anglo-Americans' attempted landings have been thrown into the sea in confusion. Negro cooks have taken up weapons and are endeavoring to protect the withdrawal of the assault troops. The scene is indescribable. All are being hurled back into the sea. The casualties are fantastic." The boy at the radio grinned. It didn't seem particularly funny to us.

From the deck of the LCT, when France was only a few hundred yards away you could still make no sense out of how it was going there. The men on the beach were little black figures against the white sand. Amongst them the sand spouted up in little geysers and the black figures seemed to be dancing about these geysers. Now and then a tiny vehicle would pop out of one of half a dozen landing craft that had beached up ahead of us—pop out and then move very slowly through the geysers and stop entirely or climb up over a dune and disappear. We were one of a very long line of LCT's, all dirty white in the morning sun. We were bow to stern in a straight line moving very, very slowly. The landing points were already jammed up and it was not noon yet.

The water was calm in where it was shallow and the line of warships which was still firing was far behind us, almost on the horizon. Overhead the fighters went by in twos and fours in long sweeping arcs. They were neither firing nor fired upon, but far up the coast we could see a carpet of gray white puffs in the sky and just above it, twinkling over it like stardust spilled, flickers of light told us that there were bombers there.

For a little while, coming in, we had heard the dull vibration of the battlewagons firing but now our own tanks in the hold below us were warming their motors and our ears were packed with the sound of them. Seen but not heard through this din, strange topsy-turvy things were going on around us. A little landing craft full of men, running alongside of us, raised itself gently in the air and with the majesty of slow motion yawed over until it was quite upside down and its open mouth, still filled with men, bit into the water and sank until only a thin line of its keel showed. The geysers that had shown on the beach as we watched, marched out to meet us. Tall plumes of white and gray water rose and fell. A little boat came toward us bobbing out from the beach and passed directly below where we stood. We looked down and saw the hurt men lying there on the bottom—some twisting, some just lying. The two landing craft ahead of us were in now and there was a little stretch of open water between us and shore. The young skipper said, "Here we go now," and the battered old LCT seemed to pick itself up and reach for the land. As we came closer, the men around the geysers of sand on the beach seemed to be playing with them. They ran about amongst them and threw themselves down on the ground and wiggled and twisted. One man, just before we touched, stood right next to a geyser and spun twice around with his arms thrown out.

All these things we saw from the deck as in a trance. When a second boat further to the right of us lifted into the air and capsized, the water around it boiled and spurted. The whole experience of the night, the big Forts flaming and crashing, the horizon burning with the cold flames of the battleships' broadsides, the wild wind and water—all these things blended into a single experience and I felt like the little girl in *High Wind in Jamaica*—I had an earthquake. Other people's experiences could never now compare to mine. I had *my* earthquake.

When we grounded and the ramp went down, the moment of childlike wonder was past. From then on it was intensely prosaic. The Colonel and I had one jeep between us, an armored jeep with a sheet of quarter-inch steel instead of a windshield and a .50-caliber machine gun on a pedestal just behind the two front seats. We had a driver and a gunner. We did not want to trust ourselves to the jeep going in, so we tied it on to be pulled ashore by the last tank off, and the Colonel rode on the back of the first tank while I climbed up on the back of the last—the one with the jeep in tow. This was in case something happened to one of us. We had a place marked on the map just inside the first ridge of dunes where we would meet with the tanks from the other landing craft. Our platoon of mechanized cavalry and the glider infantry who were to ride the tanks were to meet us there, too.

The skipper had done a good job for us in landing. To their passengers, skippers of landing craft are all divided into good skippers and bad skippers. Bad skippers edge their craft in timidly and ground in deep water so that even waterproofed vehicles may flood out or disappear entirely under the waves. Our skipper was a good skipper and he took his chances on being able to back off the sand and rammed the boat home. Our big tanks hardly splashed themselves from the ramp to the dry beach.

Our nose was in directly opposite a cut in the dunes where a roadway went through. Majestically each of the first five of our tanks dropped its nose down the ramp, waded and waddled across water and beach, up-ended over the dunes and was out of sight. Halfway over the beach my sixth tank, jerking the jeep behind it, took it into its head to pause and think things over. Sitting on top of it, while it was still on the ramp, I had made a quick appraisal of the beach ahead. Most of the sand geysers were from what I thought must be mortar fire. The mortar shells were dropping short, to the left of where we wanted to go. They did not seem worth more than a mental note that if they came closer one should drop on the far side of the tank. Just about the time the tank stopped, somewhere up in the foothills, they changed their range and the shells began going long, reaching over us.

The next thing I knew I was bounced off my vibrating steel perch by the blast of something and I was in the sand back near the jeep that was in tow. One of the men in the jeep, I saw, had been hurt by whatever knocked me off, but it was only a bloody scratch, and the three of us fell to wrestling with the tow-rope to get the jeep loose. When we got it loose I sent it ahead to the Colonel and began to pound on the metal sides of the tank to try to get the driver to pay some attention to me.

We were stopped smack in the only roadway ashore and the whole invasion seemed to be piling up behind us or swirling out of the ruts to follow the jeep around and thus get past us. Men were running clumsily through the sand, swaying from side to side from the awkwardness of their footing and from the gear they carried. All of us had big flat rubber inner-tube-like preservers around us under our arms.

My damn driver couldn't hear me from inside the tank. The tank was buttoned up. There was no way to talk into it. The mortars dropped long and dropped short, each spinning the sand into the air and breaking the air itself open with sharp concussion. Then there was suddenly that fast high note that later on I knew was the shell from an 88—but only knew it later on because when you have ever heard one close, you don't have to think or remember ever again. You will always be on your face flat before you have time to recognize anything, so instant is the connection between that sound and a reaction to get out of its way. It must have gone a long way past for I don't remember feeling it hit.

There followed a nightmarish five minutes while first I got up and pounded on the tank and then I dived back into the sand as that flick of sound came again. Men were not running past now. Everything was still on the beach around me, everyone flat. I could only think that as long as my tank was there, that gun would keep on firing until it hit it. I climbed up on the front of the tank and pounded on the bullet-proof glass in the driver's slot. Reluctantly, the hatch came up next to me and a head in a football helmet rose from it. I roared into its ear, "Get the hell off this beach." The head disappeared, the hatch closed and finally, finally, finally we began to move again.

We went up over the dune. In the shelter of the sea side of

the dune there was a long row of men scrabbling in the sand to make themselves foxholes. I sat, majestic, on the top of the tank but I could not direct it. It waddled along in the tracks in front of it, then the driver turned sharply and went down the inshore edge of the dune.

There were no geysers of sand here. Off to my left were the still waters of the inland lake which I had thought so much about. The water lay calm and peaceful. Beyond, the sloping hillsides were a rich green, with fringes of trees between the fields and woods along the skyline. A mile or two away, that lone steeple I'd seen from the sea rose higher than the trees.

A hundred yards down the beach we came abruptly on the other tanks. Their lids were up and their crews out of them, tearing off the big air scoops that stuck up like bustles on their behinds. The scoops were part of their waterproofing gear. The Colonel and the captain of the tank company and several of the sergeants were standing about grinning.

When I slid off to join them, my driver friend spun his tank at right angles, rolling one tread over a five-gallon can of machine oil which one of the other tanks had unloaded there. It sprayed me head to foot with black oil. The oil dripped off my ears and my nose and everybody laughed. We felt very fine to be ashore in the sunlight. There had been nothing to it.

There had been nothing to it because of a mistake—as far as I know the only one of the entire invasion—in navigation. The beach exit road we had come through the dunes on had been written off in the planning as too obvious to be practical; it would surely be a nest of wire and mines and other defenses. The landing had been centered north of this exit but because of a minute mistake in the navigation on the morning of D-day, the whole beach had been side-slipped south a few hundred yards from where it had been intended. This put the sub-landing area known as D for Dog in the Red sector of UTAH, dead on this exit. The first vehicles drove straight through it; the Germans had left it unmined and unguarded, apparently as an exit to the beach for the use of the local population.

Miracle Two followed Miracle One: on the far side of the dune opposite this beach exit, a single raised road ran two miles due inland across the flooded areas. The road could also be seen on our aerial photographs but, once again, no planner had had the temerity to count on its being intact when the first troops landed, so easy would such a road be to demolish. Even if it weren't mined, a hit from a field piece could have torn a crater in it which would have put it out of action. Yet on the morning of D-day, this road—this carpet leading straight to the heaven of the solid mainland—was unscratched, intact. It had been left either for the local population or for the German Army to get supplies down to the pillboxes on the beach itself.

When a half hour later, after we had the waterproofing off the tanks, our column set out across this causeway, no one even fired on us. We could hear the fire coming from the foothills and going over our heads to the beach itself, but no German commander bothered to shell the precious road. As we passed along it, we could see that a few Germans had tried to stop the first amphibian tanks when they had rolled in out of the dawn. Their bodies lay in the mud on the edge of the road or half-floated in shallow water. The causeway was very narrow and there were two turns in it. An American amphibian tank was half off the road in the water up to one's shoulder at one of these turns. It seemed to be unhurt but the crew had abandoned it and gone on on foot. We saw no American dead along the causeway and we hit the slopes of the foothills at ten miles an hour.

It was around noon and no trouble at all in sight. We should be now close to the spot from where the German guns were firing on the beach. But our orders were not to stop to look for them but to cut and run for it. Somewhere back in those hills there were the American airborne troops who, if they had not been lost in the drop, would need our tanks intact.

By the time we reached the steeple I had seen from our landing craft, something had blown the top off it. It stood in a little village square in which the sight that fascinated me most was a corpse of a German soldier in a roadway near the corner. It had been run over by so many tracked vehicles that it was ironed flat like a figure in a comic strip—really—absolutely flat, the arms of its gray uniform at right angles to its pressed and flattened coat. Its black boots and the legs that there were in them were just as flat and thin as if they had been cut from a sheet of dirty cardboard.

There was an MP from the infantry regiment ahead of us standing in the square and, without being asked, he simply pointed us a way through what looked like an alley. Beyond, there was an open road and again we rocked and roared on into France. I thought I knew the road we were on. In a few miles there would be a crossroad and the right fork would go on to Ste. Mère Eglise. We passed neither friend nor foe until after this crossroad. Then, just under the brow of a hill, we met a lone American tank. Its crew was sitting on the road beside it. The Colonel and I were in a jeep now. We had cut ahead of the column and come up to this tank. Its crew chief said it had landed two hours before and that when it had gotten to where it was, some infantrymen there had said to stop. There was something on the hill beyond. We asked, what? The sergeant shrugged his shoulders. He said the infantrymen had gone away but that his own lieutenant had come up awhile later and had gone ahead to look around and something had shot at him so that he told the sergeant to stay put until something else came up.

While we were talking, our own tanks had spaced themselves out behind us on each side of the road at intervals, as on a drill field. The six-wheeled armored cars of the reconnaissance platoon had halted just behind us. It was a lovely morning, the sun was shining and little white clouds were in the sky and everything was quiet and green all around us. Colonel Raff and I went up on the top of the hill and looked across to the next rise through our glasses. The road ran straight north. We could just see the rooftops of Ste. Mère Eglise beyond the second dip of the road.

The skipper of our reconnaissance platoon was a gay young man in his early twenties. He was asking the tankers if they realized that his was the first American scout car to have penetrated Fortress Europa. Raff beckoned him up and said, "Go down and see what you can see." The lieutenant got in the lead scout car and it crept down over the brow of the hill. The tank engines were all silent and the rubber tires of the scout car whispered on the asphalt. It went down the far slope a little way and halted to look around. Raff beckoned the sergeant of the nearest of our tank crews. "Go on down after him and cover him," he said. The tankers climbed in and started their engine. The big hunk of steel lumbered up over the brow of the hill. Then it came close to the scout car and the latter began moving again and the two vehicles dropped down into the valley. In profile, the road made a very flat "U" through the valley. When the two vehicles reached the bottom of the "U" there were two explosions in quick succession. Standing on the brow of the hill we could see the men piling out of the tank and out of the scout car and diving into the ditch on the right. Then everything was very still. And neither vehicle made a move or sound and nothing whatever happened.

What occurred next was a comedy turned tragic. The scout car and the tank which we had sent out ahead had been fired on all right, but neither had been hit and the crash we had heard happened when the scout car backed up suddenly and rammed its own tank. Both crews thought their vehicles had been struck by enemy fire and had piled out into the ditch. The first survivor was a terrified GI from the tank who had crawled all the way up the hill in the gutter. He reported that he was the sole survivor. Ten minutes later the lieutenant from the scout car came in, having circled through the fields. Sheepishly he explained what had really happened. He had stayed by the vehicles awhile to see if he could see where the shot had come from but had nothing on this score.

With such obvious evidence of high-strung nerves, Colonel Raff and I decided to send another tank forward with orders to stay out until it had positive contact with the enemy. It went past the stalled vehicles and was a hundred yards beyond when it was shot through by something big, and burst instantly into flames. Three of its crew lived.

Raff and I had been halfway down the hill behind it, watching the far brow through glasses but we could see no muzzle flash. Whatever was there was well concealed and now held its fire.

I went back onto our hill and found a stray battery of little 75-mm. howitzer cannon that had come up from the beach. An eager young lieutenant in charge was anxious to shoot them at something and seemed to have no orders except to make his guns useful to somebody. We put him out in the field on the left of the road. I told him to try to knock the hedges off the corners where the road cut over the far hill beyond the burning tank. It was an easy shot for a popgun and it only took four or five rounds to hit each corner in turn. But when we sent a third tank down to pull out its stalled mate, it was fired on again. It got back.

This time the crack of an 88 was clear and unmistakable. It was coming sharply angled from one side; the contours of the valley had thrown the sound off before. We were not supposed to engage the enemy with our little task force but now there seemed no way to get through, past the gun ahead of us, except to push whatever was on the hill out of our way. We still had no knowledge as to whether or where the 82nd Airborne Division had actually landed and, until we found out, we could only presume it was where it was supposed to be—and that was a scant two miles from where we were. There was no infantry around us; we must have passed through the assault waves or else they had turned up the coast instead of coming inland. We still had seventeen tanks, two scout cars, and about one hundred glider infantrymen—and the four howitzers that had attached themselves to us. So we made ourselves a little battle.

Raff ordered the captain of the tank company to fan his vehicles out on either side of the road and to work them forward from field to field, with the infantry riding on them. I began to direct the fire of the howitzers along the brow of the hill, seeking out likely places where anti-tank weapons might be concealed. By now it was well into the afternoon. Our tanks had just begun to move forward when the scouts of an infantry regiment that had landed after us arrived. Behind them, slogging away in long columns on either side of the road, came the doughs. Their regimental commander moved into a farmhouse back by the crossroads and he had radio communication with somebody, for when Raff and I went back to see him he gave us our first news. Everything was going fine on our beach but at OMAHA they were still on the sand and in a hell of a fight. At OMAHA they were up against a cliff; the water had been rough, and there twenty-five out of the first twenty-seven amphibian tanks to be set afloat had sunk one after the other, drowning their sealed-in crews. Now, on the beach without tanks to help them, the engineers and the infantry were in trouble.

Okay, so now would the colonel of the infantry like to take over our battle and let us try going on through by some other road? Thank you, no. The regiment's orders were to get up to beyond the crossroads and wait. But the division commander was on his way up.

Raff stayed at the command post to try to persuade the signal men to see if they could raise the airborne division for us so that we could find out where we were going. I spent my time in the jeep running back and forth from here to our own CP, which was no more than a spot on the side of a road, halfway down the hill. There we had told our sergeant to wait for us and to keep track of things. Our only communication was via a radio in the jeep through which we were supposed to be able to talk to the commanders of our tank company and our reconnaissance platoon. Our radio operator sweated over this and now and then got through to one or the other for a brief unsatisfactory exchange of identifications. Mostly I kept in touch by getting out of the jeep and running into the fields behind the hedgerows till I found whomever I wanted to talk to.

My second trip up, I found the tanks in line behind a thicket hedge, firing through it across the valley. We had only fifteen tanks now. Two more had been hit when they had ventured into the field beyond. They had located one enemy gun, dug in in the far corner of the field—but not located it exactly, for it was very sparing of its fire and only let go when it had a sure kill. Obviously we could go no further until it was out of the way and I started the glider infantrymen after it on foot.

I had a field wire down from the howitzers to just behind where we were and I kept on pointing out places for the lieutenant to try to hit. About the third shell, after we got the wire working, we had our first fun. It caught some kind of an ammunition dump which began going off like fireworks in the woods ahead of us. I told the lieutenant to keep it up and went back to report the situation to Raff. On the way back, our radio began to work again. Someone in one of our tanks off the other side of the road was talking. Even through the metallic reception you could recognize the tenseness in the voice. It said, "We have got some fellows that are pretty badly hurt here. Can you get anyone up to us? We have lost one tank. We are almost on the top of the hill and we can see enemy traffic on a road ahead. Can you get somebody up to us? We cannot move these men. They're hurt bad."

I told the operator to say we would try. The boy at the other end knew as well as I did that we had no medics in Task Force Raff. We were taking our chances in getting through without casualties and now we were getting casualties. That was that. But the regiment back at the crossroad had medics and I hoped I could borrow some. But I did not get back to the crossroad for I met the Colonel walking towards me halfway back. He was looking at the watch on his wrist. As I pulled up he said, "Do you see what time it is? Do you know where we are? They will be here in a minute. We have got to do something about it."

I said, "What the hell?"

He said, "The gliders. That field down there, right in front of the tanks. That's one of the glider landing fields. We were supposed to have taken it this morning. The gliders are on their way over. They will come down right between us and the Germans. I have been trying to get through to the command ship for an hour, but we can't raise them. The gliders must have taken off from England long ago."

Very dramatically, while he was still talking and while I was trying to understand all he said, they came in from the north. They came in in a beautiful formation of two-motor planes. Behind each, riding high on the end of the kite-string-like tow lines, were the gliders.

We had a dozen smoke grenades in the jeep—recognition signals. I began pulling the tape off ones marked "orange" and throwing them into the field by the road. There was a chance that the pilot might pick up the color and come over towards us. The smoke streamed out of the grenades like a suddenly released genie, but it clung close to the ground and blew into the hedgerows and then dissipated into thin air. It was obvious foolishness. The big formation of transport planes—there must have been forty or fifty of them in tight V's—came on as if they were on rails. They were flying two or three hundred feet high, not far above the tree tops.

As they crossed above the road directly in front of us, the lead glider let go its kite string, and all the kite strings behind, which had been tightened black against the sky, now floated loose. The gliders were on their own and at that very second we found out for once and for all what was on the hill ahead of us. Whatever else, there was a battalion of enemy infantry. The whole hilltop began to crackle with small arms fire going up towards the planes. The battalion had held its fire, waiting for us, but the glider invasion was too much for it.

All kinds of weapons were now firing at the airborne fleet. The big mother transports banked sharply in unison and began their turn back to England. The gliders seemed for a second motionless. One of the first transports to turn suddenly began smoking. It roared over our heads and thundered into a field just behind us. The column of black smoke from it reached up sharply for the sky and the gliders, which had begun to drop and turn, went through the smoke. The glider pilots were trying to find places to set their craft down. They could have had no very clear idea of what was going on below them.

The field that had been reserved for them in the plan was the field, of course, in which our tanks and the enemy's 88's were poking at each other. It was too small a landing ground for so many gliders under any conditions. Only a few of them were able to make it. For desperate seconds they beat the air over our heads like monstrous birds. Then they crashed into trees and hedgerows on each side of us. They pancaked down on the road. They skidded crazily, and stopped.

The best pilots had swung in easy glides to the flattest ground and there they slid softly to rest not a hundred yards from the muzzles of the German firing line. All our tanks began firing at once and everyone with a rifle shot it off, trying to get some lead into the woods where the Germans were and so slow up the fire on the helpless gliders. Men were scrambling from the wrecks of the gliders, running about as if in a daze.

The gliders that landed behind our lines were in worse shape even than the ones that had landed in the field, for there were no really open spaces where we were, but only miniature pastures between the steep hedgerows. Most of these had orchards in them.

In the midst of it all, a glider whose tow-plane had straggled cast off, circled once and made a perfect landing directly in front of where we knew the German 88 was. It was unscratched. Its passengers got out, appeared to dust themselves off, opened the nose and rolled a little jeep into the field. They made several trips back and forth into the glider to get additional equipment and packed it carefully in the jeep. Then, as if nothing in the world were happening around them, they got in the jeep and rode slowly across the field, found an opening in the hedge, pushed onto the road and rode past us, utterly unconcerned. Everything up the hill had been firing at them from the second they landed and not one of them had been scratched.

The battle of the glider landing was all over in ten minutes. It was without direction and there was nothing really that anyone could do about it. The survivors filtered past us, supporting the limping, carrying the wounded. There were more still alive than seemed possible. Their officers began collecting them in a field behind the howitzers.

By the time the last gliders landed it was twilight and nearly midnight. We had been very tired for a long time and Raff collected some of the pilots from the gliders, who had presumably slept in bed the night before, and impressed them into service as guards. We had drawn our tanks back onto the top of the hill and almost the last thing I remember of that first day was checking them off in the dark as they came in, and talking with the captain about spreading them around the four sides of a field that had fairly open country around it. We put them around in a circle, like the wagon train in a Wild West movie just before the Indians come. Then I got the canvas roll off the front end of our jeep and dropped it in a ditch. I was asleep on it before I could get it unrolled and then someone was kicking the hell out of me and it was a whole four hours later, and D plus 1 had begun.

I still had my stove and half a canteen of water, and I made hot coffee with Nescafé. The others had some water, too. I made coffee for Raff and the two drivers and myself. Then we got the tanks running, rolled them back out on the road and spread them out through the fields, and we got the battle going again.

The infantry that had come up the afternoon before had gone off somewhere during the night and we had the battle all to ourselves for a while—that is, it was just Task Force Raff versus the German infantry battalion we now knew was on the hill in front of us. We had pushed in both wings of its position the first day and had taken or damaged all the field pieces that had had us under direct fire. Now the Germans were beginning to use their mortars, whose fire they laid on the crossroad just behind us. That was nice because it made it comparatively safe up front, with only some small arms fire there. I didn't see it hit anybody. It was fairly obvious, though, that we hadn't enough weight of men to push the Germans off the hill or to get through.

Raff went off again to try to find someone who could tell him what the score was and my adventure of the morning was in trying to organize the pilots from last night's gliders into an infantry attack. They seemed to have spent the night here and there in the fields and were now turning up asking the way back to the beaches. They said they had strict orders to get back to England as fast as possible, to fly over more gliders; not many of them were interested in seeing what it would be like to be a doughboy. Most of them had carbines but they said they'd never fired them. They said they had been given them just before they took off and probably that was true.

Just the same, somewhere the other side of Ste. Mère Eglise there was a whole airborne division that had now been cut off for thirty hours and they would very definitely be wanting our tanks. The only chance we had to get the tanks through seemed to be to get some infantry out in front of them and maybe scare the Germans off that hill. The Krauts weren't behaving very aggressively but it had cost us four tanks trying to push through without infantry the day before.

About this time there turned up on the road an eager and energetic young captain who was there as a G-2 observer, I think from Corps. I asked him if he would take on a job and take a skirmish line through some hedgerows to the west of us. It looked as if they would lead around to behind the hill where the Kraut battalion was. There was a chance that infantry fire from an un-expected quarter might worry them about being surrounded. The captain said sure and one way or another I got him sixty or seventy men—some stragglers from God knows where and all the glider pilots I could catch. The last six or seven I had literally to catch, making motions at them with a pistol—for they had become very, very enthusiastic about carrying out their orders to get back to England.

My improvised infantry was not an unqualified success. About an hour later the captain came panting back to where I was trying to keep the tanks and the battery of howitzers usefully employed and reported that the trouble with his advance was that he couldn't decide from which end of the line he ought to direct it. He said he had originally tried going first but that, after he had gone a few hundred yards, when he looked around he found that instead of seventy he had only thirty or thirty-five men follow-ing. The more conscientious of the glider pilots had just dropped out of the line and taken off for England on foot. So then he tried stationing himself at the rear end of the column. When he did that, he claimed, the front end always got stuck some place and nothing happened at all until he went up to it, by which time, when he looked around, he found that instead of thirty-five he only had twenty-five men.

This obviously called for a reorganization. By this time I had collected a new batch of stragglers and pilots which I had been considering as my personal replacement pool. I asked the captain how far he had gotten. He said nearly past the hill and that as far as he had gone he didn't think they had been seen and that no one had shot at them. So I sent him out again with my replacements.

By noon the operation was a little better than a draw. The captain came back to tell me that on the far brow of the hill they had made contact with the enemy, who had promptly abandoned a horse-drawn 88-mm. rifle, taking the breechblock with them. So they had the credit of taking a field piece and had no casualties. When I asked him how many men he had done this with he pointed to the group behind him. There were about twelve of them. The run of the mill hadn't been very good but the twelve who had stayed were right on the ball.

About this time, Raff came rolling up with all kinds of news. We had the division commander and his staff at last, back by the crossroads. The reason we didn't have the division itself was that the afternoon before one of its regimental commanders had decided that we had the Ste. Mère Eglise front in hand, and the main weight of the American infantry attack had been sent in to the east of us—that is between where we were and the beach. It was reported as going very well and being some miles ahead of us there. Also, the missing airborne division had been contacted. Its headquarters at least had landed safely and it was about three miles from where we were, west of Ste. Mère Eglise, about where it was supposed to be.

I went back in the jeep with Raff and found a council of colonels and generals meeting in an orchard. Some outfit, I guess the division's headquarters, was moving into a farmhouse across the road. There were some wounded and stragglers sitting in the dust against a stone wall in front of the farmhouse, and thirty or forty untidy German prisoners were lined up opposite with a GI guarding them with a machine gun. A couple of miles down the other fork of the road there was supposed to be another little battle going on, in a town called Chef-du-Pont.

As we opened our conversation with the general, a soldier came from somewhere with a message on a radio blank addressed to Colonel Raff. It was from Ridgway, the commander of the airborne division, and said that his CP was surrounded, that he had many prisoners and wounded and was running low on ammunition. Would Raff please bring medical supplies and ammunition. This put it squarely up to the local division commander, for while our mission was to get through to Ridgway and the 82nd Airborne we had been attached for the landings to the 4th Division, and its commander had the right to order us to stay where we were if in his judgment the need were greater. He said to Raff, "Look here, I've got a crazy battle on my hands and I'm fighting in three directions right now and I don't know what I'm up against or what's going on." And then he paused a minute and went on, "But you pull out of there and I'll put something in to take your place. You pull out and see if you can't find some way around the town and in to Ridgway."

Raff made up his mind quickly. He said he would take the column in and that I was to get the hell down to the beach and someway get some ammunition, and some transportation to haul it in, and come back and catch up with him. Everything began happening very fast. Some kind of a medical unit was on the road behind us and while the 4th Division's infantry was taking over from Raff's tanks, we talked the officer in charge out of a jeepful of morphine and plasma, and Raff took that with him. Between us, remember, we had only the single armored jeep. So I went out on a crossroad and stopped a shiny new one which had just managed to get itself out of a glider. The driver said it belonged to Major somebody, but his major wasn't there and I was a major who was on the spot.

I went off to the beach in my captured jeep. Halfway to the beach, I passed a commotion that looked like a headquarters pulling in, and sure enough it was—a real live corps headquarters. Everyone was very friendly and excited to hear how it was going up ahead, and the G-4 lent me two two-and-one-half-ton trucks with a driver and a helper for each. So I took my nice new convoy and drove on down to the beach.

The beach was a terrific thing on the morning of D plus 1, already jammed with vehicles and equipment and with thousands upon thousands of soldiers and vehicles milling about. But the road net made sense. Without asking the way once we went through a maze which the MP's had already organized and suddenly found ourselves running along the dune road behind the beach. The beach itself was still under fire from pillboxes further up the shore which the infantry weren't able to get at. But these guns, firing through slits, had a narrow traverse and could only cover the edge of the beach itself and a few feet out into the water. Their shells sent high geysers of water up into the air and the DUKWS and the landing craft shuffled in among them.

The air over my beach was full of balloons now and as far as you could see towards England there were the hulls of ships and more ships crowding in. There were no signs on the road yet to show where anything was on shore. But the sand strip was so narrow and flat that you couldn't miss an installation. The ammunition dump that had been begun on the sand spit was spread out on the beach side of the road. It was already a few acres of small piles of boxes and crates.

The layout of everything was very nicely planned. Right next to the ammunition dump they were laying out the corpses. This was thoughtful because if the ammunition dump were hit, the dead probably wouldn't mind. While I was fussing around, they brought some in in trucks and laid them out the way it's taught in the book. These had no covering but most of the new recruits in the line came from a big hospital tent on the other side of the road and these were covered with respectable blankets.

The ammunition dump was in charge of a private first class who couldn't have been more friendly or helpful. His officer was off somewhere trying to get some more stock for the store. Not until he asked me what I wanted did I realize how thoroughly I didn't know. It just happened that my military experience had not included drawing ammunition for an airborne division, which only goes to show that a soldier should be taught everything. My friend the Pfc. didn't know either so we sat down on a box and I asked him what he had, and together we figured out what might be useful to Ridgway's Division.

We knew that they couldn't have anything very heavy with them so I bought them some 75 howitzer ammunition—the Pfc. said he was sorry he didn't have it in the fuze he personally liked best—and mortar shells and grenades. I also told him to throw in an assortment of M1, carbine, and .45 pistol ammunition. You can always use that around a battle. He didn't have everything but he and my drivers went off to fill the trucks with what he did have, hoping that the next DUKW ashore would bring the missing items.

It was then that I remembered that I had been forgetting to eat for a long time and I slogged through the sand across the road to the hospital. There, too, they were hospitable and gave me the best they had, two cold cans of C-ration beans. I succeeded in slashing myself in trying to get one of the damn things opened but a sergeant in the ward tied the hand up for me, so that for the next few days I was to gain unearned respect by looking as if I were carrying on, though wounded in action.

In the big ward tents the wounded lay on stretchers, silent and contemplative. I don't know what you would have called the place—a clearing station, I guess. The two tired medical officers were going from cot to cot kneeling by the boys there, reading the tags that were affixed to them, exchanging a few words. There didn't seem much that they were equipped to do yet. I suppose they were packaging the casualties to be loaded in the emptying landing craft and sent back to England. The 88's would have one more shot at them as they went out through the surf and then they would be away from it all.

After the beans I felt fine again. Getting the jeeps and the truck and finding my way and loading up and all had taken most of the day and it was afternoon as we started back. I swung my convoy onto the road that had been so empty when I had gone over it only the day before. Now the full two miles of it were lined on both sides by columns of slogging infantry. The infantry really were slogging here, for walking wide of the shoulders of the road they had to wade in the mud where the roadbed disappeared into the lagoon.

The road and the nearby waters were strewn with so many abandoned life preservers that they might have been confetti. On the road itself, we fitted into a long column of assorted vehicles of war which rolled slowly forward at five or six miles an hour. Beyond the lagoon, where the roads branched, there were no longer enough vehicles to fill them and we could roll again. We went back the way we had come out, through the village where the German corpse had been flattened, onto the crossroad and this time—Raff had told me the way he was going to try to get in—we took the road toward Chef-du-Pont. We took it as fast as we could and still stay on the road, because mortar fire was coming down on it and we were now very explosive. Two miles further ahead we caught up with Raff's rear guard—scout cars from the reconnaissance platoon. Yes, they thought Raff was going to make it. After I left, a sergeant from the 82nd Airborne had showed up in the flesh. He had come several miles across country, through fields, and he was now up at the head of our column leading Raff back. We went on in after them and presently had the sergeant guide ourselves. Raff had sent him back to fetch us.

It was queer business cutting through fields. It felt like being a rabbit with hounds after you. When we got to a metaled road, we looked to see that it was all clear and then bounced and jounced straight across it and into the field beyond. The roads we crossed were still German roads. Now and then we heard firing but could not locate the direction. We were not following Raff's tank tracks but were trying another way. We went on for an hour or two. I was sure we were lost but suddenly we came to a field which was unusually large for Normandy, and in the far corner we saw quite a big stone farmhouse. The sergeant said, "They're in there, but take that farm road all the way around the far side 'cause they can see into the field from some place. And go slow on the road because if it makes dust they'll put fire on it."

A little way up the road we met a ragged paratrooper. When he saw the big trucks following me, he turned and yelled down the road to some other paratroopers beyond, "Lookit. See 'em? We've been joined up." The trucks obviously looked very, very good to them and I didn't stop to explain that we had only two and that there was nothing behind us.

When we came all the way around the field to the farmhouse, we saw that a high stone wall enclosed it. At the gates of the stone wall there were soldiers standing about and one of them pointed at some trees off to one side, motioning to the drivers to hide the trucks there. They looked anxious and alert. When the motors of the trucks stopped, I heard for the first time a continuous crackle of small-arms fire off in the distance—in any direction I turned my head. There were spurts and isolated shots but the sounds made a continuous pattern.

I went past the soldiers through the gate.

Inside the stone wall there was a sight to make you stop and shake your head. There was a big muddy yard that once belonged to the farmer's household animals. Now it was carpeted with several hundred German soldiers and officers in various states of disrepair, lying down or sitting up silently. Not a sound came from the whole big puddle of them. They lay like gray green water in a sump, quite still. Around them, on the shores of the puddle, sat a circle of muddy desperadoes with pistols and Tommy guns pointed at the pool of Germans. It was quite a tableau. The boys who were guarding the Germans were all wounded or hurt, which was why they were sitting down. But each had at least one good arm in which he held his gun. The wounded were guarding the prisoners because the division didn't have enough unwounded to spare any able-bodied guards.

I went past the pool of prisoners to the house, thinking Ridgway and the headquarters would be there. But inside the house there was only another nightmare. There was a big room with a stove set in the wall on one side but all the other furniture cleared out of it. On the floor, from wall to wall, packed solid, arms and legs over one another and intertwined, there were badly wounded paratroopers. They were not silent and the room was alive with the kind of sound that animals make when they are hurt. Amongst this wreckage there climbed carefully two French women, a mother and a daughter, I think. One had a kettle of hot water in her hand and was going to do something with a medical officer who was standing in a far corner. I don't know what the other was doing. They were being helpful.

The medical officer saw me and picked his way across the room. He told me that Ridgway and the division headquarters were in the orchard on the far side of the farm-yard. I told him I had come in with ammunition. He wanted to know if I could take some of his wounded out.

I said, "I don't know. Why not?"

He said, "Look at them. There are two hundred and fifty around here somewhere. They are all over the house. I'm out of every-thing again. We are tearing up sheets and things."

He waited a minute and said, "I've got to get some of them out."

I said, "If it's all right, when they've got the ammunition off I'll bring the trucks down here and see if I can't take some out for you." He looked like a man getting the first good news he's had in a long time.

I went on out of the house past the prisoners. One of them was on his feet and was trying to get something across to the guards—in German, of course, with gestures. He looked as if he were ask-ing permission to go to the toilet. The guard he spoke to had only one good arm. He looked mad and he leaned forward with the arm he had in working order, holding a Tommy gun. It was heavy and it wobbled. A German officer lying near the German boy struck him in the leg and the other Germans near by yelled at the boy to sit down. He backed away from the guard and went down on his knees. One of the other Germans pushed him over sideways as if in disgust and everyone was silent again.

Beyond the prisoners there was another opening in the wall and beyond that there was a pretty orchard that was just coming into bloom and the evening sun made it sparkle. There was nothing to be seen in the orchard except one body under a blanket, and a jeep with a thin radio antenna in one corner, and a group of officers standing near a hedgerow opposite. One of the officers was Ridgway and another was Raff. Raff had gotten there an hour or so before me. His tanks were already out somewhere, working.

There might be ten thousand men in an airborne division reinforced. Ridgway figured he had about twenty-five hundred with him or in touch. He did not know what had happened to the rest of them. We presumed they were lost—had been scattered in the drop and landed too far away to be of help. We were wrong, because in a week most of them turned up. But their radios had been smashed in the drop, or had gone out of whack for some other reason, and they were then out of touch. All Ridgway knew at the time was that he only had a quarter of his division with him and a lot of them had been hurt coming down in the hills of Normandy in the dark. He had no clear picture yet of who was around him but he was in good heart. He had parachuted himself the night before, and his staff with him. Most of them were there and the G-4—the supply officer—was excited to learn what I had brought. We went off to get it out to where the guns were. Apparently the Pfc. and I had been fair shoppers, for what they needed most were the 75-mm. howitzer shells we had. The 82nd landed its light artillery successfully but had had to stop firing some hours before when their last rounds had been expended.

I have one other memory of the 82nd Airborne CP on D plus 1. It was after I got back from handing over the ammunition trucks. We were all standing where I'd first met Ridgway, ten or twelve of us, in the orchard a few yards in front of a hedge under which there was a ditch which was serving as bachelor field officers' quarters. The sounds of firing still came in from all four sides of us, now further away, now nearer. Every little while as we talked, a small party would come in from one side or another of the orchard. Each party consisted of two or four or five very badly frightened German soldiers with their hands so high in the air above them that they looked as if they really were reaching for something—and behind them one or two, but never more, grim and tattered doughboys.

Grim and tattered is exactly what a paratrooper looks like after a night drop into trees and hedgerows. These looked particularly ferocious and you could tell that they were still angry and did not want to be obeying the orders to bring the prisoners in. The word had gone round that the Germans had been shooting parachutists as they hung in their harness, after their chutes had tangled in trees and brush, and also that the Germans had been cutting them out of their harness and, instead of taking them prisoners, hanging them by the neck. So these boys were playing for keeps. But they still kept bringing in the prisoners as they cornered them or overcame them.

It was almost night of the second day ashore. Raff and Co. had helped but had not really relieved the division. Quite obviously, whether what was left of the airborne division would survive was a near thing. The thought was in all our minds.

Then suddenly, against the even unevenness of the rifle fire, came that familiar sharp high whining crack and on top of it a sharp concussion, very close. We stood under one row of apple trees. Down from the row beyond us, drifting as if a bad boy had shaken the limbs to knock the blossoms loose, came leaves and twigs floating down. This I saw clearly over my shoulder as I disappeared into the ditch under the hedgerow. There were two more cracks in quick succession and I stuck my helmet up over the edge of the ditch and looked out. I looked to the right and I looked to the left and all along the ditch there were other helmets like mine now, poking up to peek out. And in the field we had left so suddenly there was now only one man standing and that was the General. He was standing there quite alone, bareheaded, and looking down at his staff and his visitors.

What he said quite calmly was, "I *thought* they were ranging on that radio. You know, I think we ought to tell them to move it. They might get hurt over there."

It doesn't sound much telling it but it was really one of those moments. Cut off, dwindling in strength, not knowing what next, there was a tension there that could have been snapped by the enemy's locating the CP—where all the wounded and the prisoners were, and the commanding general and his staff, and his communications. One flicker of indecision and that whole tenuous thing you write about as morale would have broken like a glass dropped on stone. It was obviously a crazy thing for the commanding general to do—to stand there without even a helmet on and let the 88 fire break around his head. But it was one of the things he had to do, and it was superbly right to do it, and Ridgway did it with grace and dignity—and great courage.

The 88 kept on firing; its bursts were now long, now short. After a few more shells, it was obvious that its gunners did not really know where we were but were simply ranging around looking for us. The dangerous moment was past. The show went on.

I thought to myself, We are here to stay. OVERLORD is going to work.

PART TWO

CHANNEL TO VICTORY

7   The Conference Table vs. the Atlantic Wall

THE first six days in Normandy belonged to the OVERLORD *
planners—as the life of a baby belongs to its mother during the
very act of its violent birth. During those six days there was
nothing the doctors on the far shore could do about the infant
invasion except to wait for it to struggle from the landing craft.
They could not speed its birth, nor slow it; could not even alter its
direction or maneuver it. For six weeks thereafter, the invasion
was still a very young child whose life depended upon the daily
sustenance it sucked from the beaches, but after the first week
there were things that the generals could do about keeping it alive
—after they had come ashore from their command ships and their
tents had been set up for them. Through its infancy, however, the
survival of the invasion depended upon its prenatal health, the
soundness of its growth as a living but still unborn thing in its
womb in southern England. As during the birth of every living
thing, its ultimate existence also rested on the will to live of each
individual cell that composed it. Without the struggle of the individual soldiers who crossed the beaches and went into the rolling
hills and fought there, each for his own individual survival, the
whole invasion, however beautifully planned and marvelously put
together, would have been a child born perfectly formed but dying.

* You will sometimes hear this operation referred to as NEPTUNE.
OVERLORD was the overall plan for the trans-Channel invasion of Europe;
NEPTUNE was the code name for the assault phase of OVERLORD.

With these thoughts, the metaphor ends—for in Normandy, of course, there were not one but three invasions—and the first problem of their survival was to join them into a single effort which would be greater than the sum of the three individual efforts. Specifically the British landed to the east on beaches of their own, the best known being called JUNO and GOLD. Some miles to the west of JUNO and GOLD, another self-contained force, this one of Americans, went ashore at the foot of some steep sand cliffs, on a beach that was known as OMAHA. All of these beaches were solidly on the coast of Normandy where it runs east to west, parallel to the south coast of England.

A little further to the west, beyond OMAHA, there is a town called Isigny which is at the mouth of an inlet. At Isigny the coast of France makes a right angle turn and juts thirty miles due north into the English Channel to form what is known as the Cotentin peninsula, on the tip of which is the port of Cherbourg. This peninsula is easier to remember if you simply think of it as the Cherbourg peninsula. A few miles down the Cherbourg peninsula from Isigny, there is another beach which the Americans called UTAH. The American assault force which took UTAH was as self-contained as the other American force at OMAHA or the British around JUNO and GOLD.

All three assault forces had initially similar missions: to land, to force and reduce the coastal defenses and to proceed far enough inland to protect the landing beaches from enemy fire. So far each was on its own. Immediately thereafter all three were to press out on both flanks. So pressing out, JUNO and GOLD would be joined with OMAHA, and OMAHA would reach around the corner at Isigny to meet UTAH. After this juncture, the Anglo-American beachhead could be said to exist.

The first further responsibility, beyond the establishment of the beachhead, fell to the forces which landed on the Cherbourg peninsula at UTAH. This was to take the port of Cherbourg. It might be done in one of two ways—either by immediately turning north, to drive twenty-five miles, or by first going straight inland from the beach, twenty-five miles across rolling country to the Atlantic side of the peninsula, thus isolating it from the mainland of France. With the peninsula thus denied enemy reinforcements, it could be whittled down and the port taken at the American commander's pleasure.

The capture of the port of Cherbourg was a fundamental requirement in Plan OVERLORD, but the pre-invasion planners had left it to the field commander to decide how the attack should be handled. On the subject of exploiting the balance of the beachhead, the planners had had to be even more vague. They stated as an axiom that a second major port would have to be taken within sixty days, but left it to the commander in the field to determine whether that port should be Le Havre, at the mouth of the Seine forty miles away to the east of where the British landed, or Brest, a running two hundred miles, first due south and then around the corner out along the Brest peninsula towards the Atlantic.

After taking Cherbourg and either Le Havre or Brest, the planners suggested that the field commander might be interested in moving on Paris. After bringing up this exciting possibility, the OVERLORD planners ran abruptly out of imagination and, apparently terrified by their own temerity, hastened to urge that the field commander knock off for at least three months—while supplies piled up behind him and he rested, refitted and regrouped his forces.

On the subject of who should be in command in the field, soon after the landing the crisp clearness of OVERLORD's allocation of responsibility for the assault also fell away sharply into vagueness. General Sir Bernard Montgomery was to be in unquestioned command of all ground forces during and immediately after the assault, restricted only by the clause which denied him the right to place "forces smaller than a corps" of one nationality under the command of another nationality. But it was foreseen that one day the American forces in France would be so numerous, and the area of the whole occupation so large, that this form of command would be inadequate. On that date, the commander of the American forces would no longer be responsible to Montgomery but he and the senior American commander, now co-equal, would both be responsible to the Supreme Allied Commander. But no date was stipulated for this major alteration in the command. It was simply left that it should take place when in the judgment of the

Supreme Commander the situation warranted. The OVERLORD planners were farsighted enough dimly to see Paris beyond the mists of the Normandy beaches. Presumably, although it was never directly so stated, they felt that the British Commander-in-Chief should continue to have the Supreme Commander's power of attorney until the German armies in France had been destroyed and the capital of France taken. Montgomery's staff officers certainly so assumed.

Whatever the future was to hold, however, there was no question but that Montgomery commanded the Allied ground forces on the Continent after they emerged from the toils of the landing itself, during which no individual could impose his will on the battle and only the effectiveness of the plan itself, and the courage and resourcefulness of the individuals who executed it, determined whether there would be any Allied army in Europe to command at all. After there were armies in France to maneuver —two of them to be precise, one British and one American— Montgomery began issuing orders and the big show was on.

All military plans begin with an appreciation of the enemy situation. The military term "appreciation" involves an estimate and an analysis. What has the enemy got in front of you, where has he got it, what is he likely to do with it? The things he *can* do are called his capabilities. In European armies, the things you guess the enemy is likely to do are called his intentions. The American Army does not approve of guessing and is against the listing of intentions. But American staff officers do weigh the likelihood of the enemy's taking advantage of the various capabilities.

The whole picture of what the enemy is up to is put together by the Intelligence advisors on the commanding general's staff—called the G-2 section in the American Army. It is based on information gathered from first-hand reports in the field—what's been seen and heard in the front line—on the interrogation of any prisoners that may have been taken, on aerial photographs and visual reconnaissance from aircraft, on the information which may reach headquarters from line-crossers and agents behind the enemy lines, from what can be learned by monitoring (listening in on) enemy radio channels—or by tapping his field telephone lines if they can be reached—and even by analysis of the enemy's high level pronouncements and public communiqués. All this is salted down with knowledge previously gained.

An army's appraisal of the enemy is continuous; G-2 goes in business with a reasonably complete knowledge of what troops the enemy has at his disposal, knows each unit by name, number and composition. Throughout the war, G-2 keeps track of each unit, studying its individual capabilities, its successive commanders, noting its casualties, and the reinforcements that have been given to it, how well outfitted it is, how much ammunition it's got and, very important, its day-to-day morale.

On the morning of the invasion, the enemy's coastal defenses— his famed Atlantic Wall—had the capability of inflicting very heavy casualties on its attackers. From his immediately available reserves, the enemy commander easily could bring up sufficient field forces to outnumber us. The initial assault was on a seven-division front—not counting the airborne divisions—but it would take two days for even all the elements of these assault divisions to get ashore. The build-up race between the Allied landing craft and the German troop trains was demonstrably an unequal one. At any time during the first six days, the Germans were capable of throwing a dozen fresh divisions in against the Allies, the latter fighting with only the supplies they brought ashore with them, without over-all command and control or communications, and without any ability to maneuver. The enemy's intentions, of course, were to throw us all back into the sea—if he could.

The first waves of the Anglo-American invasion, however, were not annihilated and thrown back into the sea (as the German radio had gleefully broadcast from the safety of Berlin on the morning of the invasion). Only under the cliffs of OMAHA, in fact, had there been even a momentary delay. There, the first assault waves of Rangers, engineers and infantrymen of the American 1st Infantry Division had been pinned on the beach below the cliff for six hours until the destroyer screen swung in close and battered the pillboxes set into the cliff with direct fire—and the foot soldiers had scrambled up the sand, some of them led personally by full colonels and brigadier generals. The battle-cry was, "What the hell, we might as well die up there on the cliff as down here. Come on, let's go." After scaling the cliffs, the force on

OMAHA made a clean breakthrough and on D plus 1 were only halted by orders from Montgomery himself.

Both on British GOLD and American UTAH the assault waves had battered through and over the thin shell of obstacles and fortifications on the beach and were several miles inland by noon of the first day. The preliminary air bombardment and the shelling from the naval guns had knocked out few of the concrete emplacements but they had stunned and scattered the Germans who were strung out along the shore. There were no shock troops there but only older men who had been in an occupation army too long, and the Germans had in their ranks too large a percentage of unwilling comrades impressed into service from the conquered territories of eastern Europe.

More important still, there was the miracle that the Allies had achieved complete surprise—surprise that was strategic as well as tactical. The element of strategic surprise lay in the fact that the Germans considered the narrow crossing at the Pas de Calais the most likely avenue of approach and had given the beaches of Normandy only second priority. Moreover they did not really expect the invasion at all for another month. Thus they had concentrated on the defense of the Pas de Calais and had been lulled by our incessant maneuvering into the happy thought that we were not ready.

Tactically, the Germans had a right to expect at least a day or two's warning before we showed up. Even this had been denied them by the happy circumstance of a solid cover of low cloud over the Channel for the two days preceding the landing—when the Channel itself had already broken out with a rash of our shipping. The cloud cover was not so low but that a reasonably energetic Luftwaffe could have flown under it but the Germans' Channel reconnaissance had long since deteriorated into routine flights at high altitude. On June 4 and 5, seen from a thirty-thousand-foot altitude, the Channel was covered with an impenetrable blanket of cloud. Thus the Allied armada crept upon the shores of France unnoticed.

When the Allies struck, the bewildered forces of the Atlantic Wall, stunned and surprised, fell back in a confusion that was even greater than the confusion inherent in the landing forces'

first few days ashore. The confusion in the Germans' higher headquarters seemed even greater. At long last, the sacrifices of the
Dieppe raid paid a small dividend. Dieppe had frightened the
Germans for a few hours and the whole coast had been alerted
for a full scale invasion. Subsequently everyone's face had been
red—when Dieppe had been identified as no more than an Allied
raid. In June, when the first reports of the approaching Allied
fleet reached the headquarters of Colonel General von Kluge,
Commander-in-Chief West, first the map-room orderlies and then
the junior officers, each in turn, hesitated to sound the alarm and
wake their superior officers until the first flashes had been confirmed. Actually six hours seemed to have elapsed before a
telephone was lifted. Under Von Kluge, Field Marshal Rommel
was in command in Normandy; on June 5 he was amusing himself
in Berlin.

Even after the German command had belatedly pulled itself
together, it seems to have suffered from a "This-can't-happen-to-
us" reaction. By the time it recovered, the opportunity to strike
the separate Allied beachheads before they were consolidated was
gone forever. Armed forces are like that; they are at the mercy
of the decisive reactions of their commanders. Without the necessary orders, nothing happens—regardless of how alert and able
the junior commanders and their forces may be.

With the one horse already stolen, the Germans now strove
to get the lock back on the barn door to save the rest of the stable.
The first enemy command decision with which Montgomery had
to contend was not, as everyone had expected, an order to counterattack the beachhead in force but was simply a resolve to contain
the beachhead—to keep its expansion within reasonable limits—
until the Allies' further intentions were clearer.

In order to contain the beachhead, the enemy began moving
up his immediately available reserves as rapidly as possible, but
instead of launching even local attacks he contented himself with
forming his troops into a continuous line, ordering them to dig
in there. It was soon apparent that he was unwilling to draw on
the troops he had available on the Pas de Calais. Would our landing in Normandy be our only, or even our main, effort? He made

no move whatever to bring troops across Germany from the Russian front.

In disposing the troops he did bring up, because of the nature of the terrain the enemy had to group most of his armor around the eastern end of the beachhead in front of Caen—for here the Allies had landed close to the plain which leads down to the Seine. If Montgomery were to break through here, cross the Seine, take Le Havre and proceed eastward, the Germans' whole force in France would be in danger. An Allied drive up the Seine valley would cut off most of them.

About the rest of the Allied line, the enemy felt more secure. No flat ground beckoned the Americans on but only many miles of that unbroken hilly country which the French call the Bocage. It is terrain so easy to defend that it might have been dreamt up for that precise purpose.

In the handling of the Bocage country lies the whole secret of the strategy which took France back from the Germans.

It must be understood that the beaches chosen for the assault lay along a strip of coast line backed by a semicircular bulge of a very special terrain, unlike the terrain in any other part of France. It was this bulge that was known as the Bocage country. The Bocage country began just east of Caen and its perimeter swept south, away from the beaches in a shallow arc sixty or seventy miles inland. There it turned west toward the Atlantic, and it reached the mouth of the Channel at Avranches, just where the Brest peninsula begins, in the very crook of the elbow of the Brest peninsula.

Beyond the perimeter of the Bocage country, France is flat. Inside the perimeter, the ground is broken into a continuous succession of tiny hills without marked ridge lines. These hills themselves are cut into minute fields, each handkerchief size field surrounded by dense hedgerows which grow up out of ridges. Even without the hedgerows on top of them, these ridges fence in each field as securely as a New England stone wall. The exact pattern varies. Many of the little fields are also surrounded by ditches three to four feet deep and the hedgerows rise between the ditches of adjoining fields. Some have double rows of trees and ditches, with an embankment between. The hedgerows them-

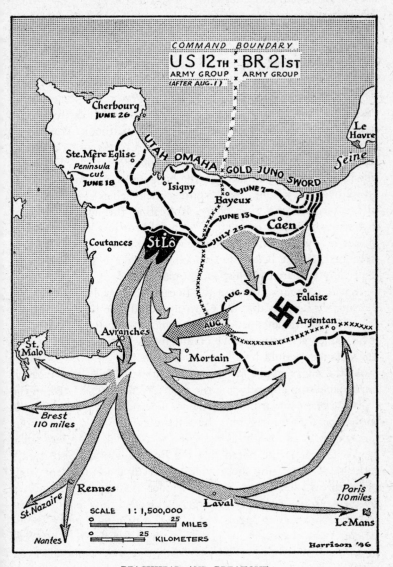

BEACHHEAD AND BREAKOUT

selves are dense and continuous and the Bocage country they characterize is also sometimes known as the hedgerow country.

There are few of the long straight arterial highways that characterize the rest of France in the hedgerow country. The roads are narrow and winding. But it is the endless succession of tiny fields separated by dense hedgerows that makes the country ideal for defense. The combination of the hedgerow and the embankment—often with ditches thrown in—constitutes an earthworks as efficient as if built to plan out of a military textbook. You cannot see through the hedgerows from one field to the next, and each may conceal a weapon large enough to stop a tank. The tanks themselves must lurch through the hedgerows, up-ending as they crash over the mound, thus exposing their bellies as if they were paper targets on a rifle range. Retreating through the Bocage country, the enemy can defend each field for just long enough to inflict heavy casualties on the attackers and then drop back unseen to the next hedgerow, which waits like a switch position especially prepared for just such a maneuver.

It was, of course, because the Bocage country lay back of the Normandy beaches that the Germans could take the risk of leaving them lightly defended. They reasoned correctly that an enemy who gained a foothold there could always be slowed down until the defenders could bring up reinforcements.

At the edges of the hedgerow country the hills that make it formidable stop abruptly and the plains stretch—southward, to the Loire River; eastward, to the Seine. The military game of landing on beaches leading into the Bocage country is to fight your way out of it as rapidly as possible and to break loose into these plains. (It should be noted that the Bocage country also does a nice job of protecting those who have secured a lodgement from being thrown out of it.) So Commander-in-Chief Montgomery's problem, as soon as sufficient forces had landed to give him troops to command, was to break out from the Bocage country somewhere. With the Germans concentrating their defending forces in such a tight circle around the Allies, the prize was made even more desirable. A real breakout anywhere would not only set the Allied armor free to race across the plains but would also turn the whole German line. It was an odds-on bet that large portions of it could be encircled—for if one cannot advance rapidly in hedgerow country, neither can one retreat rapidly through it.

By the end of the first week ashore, enough information had come in to Montgomery's 21st Army Group Headquarters for his Intelligence officers to estimate that the Germans had committed their entire immediately available reserves. It was at that moment that Montgomery made the bold decision to defeat the German army facing him immediately, with his own British Second Army and without any assistance at all from the Americans to the west of him.

Vitally important to Montgomery in making his decision was the spectacular success of the Allied tactical air forces in what is called "isolating the battlefield." To isolate a battlefield by air action means flying over the enemy's front line to attack the communications in his rear. It means cutting vital railway bridges, bombing out road centers, scattering dumps and even strafing columns on foot when the enemy's troops have been forced out of their trains and trucks. The isolation is never water-tight but operates to limit the rate at which the enemy can reinforce his troops in the front line. In Normandy, this isolation of the beachhead area was vital because the action on both sides was limited by the respective rates of reinforcements—the Allies across the beach on a timetable that could not be materially altered, and the Germans across the excellent road and rail net of France.

The key to the isolation of the beachhead areas was the destruction of the bridges over the Seine, for without them the German reinforcements from eastern France had to make a long detour through Paris to reach the battle. The fighter bombing of the Seine bridges made military history over night; every single bridge over the Seine from its mouth to the capital was successfully blown apart. Such a thing had never been done before. Thereafter, German reinforcements continued to come up but they were limited to a trickle coming across the Seine in ferries, or over temporary ponton bridges which had to be hidden by day. Coming by rail, soldiers had to detrain as far away as Paris and walk or bicycle from there on, their supply convoys creeping after them by night. To accomplish all this, the Allied air forces had, of course, first to battle the Luftwaffe back from the front so that its nearest useable airfields were some hundred miles to the rear. Thus handicapped, when enemy fighters came to the front they found themselves outnumbered and outfought.

All this advantage Montgomery had to work with. He saw the situation map before him as if it were the map of another El Alamein, with an enemy wholly committed and without the power to bring reinforcements to the battle. His resources thus limited, the Hun could be out-maneuvered, defeated and destroyed. On this reasoning, Sir Bernard proposed to fight a battle of his own making at Caen. Following victory here, The Master's armor would be ready to break loose into the Seine Valley.

The first fundamental idea in the OVERLORD plan—that before everything else the Americans should capture Cherbourg and get that port solidly behind whatever offensive was to follow—Sir Bernard now described as of secondary importance. When asked about it, Montgomery's Chief-of-Staff actually made the statement in a staff conference that Bradley and his Americans "would certainly be required to take Cherbourg—but simply as a matter of discipline." Churchill's description of Montgomery had been accurate: if he was magnificent in defeat, he was also insufferable in victory.

By the morning Monty's Chief-of-Staff voiced his sentiments, General Bradley had made his own decision to take the long road to Cherbourg—to cut the peninsula first and only then to push on to the port itself. The first attempt to drive across to the sea had come to a bloody halt in the hedgerows, a few hundred yards beyond where it had jumped the day before. The commander of the division concerned was relieved, and a second division which had landed after the assault moved up to strike. At the other end of the line, where the British and American forces joined—along the so-called international boundary line between the two armies —the American infantry was some miles out in front of the British and complaining that its flank was not being covered. But Montgomery made no use of it in planning his Caen attack. He did not feel that he needed the efforts of any Americans.

Other considerations must have moved him in making his decision, as his quick blue eyes scanned the situation map which was spread before him and he thought of the situation as it was that day, and of the changes that were bound to come about if he did not act now. His was, as his officers had told us the day we joined his staff, a British headquarters. His 21st Army Group was composed of one British and one Canadian army. As these armies had gathered on the southern shores of England, they were at their maximum strength. From Canada would only come replacements, to maintain the divisions already in the field. The British Government, for reasons of its own, had its manpower spread all the way across from the Mediterranean around to the Far East. From England itself, as well as from Canada, there would come only replacements, no newly formed divisions. Even these replacements would be inadequate and the British foresaw the day when they would have to break up some units to keep others at full strength.

On the other side of the international boundary, the American forces were already outgrowing the forces of the Empire in relative strength. The invasion had waited for only enough American divisions from across the Atlantic to match the available British strength. Behind these divisions, whole armies were queued up— were already landing in the United Kingdom, were crossing the sea, were embarking, were training, were being activated. For the strictly immediate present, the advance guard of this great force was under General Sir Bernard Montgomery's command. If the destruction of the German Army was to be a wholly British victory, it had best be now, when the Empire forces in France and immediately across the Channel from France were stronger than they would ever be again—and before the Americans overshadowed them by sheer weight of numbers. And here on the map was an overwhelming victory waiting to be won—for, apparently, the lightest of casualties, so overwhelming had Allied superiority suddenly become.

Montgomery's principal officers and Montgomery himself were a unique combination. They had never been beaten. They had come into the war at the end of an almost unbroken succession of defeats administered to their countrymen. They had come into it in Africa, at the very gates of Alexandria—taking over the last line of defense before all Egypt fell—and, after Egypt, the oil in the Middle East. They had three assets with which to meet the crisis. They had, first, the fact that their enemy was now a whole desert away from its nearest supply port and had to fight with what it had with it in the field. They had, second, the big new American tanks and trucks which had come to replace the cast-offs with which the Mediterranean armies had always fought before. They were operating in the first economy of military plenty which the Mediterranean had known. And, finally, Monty's army got a taste of its commander's cocky confidence. To troops who had been beaten so often, this was a nourishing as well as a heady wine.

The times were made for Montgomery in Africa. What he had to offer—his decisiveness, his discipline, his intolerance of muddle-headedness in his own officers, his disrespect for bumbling higher authority—but above all his supreme confidence in himself, his hard egotism—all these things made new men of the officers who had come so close to destroying Rommel so many times—only to be frustrated by stupidity in high places, by uncertainty and by lack of equipment, and by the open conflict of political with military aims. Monty had made new men of his troops, too, for they felt his vitality and his impatience to get on with it—and he brought them new weapons with which to fight. With these tools and this spirit Montgomery won on the battlefield of El Alamein.

It is true that the tools had been on their way long before Montgomery took command, and that Rommel had been fighting for as long as the British on almost as thin a shoestring at the time he was beaten. But Rommel had never been beaten before and, with the Eighth Army, Montgomery beat him. With Rommel's defeat at El Alamein, the whole tide of the war in the West seemed to set for the Allies. Rommel was on the run—and at the end of the run there was the vast weight of force from the western continent waiting in Tunisia to finish him. All this had had its effect on Montgomery and his headquarters.

The manner of the death of Rommel's Africa Corps is important to know, too—to understand Montgomery at Caen. You have to recall those days before the victory in Tunisia when the Americans had fallen back in confusion, scared by a skirmish that was hardly more than a bluff. Presently the Americans under General Patton were to hold, in the classic simile of one communiqué, "the walls of the cylinder through which the piston of the Eighth Army" drove the Africa Corps. And Bradley's infantry and armor were to go in through the desert hills to kill and capture one hundred and fifty thousand Germans at the tip of the Tunisian peninsula. But it was in confused recollection of the early days of this action that Montgomery had made the remark which set off a historic feud.

It happened after the campaign, when Montgomery had called a conference of his principal commanders and asked each to address their assembled staffs on how victory in Africa had been won. It was a stimulating session and General Patton attended it as an observer. After it was over, a British officer asked Patton if he didn't think it a fine show. When Patton's comment—to the effect that there had been too much talk to entertain him—was relayed to the British commander, Montgomery's reply—the words were memorized in American Headquarters—was, "The next time I see Georgie Patton I'll have just three things to say to him: Get out of my way, take your troops back and train them —and leave me your petrol." *

The crack about training had a particular significance because after the Americans' defeat at Kasserine Pass it had been seriously proposed to the Americans (by Field Marshal Alexander's officers) that plans for the campaign be altered while American troops were given further training before being returned to the front. It was this situation to which Terry Allen, then commanding the American 1st Infantry Division, referred when he told his troops before El Guettar that he wasn't kidding, not only the honor but the whole effectiveness of the American Army in the field depended on how the 1st Division performed that day against a German Panzer division. El Guettar was a miniature American victory which followed Kasserine Pass.

To the American command, the early setbacks were a worrisome but wholly natural part of the process of hardening new formations in battle, an integral part of the metamorphosis of

---

* After France had been liberated, Patton is said to have proposed sending a five-gallon can of gasoline to Montgomery. The messenger was to remind the Field Marshal of his stipulation and to report, "Sir, General Patton's troops are now trained; he hopes you feel he is far enough out of your way [Patton was several hundred miles ahead of Montgomery at the time]; and here is all the gasoline the American Army has left over."

green troops into veterans. On Montgomery, they made an indelible impression, an impression still clear and sharp in Normandy when he thought in terms of "requiring Bradley to take Cherbourg as a matter of discipline."

All this quick past lay immediately behind the British Commander-in-Chief as he gathered his forces on the beaches of Normandy just outside the little French city of Caen. It affected the viewpoint of the staff to whom he was The Master and who were cast in the same image. Now was the moment to take the offensive, when the blow could be struck against an enemy as committed as he had been at El Alamein, and struck with British forces under a British headquarters, for British credit and prestige. There would be other German armies in Europe to defeat after the army at Caen was destroyed, but these The Master would take in his stride, piecemeal, one at a time, using American troops then, after he had taken them in hand. There would be no question of his retaining command of the American forces after the initial victory. Sir Bernard would strike at once.

The result of Montgomery's decision was the battle of Caen—which was really two battles, two successive all-out attacks, continuing after Caen itself had fallen. Beginning in mid-June and ending nearly a month later, it was a defeat from which British arms on the Continent never recovered. It was the first and last all-British battle fought in Europe. As he had feared, Montgomery was never again able to gather sufficient Empire forces under his command to fight alone but thereafter had always to borrow troops and supplies to gain the superiority without which he would not even plan an attack.

Montgomery finally took Caen—so tardily that to the watching Americans Stalin's cable of congratulations to Churchill seemed a masterpiece of irony. It said simply, "Congratulations on your brilliant victory at Caen."

Montgomery took Caen only after two all-out attacks, each one involving the full employment of the strategic air force on tactical objectives. He was stopped just beyond Caen after practically destroying the British Armored Corps by running his tanks in successive waves head on into German 88 fire. He failed to destroy, or even to defeat, the German army opposite him. After

Caen, he could not even attempt to break out of the Bocage country. His forces were exhausted.

The British troops involved at Caen were the Empire's best and the story of the armor charging at Caen was tragically similar to the story of the British Cavalry as immortalized in "The Charge of the Light Brigade." The Germans met Montgomery's attack by depressing the barrels of the anti-aircraft batteries which saturated the Channel coast, using them for direct fire from behind hedgerows. Montgomery's tacticians had counted on only field artillery opposition from the Germans' ground forces; when the ack-ack batteries joined the battle they were undone. They had also expected the strategic bombardment to cause even more disruption than it had.

Most of all, however, it was the hedgerow country that lost Montgomery the battle of Caen—the hedgerow country that beat the men who had learned their trade on the flat desert. The hedgerows won over the individual courage and brilliance of soldiers who had survived Africa because they were both brave and brilliant but who did not understand the terrain in which they now fought.

This I know from personal observation because at the conferences that planned the battle of Caen the minority opinion (led by a young American colonel named Bonesteel) predicted what would happen to armor in hedgerow country but was overruled. For my part, I had only to watch and wonder—so sharp was the difference between the men who said it will happen in such and such a way at Caen and the men who said, "No, it will happen so and so." I listened to the argument and I heard Bonesteel's prophecy that the tanks would be destroyed. I have no way of knowing whether both sides were ever put up to the Commander-in-Chief. Montgomery's staff was not invited to protest Montgomery's plans. But I do know that before the orders were issued to engage in the battle of Caen, the argument as to why it would fail had been developed and vigorously expressed on what the British called "lower levels."

While the back of the British armor was being broken at Caen, the American infantry began the reduction of the Cherbourg peninsula the hard way, without either spectacular aerial bombardment, massed armor or even heavy artillery barrages—on foot. To Bradley, the Bocage was an infantry problem and there was no short cut to victory.*

Scrabbling from hedgerow to hedgerow, up hill and down dale, the infantry which had landed at UTAH pressed the attack to cut the peninsula. They cut the last German north-south communications at Barneville-sur-Mer, twelve days after the landing. It had not been too tough a fight because the Germans were still off balance; one division, the veteran 9th Infantry, had done the job, with two others protecting its flanks. Bradley immediately wheeled a corps of three divisions north and in four days this force had marched and fought its way to the perimeter defenses of Cherbourg. There followed another four days of fighting, this time with a real artillery and air bombardment, and the first fortress city of Europe fell on June 26.

The march up the peninsula had involved the most ruthless destruction (of the towns the Germans chose to defend) that the whole campaign was to see. The taking of the port itself was an impressive feat because it was surrounded by a semicircle of rugged hills and these were heavily fortified with steel and concrete. The speed and violence with which they were attacked was what counted. The German garrison was bewildered by the shock of it. I remember some of the German nurses who were captured in a hospital there. They could not get over the confidence of the Americans—"All of you seem so *sure* you will win." One said she was unhappy she had been born a German.

Bradley had used less than half of his forces in the reduction of Cherbourg but he had plenty for his other divisions to do. Their first mission was to keep the Germans from consolidating their positions anywhere along the line. The order was to attack constantly, to keep driving inland, away from the marshes and the flooded areas back of where the peninsula joins the mainland. The

---

* An important contribution to the solution of the Bocage problem was a tank-dozer—the tank rigged with a heavy scraper blade like a snowplow or a bulldozer. Such armored vehicles pushed down hedgerows and filled ditches to make passages through these obstructions. They were impressive proof of the adaptability of American arms. But the best medicine for the Bocage hedgerows remained good old-fashioned firepower.

attacks were unspectacular; some of them were obvious and heavy-handed—unimaginative line bucks, involving heavy casualties. But through the weeks they edged forward until, by the time Cherbourg fell, they had spread some miles south from the base of the peninsula. Now the Americans had room to maneuver, with a net of good roads behind them and the enemy pushed well away from the beaches—and from the dumps and the airfields that were opening up behind them. When Cherbourg fell, Bradley had thirteen divisions ashore, only six of them in the line after the surrender of the port—which gave him an unemployed striking force of seven divisions. He was all set to go.

Throughout the campaign to take the peninsula and to broaden our hold on its base, Bradley remained under the nominal command of Montgomery. However, after venturing the opinion that what the Americans did was of academic interest only, the British Commander-in-Chief had left the American Army Commander to his own devices. It was only after his defeat at Caen that Montgomery awoke to the fact that his own failure, plus Bradley's success, had cost him the command of the ground forces in Europe.

Eisenhower's Supreme Headquarters may or may not have wanted to create an American command the equal of the British so soon—the change required the Supreme Headquarters to become operational itself, if only to co-ordinate the two efforts. But Montgomery had shot the British bolt * and the American forces had gone ahead on their own—on Bradley's initiative—and were set up with plenty of troops and plenty of room to maneuver in. SHAEF had no choice.

Montgomery made one more bid for his right to command. He proposed that the American forces swing on a British pivot from the vicinity of Caen and sweep the Bocage like a broom. He not only proposed it; he issued orders that it be done. But by the time these orders got through to Bradley's headquarters, the latter's plans for a battle that might win the war were already before Eisenhower. It was an unequal contest, between the ideas of a

* So dramatic was Montgomery's failure that the British Chiefs of Staff themselves actually encouraged Eisenhower to crack down on him. The Supreme Commander, however, contented himself with a note urging his British Commander-in-Chief to remain on the aggressive.

man who had just been defeated and had nothing of his own left with which to fight, and the proposals of a victorious general with fresh troops. Eisenhower took back the unrestricted power of attorney he had given Montgomery for the assault and the first act of the command and control drama on the Continent was over.

As Supreme Commander, now about to take command, Eisenhower did not give Bradley the powers Montgomery had had. He did not even release Bradley from Montgomery's operational direction—on paper. He simply let Bradley get away with doing what he pleased, despite the papers. But there was no doubt about what had happened: the senior command in the field had passed from the great Montgomery to the humble Bradley.

Eisenhower himself could not take active command in the field if only for the reason that his headquarters was not designed for it. The staff which had been given him—he picked only a few of its members—was not a field staff. It was never meant to be and was not organized as such. It was built to co-ordinate Anglo-American war efforts in the theater of war, not to run battles. It was constructed to be informed of decisions, not to make them. Decisions as to strategy would be made on higher levels, by the Combined Chiefs of Staff of the two nations and by the heads of the two States. Tactical decisions, SHAEF would have to accept from its field commanders. It was set up as a super de luxe, polylingual go-between, complete with WAC's, ATS's, MP's, PA's and brass enough to start a foundry.

All these things SHAEF was in the beginning and remained till the end, even though, later in the campaign, history sought vainly to give it a more active role. After it was all over, and all the fighting done, and the dead buried, and the PW's sent home, SHAEF had its picture painted by its own public relations officers—on a metaphorical white horse, brandishing its saber and leading the Allied nations into battle. But nobody who had been in the field was fooled.

At the time Bradley took Cherbourg and Montgomery lost his armor at Caen, the SHAEF headquarters was frantically trying to collect itself in England, preparatory to moving to the first convenient location either army could capture for it in France. Eisenhower himself had received the Combined Chiefs of Staff in their august persons on the beachhead on D plus 5 and explained to them what Montgomery said he was going to do to the Germans. When Montgomery did not do it, Bradley became Eisenhower's senior field commander on his, Bradley's, record since D-day, and for want of competition—for Montgomery's planning was now as tired as his troops.

At the time that Bradley inherited the active command in the field, his army was drawn up along "St. Lô Road"—one of those rare arterial roads that cut through the Bocage country, this one running from St. Lô almost due west toward the Atlantic. Having cautiously fought his infantry from one limited objective to the next for nearly two months, he was now to execute plans for a battle even more ambitious than Montgomery's at Caen.

To begin with, the battle of St. Lô called for an all-out infantry attack on a relatively narrow front—about five running miles—and this attack was to keep going until it cut clear through the German defenses. Having forced a gap in the German perimeter defense, Bradley would then break loose his armor beyond it. It was a play of great daring, for the armor could not *immediately* break loose into the plains, which were forty miles beyond. Having gotten into the German rear areas, our tanks would still have to run the gauntlet of those forty miles of unbroken hedgerow country before they could come out on the nearest flat land at the base of the Brest peninsula. They would have to rely solely on speed, on getting through so fast that the Germans, racing backwards, could neither catch up with them nor bring up reserves to cut them off anywhere.

The plan for the attack phase of the battle was called COBRA—because the two armor-reinforced-by-infantry columns, which were to do the running through the hole made for them by the infantry, were each nearly one hundred miles long and so had to be coiled behind our lines, coiled to strike. When I first heard the name I thought it was an apt one but hoped the Germans didn't have a mongoose in their army. There was a story current that a planning officer on the First Army staff, thinking that the streaking columns would turn and wrap themselves about the German army, had wanted to name the plan for a snake which crushed its victims—but that the only snake whose name he could remember was the cobra. Actually, the name COBRA fitted well because the savage lashing out it called for was part of a larger plan of Bradley's called LUCKY STRIKE. The lucky strike would be the break-through to encircle the whole of the Bocage country and free France.

This was the measure of the ambition of the plan that Bradley had begun dreaming up when he was still in England, and which the veterans of the staff he brought with him from Africa had been working on ever since. It is hard, looking back from the hindsight of a victorious campaign, to recreate the atmosphere in which Bradley's plan was created and the battle begun. Relatively few of his troops were yet veterans; his husbanding of his armored divisions had been wise but it had meant that they were still without battle experience in France. Fourteen days after the original landing, the American beaches had been turned into shambles by the historic storm of June 20. The Cherbourg harbor had only just been cleared of mines and could contribute practically nothing to Bradley's supplies. The German propaganda radio had already begun to make capital of what it considered the stalemate around the Allied beachhead.

Bradley had no evidence whatever that the Bocage country could be forced without casualties he couldn't afford, and an armored blitz through the terrain that lay ahead looked almost like madness, especially after Caen. Yet Bradley proposed to use the entire resources under his command in the most intricate of maneuvers, involving the highest degree of co-ordination in the field and demanding a brilliantly effective supply system, to strike a single decisive blow!

The statistics on the casualties it had required to force a mile of Bocage country were against him; his plan violated at least one basic military principle in that it cut its flying column fifty miles deep into enemy territory without providing flank protection of any kind on the ground. Bradley said it had never been done before but that it could be done this time because he had the air to protect his flank—aerial reconnaissance to tell him where the enemy was and fighter bombers to break up any mass movement against him. The logistics—the supply factors—were against him, for when his armored columns finally reached the plains they would have to be fed ammunition and gasoline and food through the narrow tube which was a single road down the Atlantic edge of the Channel coast from Normandy to the Brest peninsula. This road would be already choked with the vehicles of the advancing army itself. Bradley said it could be done if the advancing army got out of the way fast enough.

It was just before the battle of St. Lô that the group of us who had been with Montgomery since March came back to Bradley's headquarters. Our time as observers on Montgomery's staff was over. We had gone there originally so that when Montgomery released the Americans to their own command, we might bring a working knowledge of The Master's plans and intentions back to the American headquarters. Actually, by the time we returned to the fold, Bradley had already been operating on his own for some time. He had been using the First Army's staff and it never quite recovered from the fact that it had thus once been senior in the field. For ever after, it was inclined to regard the now senior 12th Army Group Headquarters as an interloper.

Back with Bradley, at first we had nothing to do but acquaint ourselves with the plans already made for him by the First Army's officers. These plans included turning over part of First Army's troops in the middle of the battle to the Third Army Headquarters which had been waiting in England and was now to take the field under General Patton. Third Army was to set up shop just after the break-through and to take responsibility for the exploitation when the armor reached the plains. The First Army would then remain under the command of Courtney Hodges, who had been trotting around at Omar Bradley's heels since the preparation of the invasion in England. The American Army Group Headquarters, which had so long been run by its chief of staff, would at last have Omar himself for its commanding general. Thus the pattern of the American command which liberated France was finally set, with Omar directing from his own 12th Army Group Headquarters, having the First and Third Armies under its command, the First under Hodges and the Third under Patton. All of this had been worked out before St. Lô, had in fact been planned by Bradley before he left Bristol—completely planned except the exact time and circumstances, which could not be foreseen until the beachhead had been established, and the enemy had committed himself to fighting a containing action, and Montgomery had failed to break the deadlock at Caen.

Everything was very cozy on the Continent the week before the battle of St. Lô started. Except for the Cherbourg peninsula, the beachhead was only fifteen or twenty miles deep. All the headquarters were close together, sandwiched in amongst the batteries of 105's and 155's which were continually landing and getting in place and opening fire.

With a jeep, you could view the whole campaign on the Continent in a morning, for the roads (in the American sector at least) were amazingly free. It was all one-way traffic around the beaches, to the miles of dumps that spread out through the orchards and back. The first big fighter field on the edge of the road near Isigny was actually under enemy artillery fire for a while, and the heavy P-51's rose up from the far end of the field and let go their wing bombs before they were out of sight, banking sharply and coming in to land and load up again. For liaison planes, each of the big headquarters had its own landing strip, lanes leveled through hay fields from which the posts the Germans had set up to prevent glider landings had been pulled.

From a little L-5 liaison plane flying along the coast, you could look through one window out over the invasion fleet, riding at anchor unloading supplies—hundreds upon hundreds of vessels, with the little DUKWs and landing craft shuttling back and forth amongst them, spewing up little white wakes. Flying just above the level of the balloons that rose from almost every ship at anchor, you could see the convoys coming in over the horizon from England in stately procession. Through the other window, looking over the rolling green hills, as far as you could see, you could follow the battle line marked out by the steady puffing of white and black smoke. Shells were bursting almost continuously even over the quiet parts of the line.

We had a hell of a lot of artillery and plenty of ammunition there close to the dumps and the job was to find profitable targets to shoot at. Shells tore the tops off trees and sploshed craters in the soft ground. Most of our roads were technically under fire but the Germans only shot back when they thought they could hit something. The beachhead was narrowest beyond Carentan and signs warned that bridges there were being shelled, so you went over them in a jeep at forty or fifty miles an hour; but not many people got killed in the rear areas.

Only at night was there real excitement. Each evening after sunset, as if it were a lighting cue in a stage production, when the color left the sky, the enemy aircraft came in. Far off, the sharp slap of antiaircraft fire broke in on the steady rumble of the big guns and then, within seconds, all hell broke loose. Everything in the beachhead went off—37's, .50 and .30 machine guns, BAR's, M-1's—and everyone seemed to be firing tracers, making crazy patterns that did not focus in the sky because nobody had any idea where the enemy aircraft were.

If you were near the beach, it was fantastic; the decks of hundreds of ships lit with flashes from the muzzles of thousands of guns and the sky was all interlaced cobwebs of sparkling light. Everything was in motion.

Then there would be a long, high whiiish and then a fat man fell in a bowl of jelly and the ground shook and a short, dull sound came through under the excited cackling of the small arms fire. Sometimes after the fat man fell in the jelly, flames would rise into the sky and you would know a gasoline dump had been hit. Sometimes the whiiish rose to such an awful crescendo that you threw yourself on the ground in terror. Those would be rockets and there is no describing the sound they make when they pass close to you.

Once a night fighter shot up an enemy aircraft right over my head and that was a terrific sight. The two craft were hardly higher than the trees, and first I saw the tracers from the night fighter, which stood out from the other tracers because their line of flight was flat and they were so close they made an angry noise. The planes, too, threw great waves of sound at the ground—from their motors and the rush of their great bodies through the air and the blast from the night fighter's guns. The enemy aircraft lit up in flame so suddenly that it seemed almost to explode. Yet it didn't explode but in fractions of a second tore flaming into the ground half a mile beyond me. The nights on the beachhead were eery things.

When the plan for St. Lô was complete, we knew that it was either going to stay eery there for a long time or else there would be no more beachhead, for the American army was moving out for a show-down. It was supposed to start on a Saturday, which was the twenty-fourth, and another officer named John Watson and I did some homework on a terrain map and picked out a rise of ground a few kilometers northwest of St. Lô. We figured we could see the start line of the jump-off itself from there. We took two jeeps and went up to the place early in the morning. The infantry were to attack at three, I think; we knew that the big air show was to come first.

If you have any doubt about how casual a battlefield is, I can give you the fact that we rode through the whole American frontline position and got beyond the advanced scouts to within, I think, two turns of the road of the Germans, not only without being stopped, but actually without seeing anyone. The week before, four German colonels had come down from Paris to look around and had similarly driven through both German and American positions. They pulled up in some bewilderment in our rear areas, thus making it from the fleshpots of Paris to the PW camps of Normandy in something under five hours without the least physical inconvenience.

The only reason we didn't make this trip in reverse is that we finally caught up with a Mark-IV tank which was still burning and this seemed to call for a certain amount of consultation. The tank was burning in the square of a tiny village that now had neither inhabitants nor even any buildings but only the partially demolished façade of a church and a stone well. While we were talking it over by the well, two American boys in another jeep caught up with us and were about to whirl away off a road that doubled back to our right when we stopped them. It was they who told us that the 30th Infantry Division's front line *had* been where we were but that the division had pulled back two miles that morning to make room for the aerial bombardment. When we picked our way by compass and consultation back to the hill we had chosen, a company of infantry was on the lee side of it going over their grenades and their ammunition and sorting themselves out for the attack.

A sunken road cut across the brow of our hill. At one end of it was a burned-out German tank, and the ditches on either side of the road were filled with discarded German equipment, muddy junk. We spent the day amongst it, watching the battle warm up.

This was the day the battle warmed up but didn't come to a boil. There was the artillery preparation and the air show came off, but for some reason back where we had come from they didn't like it, so the infantry attack was put off for twenty-four hours. It went the next day after similar preparations.

The things I remember about the St. Lô attack are the panoramic effects of the scene as a whole and the air show, which was in three acts, heavy, medium and fighter bombers in succession.

The scene as a whole had the quality of a battlefield sketched in an illustrated history of the Civil War. Our own troops were trying to show our aircraft where they were by setting off smoke grenades. The smoke was a muddy purple red. We could hardly see it from a mile away and we knew it would be no good to the aircraft but it hung over the fields and little patches of woods and lay in the valleys the way the pictures suggested that the smoke hung over Civil War battlefields. When occasionally, through glasses, you could see a few men moving here or there, you could not identify their uniforms but only knew they were men carrying rifles.

We could see the German artillery firing from the hills beyond and hear our own behind us. Both were firing what's called counterbattery—that is, they were shooting at each other, ignoring any targets in between. The shells arched directly overhead and I came upon an optical phenomenon which was new to me: looking through field glasses, you can actually see shells in flight. I was looking into an almost cloudless sky to see if there were any signs of the Forts and noticed small black objects skittering across the vision of my glasses. First I said to myself, "There are a hell of a lot of birds around here," and then I recognized the shapes and caught on to the fact that I was watching the shells going back and forth—our shells going forward and the German shells coming back.

We were within easy mortar range of the German lines. We had been standing on the wrecked tank where we were presently joined by an army cameraman who also recognized the advantages of this viewpoint. After a while, we got down off the tank and lay in the ditches to watch through the hedgerows. It wasn't a bad idea, because the third or fourth wing of Flying Fortresses dropped short and removed a whole panel of six or seven Bocage fields from France, no more than a city block away from us. This was a terrific thing, too.

The first Forts had been a twinkling canopy over us, their wings sparkling in the sun, way up. Their heavy bombs had gone down in what are called carpets, churning the enemy-held fields into a froth of flame-lit smoke and dust. The Forts were much too high up for us to have any warning that one batch were going to let go short. This particular carpet of bombs came slanting down over us like a whole fleet of express trains gone mad in a nightmare, converging on where one lay.

My driver claims that the foxhole he was in blew fifty yards into the air and shook him out of it up there, leaving him to find his own way back to earth again. I can't vouch for this. In my section of the road, it felt as I imagine it would feel to hit a rock in an outboard motorboat going sixty miles an hour. My eyes were just level with the top of the embankment and I was looking through the slit made by the top of the embankment and the rim of my helmet—hoping to see where the bombs would hit behind the German line. Instead of that, I saw what seemed to be the whole hillside directly in front of me rise in a single sheet of violent orange flame which seemed to burn for solid minutes before mud and debris began splattering around me. The earth shook so that I remember trying to hold on to it.

The short salvo from the Forts hurt no one.* It was kind of a Coney Island experience—a Super-Roller Coaster, Crack-the-Whip and prat-fall-through-a-trap-door sensation. But it certainly enlivened the morning. The feature of the afternoon was a flight of three fighter bombers who were also off the beam.

* It was the following day that Lieutenant General Lesley McNair was killed by a short salvo from a formation of medium bombers, just north of the St. Lô road.

They were off it by ninety degrees and, instead of running down parallel to our front line, bombing along the straight St. Lô road, they had obviously confused a north-south highway for an east-west one and came sliding in straight through the American position. This was not so amusing, for fighter bombers can hit individual vehicles—or just plain individuals. These three saw a small American ammunition dump the other side of the road from us and an American battery—and plastered both.

From the sunken road, all this was happening while John Watson and I were having a violent argument over whether the fighters were or were not enemy aircraft. I had been watching them with glasses and I saw the parallel white bands on the bottoms of their wings, and even a star on one, so that I *knew* they were ours—and that it was damn silly to take cover because they were only buzzing us on their way home. John, who was not using his glasses, saw their sawed-off wing tips and the purposeful way in which they dove on us, and swore they were Focke-Wulfs.

The rest of the hundreds of fighter bombers were in the groove, and for an hour we watched them come in smartly in threes, peel off, and slide down towards the ground, not diving steeply but on a flat, even course. Then we could see the two little bombs drop away. The bombs seemed to fly for a long time just below the plane and parallel to it, gradually bending towards the ground and finally striking it sharply, throwing up little plumes of commotion.

I think we would have gone home after the fighter bombers' near-miss, but by this time the German artillery had given up trying to hunt out the American batteries and was laying on the crossroad a quarter of a mile behind us. We could hear the shells whine in and strike. Late in the afternoon they let up. We climbed into our jeeps then and went down to where we lived in an orchard a few miles from the shore, and were warm and snug in our foxholes before the evening musicale began.

There have been many unpleasant things written about a foxhole which, when floored with six inches of cold water, is certainly one of the world's most uninviting sleeping places. But on a night when the air is filled with little pieces of flying steel—a nice warm summer night when you have plenty of blankets and a shelter tent over the foxhole to keep the dew off—a foxhole is a lovely place in which to sleep—and if it's three feet deep, the only thing in the world you would like would be for it to be six feet deep. And you promise yourself that you will dig it six feet deep tomorrow, but in the morning the sun will be shining again and there will be only the rumbling of one's own artillery and that soothing lullaby of sound which is the sound of the shells going *away* from your guns *towards* the enemy. So you say, "What the hell. If I dig it any deeper, I'll only have further to climb out in the morning."

And so we'd seen the false start at St. Lô, and the next day the real thing began.

Bradley's plan for the breakout worked beyond our fondest dreams. The subsequent battle was, without question, the greatest battle up to that time ever fought by American arms. In effectiveness, the only comparable Allied land battle in the whole war was to be Bradley's later encirclement of the Ruhr. The battle of St. Lô won France; the encirclement of the Ruhr finished the Third Reich. Both of them were 100 per cent Bradley battles, and each was fought by American troops without assistance from any ally. It seems to me that the American people have a right to know that they produced the commander, and put the armies in the field, who were to win battles comparable in every way to the most brilliant victories ever fought in Europe by Napoleon or any other general.

No one can write about war, now that atoms and rockets have changed it all, without the strong feeling that everything that one saw and experienced is already so obsolete that to analyze its tactics and strategy is like studying how the archers at Crécy conducted themselves. It may be interesting to historians but it belongs to another world. Bradley's campaign in Europe is likely to be the last great campaign ever fought with such antiquated gadgets as armored vehicles on tracks and wheels, internal combustion engines, breech-loading weapons that have to have ponderous carriages to catch the recoil, aircraft that can only fly a few hundred miles an hour—and drop only tiny little ten-ton bombs, hardly big enough to smash up a single good-sized suspension bridge. Recoil-less cannon that a man can hold in one hand, shells that emit their own radio waves and explode themselves when they find the target they seek, propellerless and pilotless aircraft flying faster than sound—all these we had by the end of even our little war. And already, these are obsolete. Everyone agrees that there is a new world now—a physicist's world. Yet the whole fate of the world which is just being born hung, for a single second in eternity, on Bradley's success with his obsolete armies.

The week after the first Allied soldiers set foot in France, the Germans launched their first long range automatic missiles—first the pilotless bombs and then the stratosphere rockets. We already knew that the German scientists expected to win the war with these and other weapons still secret. Now we know even more about the German State under Hitler. We know that he saw the last year of the war as a race to make all our weapons obsolete before our superior weight of them could crush him. We know that until the very end, until the Russians were actually breaking into Berlin—with Silesia, the Ruhr and the Saar all lost—Hitler had a project for ultimate victory, a project which if he could have had only just one more year he might have fulfilled.

Parts of his project for victory Hitler had already almost fulfilled. He was successfully equipping his submarine fleet with devices which thwarted the anti-submarine techniques that had taken the Allies years of patience, skill and bravery to develop. Already his submarines could breathe under water and counter many of our locating devices. Mass production of jet aircraft, one hundred miles an hour faster than our fastest fighters, was well under way when the end came, even though the organization that flew them had been battered into such inertia that the technique of using this superior speed effectively had not been mastered. When we captured the experimental stations where the rockets were being developed, the scientists were still hard at work.

It does not look now as though it had been a close thing, as you wander through the ruins of Frankfurt or Berlin—but it *was* a close thing, just the same. At the time of St. Lô, it was a very close thing. If Bradley had lost there, had suffered a major defeat, no man could have foretold the extent of the disaster. A whole German army was still being held in reserve on the Pas de Calais peninsula. However successfully we disguised the fact that the Germans had really nothing to fear at Calais, we had neither the men nor the landing craft to launch a second invasion. If, in the month of August, a defeat for the American Army had followed the German defensive victory at Caen, even the orderlies on the German General Staff would have known that they could safely strip the rest of the coast of northern France to strike at us in the beachhead. Our momentum would be gone; we would have more and more troops coming from North America to pour into Normandy but we would have no room in which to deploy them, and when our beaches lost their usefulness in the winter weather these troops would be a liability. Cherbourg alone could not have supplied even the forces we had ashore by midsummer.

What makes a commander-in-chief great is understanding all these factors, projecting events into the future on the limited evidence he has on hand. Bradley's greatness emerged now in his dual appreciation, first, of the fact that the relatively untried American armies were strong enough, with the superiority we had in the air, to bet everything on a single decisive battle and win and, second, of the truth that this battle had to be fought immediately, could not wait until we had more troops ashore or pause for more supplies, but must be fought now.

The COBRA struck on July 25—after the first false start it struck with everything it had. On the twenty-fifth, all morning long the sky was again a silver sparkle of aircraft—first the Forts, then the mediums and finally the fighter bombers, swooping in long graceful inclines and letting fly their bombs like tiny darts. In the afternoon the infantry went, three divisions abreast, slogging steadily over fields which were now so pockmarked with craters that there was a hole to jump into every few feet. The infantry went on and on into the hills and then the long columns of armor began to move. The roads for miles and miles around were jammed with vehicles twisting and turning, up and down this side road and that alley, as the MP's strove to keep the skeins from tangling.

St. Lô was an infantry battle through the first night and the next day and the next night. By the third day the infantry was through five miles of successive German defensive lines; the armor was right behind them and now it began to go through. The dusty nose of the lead column found the arterial road south and the drivers began to run for it. Ahead of them, on the road itself, there were retreating German columns. The American fighter planes wheeled over these columns in twos, threes and fours and peeled off and came down along them. Four days later, the road was still smoldering from the wreckage of their vehicles.

The advance platoons of the first American armored column went through the rear guard of the retreating German left wing. The liaison planes—the little Cubs with the putt-putt motors—took over the direction of traffic and flew up and down the column, keeping track of it. They caught the spirit of the chase and dove down with the fighters. The kids that flew them fired Tommy guns out the open windows. One of them rounded up a batch of prisoners, leaning out of his canvas cockpit and covering them with a .45 pistol.

The pay-off of the St. Lô battle was a piece of terrain known as "the high ground east of Avranches." Avranches is a town in the hollow of the elbow made by the Brest peninsula jutting out towards the Atlantic. Avranches stands on a small hill. Beyond the hill on which Avranches stands, to the south, stretch the plains which lead—to the west, towards Brest; to the south, towards St. Nazaire, at the mouth of the Loire; to the east, along the southern edge of the Bocage, to Chartres and Paris. Immediately east of Avranches there runs a ridge. Whoever is on this ridge commands the gateway from Normandy into central France, through Avranches. The American armor went past Avranches just five days after the attack jumped off. The next day, American infantry, following in trucks, was on the high ground east of Avranches—and the Germans were cooked.

The first of the "Hitler battles" followed—the first of the battles which we now know were ordered personally by Hitler. The British had been making a play to salvage Montgomery's lost reputation at Caen by describing the operations of the Second British Army there as a successful sacrifice play, aimed at keeping the German army off our backs. The facts did not support this when you took a G-2 map and counted the German troops, battalion by battalion; the forces opposite the Americans were actually slightly stronger than the forces the Germans kept on the Caen end of the line. The Germans, however, did have to hold a higher percentage of armor in reserve at Caen, to protect themselves against a break-through into the Seine valley. The minute the Americans broke through at St. Lô the Germans should, of course, have used this armor to cover the retreat of their counter-beachhead army back across the Seine. They were strong enough to get it out. It was still very much intact. Its morale was reasonably good and there was time, while we got through to beyond Avranches and then decided what to do next, for them to swing back, pivoting around Caen. This was the maneuver the textbooks would have called for and, had it been successfully employed, it would have given the Germans an army with which to strike back *after* the break-through, when we would be at our most extended.

Instead of following this course, Hitler took every mobile unit in the line, withdrew all his armor from opposite Caen, and raced the whole force due west, committing it in one all-out attempt to cut off the American break-through at Mortain.

Mortain is a town in the Bocage hills, near the Atlantic coast, just east of Avranches. Here Hitler bit at the jugular vein through which the new-born Third Army's life blood pulsed. He bit with four Panzer divisions for teeth and he gave it everything he had, with the Luftwaffe thrown in.

The American corridor at Mortain consisted of that single road which ran down the coast to Avranches, and a few miles of hills inland of it. We could see the German attack coming, for the weather was fine and their armored columns had to trundle west and south around the beachhead perimeter. Bradley put the 30th Infantry Division in the line and earmarked two other divisions to stand by with reinforcements. The big decision was to let the Third Army keep on going through the gap; Patton was already screaming for more troops to exploit the break-through to the south. The road down the coast was a sight to see, sixty miles of traffic, bumper to bumper. It rolled south night and day. By day it passed under a net of protecting fighters; by night it was lit by the flares the Luftwaffe came to drop. It traveled then under a canopy of ack-ack bursting amidst the raiders.

As they came up from the east, the German tanks went into action at Mortain without stopping to regroup. They had only a few miles to go to bring the Avranches road under direct fire, and a few miles more to cut it entirely. But at Mortain, Hitler learned what Montgomery had learned before him: that you can't fight armor against infantry in hedgerow country. Moreover, his troops were having their first taste of American artillery on the defensive; it threw steel so fast that some of the captured German soldiers thought they had been meeting automatic fire.

American artillery specializes in what is known as a serenade. This is a scheme of control by means of which the guns of various calibers, located various distances from the target, fire on a split second schedule which brings all their shells in over the target at the same time, the near guns waiting until the shells from the long range guns are well on their way before sending their own missiles in pursuit. The men of the 30th Infantry Division, and the serenades from the guns behind them, stopped the four fearsome Panzer divisions at Mortain without yielding enough ground to make an honest headline in an afternoon paper.

The battle lasted three days without interruption. When it was over, an American army had passed within the sound of its firing, down over the single road along the coast, swept over and around the hill town of Avranches, and debouched into the base of the Brest peninsula below.

To understand the freedom of action which Bradley had achieved by thus shaking the Third Army loose into the German backfield we must leave the story of the Anglo-American arms to pay a moment's tribute to the resistance forces within France. An underground army is such a romantic thing, and is so automatically the subject of extravagant praise in wartime propaganda, that almost everyone who came in contact with them for the first time was astonished by the solid efficiency and hard accomplishment of the anti-German forces in France—and later in Belgium. In a field headquarters romantic talk has to be distilled down to its factual contents. In France, we were respectful of but not impressed by stories of individual heroism, of hopeless battles fought for principle only; novelists could deal with them later and Movements would make martyrs of the dead. But what cut ice with us was the fact that when we came to France the resistance was so effective that it took half a dozen real live German divisions to contend with it, divisions which might otherwise have been on our backs in the Bocage. And it made the most cynical sit up and take notice when we learned from German field officers that the Germans in central France were truly terrified, had to live under arms, could not move freely, had lost all control in sizable sectors even before we came.

Caught between the devil and the Resistance, the German High Command had finally to draw on its police divisions in central France to reinforce its army in Normandy. As the Germans thinned their forces on police duty, the effectiveness of the Maquis increased in geometrical proportion. In the plains south of the Bocage country and beyond, the Germans had no troops left to block the roads and harass our advance. The French resistance had neutralized or defeated them.

To an army on the advance, there is all the difference in the world between being able to roll through a town after smashing a single road block and having to stop to hunt out the half a hundred enemy who can fight you house-to-house with automatic weapons, and who will swarm in on your supply trains if you by-pass them. From St. Lô to the German border, we never had to worry about a town in our rear. Let one American vehicle appear in even a sizable city and its inhabitants would have the German garrison dead or disarmed a few hours later. The Maquis' traps were all set and their jaws sprang fast and savagely. Every scout car making an advanced reconnaissance was not one pair of eyes but a score— "There are Germans in that woods, perhaps a thousand of them, but they have no vehicles; over beyond that hill, around the turn, there is a tank trap; but you have nothing to fear going down *that* road; Uncle Henry was there this morning and the Germans went last night."

The effect on the morale of an army advancing so, amongst friends, is a mighty imponderable. To each individual soldier it means that if he strays there are friends to set him on the right path again; if he is surrounded there are people who will hide him until he is rescued. Such friendship is not the false friendship of the conquered, impressed by might, but the meaningful friendship of men and women who hate your enemy even more than you do.

It would be an empty history of the campaign in France and Belgium that tried to credit the success of the Allied arms in those countries to the Allied weight of guns and aircraft alone. It was a military fact that the French were worth at least a score of divisions to us, maybe more. Two great confirmations were later to come; the first, positive, when a big German garrison in Paris was beaten before even a single Allied soldier arrived and the second, negative, when we found out what it was like to fight over the enemy's border with no longer any friends beyond our own lines.

All of which is part of the explanation why, in France, there was such a special premium on breaking through the crust of the German field armies. A resistance movement can only whisper about its plans when an enemy field army is sitting heavily astride its villages; in advance of a liberating army, however, it can spread death, depression and confusion among the retreating enemy.

Through the confusion wrought by the French resistance, the American armies cut like hot knives—once they were free to roll beyond Avranches.

8   The Conference Table vs. the Wehrmacht

THE campaign that followed the breakout into the Brest peninsula was a little messy—that is, there was a high degree of opportunism in it, and considerable conflict among higher headquarters as to what to do next, and large events followed rapidly, one upon another. One of the original objectives of breaking out below Avranches was to secure that famous second port demanded by Plan OVERLORD; this time Brest. (There was also the cockeyed idea of making a brand new billion dollar port on the south coast of the Brest peninsula, at Quiberon Bay. It was the dream of the supply services, its code name was CHASTITY, and its chastity remained intact.)

General Patton's first orders were to get to Brest—as with Cherbourg, either by cutting the peninsula and then proceeding down it or by lighting straight out for Brest and to hell with the flank— at his option. Patton immediately did both—and neither. The first armored division to go through the bottleneck, past Mortain and Avranches, was the 6th Armored Division. Patton sent it roaring around the corner, by-passing the fortified harbor of St. Malo just beyond Avranches. It ran out along the north coast of the peninsula. You could follow its trail by the wrecks of the vehicles it had lost to the few anti-tank guns the Germans had left behind them—and by the ranks of cheery faces in the little Breton villages through which it had hurried, leaving only the memory of its dustgrimed faces. The 6th Armored was so small a force racing over so long a route that it could not even spare MP detachments to guard its rear.

The second division to make the dash south was the 4th Armored Division. Patton kept it going on south, told its commanders to capture Lorient and St. Nazaire, the big ports and submarine bases on the south coast of the Brest peninsula. Like the 6th Armored, the 4th went in for liberating France on a wholesale scale—and, like the 6th, left smiling faces but no rear guards behind it. Both divisions reached the outskirts of their objectives —and pulled up there, screaming bloody murder on the radio for gasoline and ammunition which they never got. Communication lines had long since stretched to absurdity and here they snapped clean.

At Army Group Headquarters, to find out where Georgie's armor was, we had to monitor the tanks themselves. To hell with fancy codes and military phraseology. His commanders were now so mad they were screaming in good, crisp and sarcastic American words to this effect: "Out of gas, ammunition and food. We can live on the country, but please reply with instructions as to how to manufacture gasoline and ammunition." Or: "Am in the outskirts with a whole German army in front of me and nothing to shoot at it. Did the impossible days ago. What are we supposed to do now?"

Meanwhile whole battalions of Germans, cut off only theoretically by the Americans, were being chivied by the French Maquis, hounded southward straight across the roads which the armored columns had taken. They lived by capturing American supply trucks, and soft-skinned vehicles now had to be accompanied by armor when they tried to get through. Not many tried —for by the time Georgie had his armor on the outskirts of Brest, the Commanding General of the Third Army had other things on his mind. Georgie had forgotten all about Brest; he decided that Paris was the place to take—and so did lots of other people.

Georgie had firm and unqualified orders to take Brest, and on a Monday had boasted that he would bathe there on Saturday night. On Saturday afternoon he called up Omar Bradley and told him that Third Army troops were actually in Brest. This was typical of General Patton, and Bradley would have been in a hell of a mess if he had believed him. The troops Patton had in Brest consisted of a platoon of cavalry which spent about half an hour

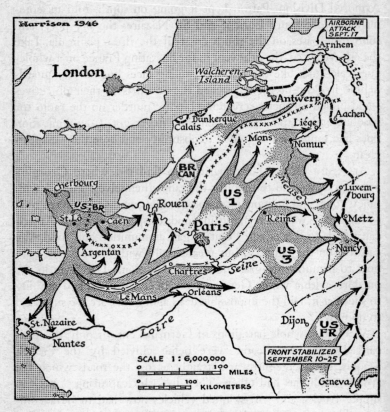

BEACHHEAD TO GERMANY

there before skedaddling back into the hills. It had bumped up against probably the most strongly defended port in western Europe, entering an area which had recently been reinforced by one of Goering's parachute divisions under command of the general who had taken Crete. Eventually Brest was taken—forty-six days later, by a whole new army and after virtually all of France had been liberated. Three whole infantry divisions did the job, re-inforced by armor—and aided by several afternoons' work of the strategic air force, and even a naval bombardment. The original attack had been a trifle out of scale.

Brest was the great boondoggle of the American campaign. It was a sour heritage from Plan OVERLORD, or a bloody sacri-fice on the altar of prestige—whichever you care to call it—because for months of effort and thousands of casualties neither a single soldier nor even a pound of American supplies was ever landed there. By the time Brest was taken, there was no need for it.

To the south, St. Nazaire and Lorient were never taken. By the end of the war, when they surrendered during the collapse of the German State, they had raided the surrounding territory so successfully that they still had supplies sufficient to have held out for at least another year.

While the 6th and 4th Armored Divisions were stranded out-side the German fortress ports, Patton was walking up and down outside the caravan trailer that Bradley used for a field office. Patton, as I have said, now had his mind on Paris and was dancing up and down like a little boy wanting to go to the bathroom, trying to get Omar to turn him loose. If he had not had his bath in Brest, he was going to have his champagne in the capital of France. But in the meantime there remained to be dealt with the now somewhat battered German counter-beachhead army, stuck tight in the Bocage country after its mobile strength had been frittered away by Hitler's interference at Mortain. Its high command was badly demoralized, with the defeat at St. Lô coming only five days after the Prussian generals' unsuccessful attempt to assassi-nate the head of the State and the latter's subsequent purging of his professional advisers. It was now that Montgomery emerged briefly from the doghouse to try to get Eisenhower to persuade Bradley that he should forget both Brest and Paris and concentrate instead on encircling the Germans in the hedgerow country and destroying them there.

Bradley's original objective in breaking out was neither the shallow envelopment that Montgomery now argued for, nor Patton's wild lunge at Brest, which had been hardly more than a respectful nod over the shoulder to the Supreme Command and its OVERLORD plan. Nor was Bradley impressed by the politico-romantic notion of liberating Paris before the German armies in France were well beaten. What he had envisaged was a wide envelopment which would bag not just a few German divisions near the beachhead, but all German units west of the Seine. This called for an envelopment which would swing across France from Avranches to Chartres and Orléans—and thence down the Seine to its mouth. Orléans, south and a little west of Paris, stoppered a bottle, the sides of which were the Seine and the Loire rivers. The Seine and the Loire would be formidable obstacles to the enemy retreat, with their rail and highway bridges blown up. From before he got to France, Bradley's eye had been on plugging the Orléans gap. But so startling had been the victory at St. Lô, and so decisive the defeat of the counterattack at Mortain, that there now followed a brief moment of delirious embarrassment of military riches.

To capitalize on these riches, Bradley had effective freedom of action. He was still nominally under Montgomery but so enormous was the prestige he had suddenly acquired that not even the Combined Chiefs of Staff themselves would have the confidence to gainsay him. But he had to make his decisions fast, and on a confusion of advices—with Patton screaming Paris, Montgomery yelling "encirclement in the hills," and his own supply people reluctant to say he could go ahead at all without that second supply port which The Plan had believed to be a fundamental condition of success. At Supreme Headquarters they were in a near panic lest the American field commanders let their enthusiasm outrun their common sense. Eisenhower's contribution was to keep saying, "Don't forget Brest." He was a very busy man now, with the French as well as the British on his hands, and his headquarters moving.

In this dilemma, Bradley chose to do three things at once. He felt that he was rich enough, and that the German Army was near enough demoralization, for him to get away with all three. He got away with two, and almost with the third.

The first thing he did was to go for the ultimate objective of which he never lost sight; he drove on Chartres to close the

Orléans gap and to start the big envelopment. Chartres led not only to the Seine, eventually, but en route gave him Paris itself without his having to strike a blow for it—the citizens of Paris rose and liberated themselves before the Americans were even within immediate striking distance of it—in fact the Americans had already moved to by-pass it to the south.

Bradley's second move was his concession to the British Commander. This called for the shallow encirclement of a portion of the German Army by means of a double envelopment, in which the north pincer was British and the south pincer American. The pincers were to close at Falaise—and came so near to closing that for practical fighting purposes the encircled forces were disposed of.

Bradley's third operation, the final drive from Chartres down the Seine to bottle up the entire German force in Normandy, he had partially to sacrifice to Montgomery's ambitions at Falaise. Bradley drove a corps down the Seine, went on to the far side, and secured crossings not only for his own army but also for the British, who were thus handed the gate to Le Havre and the rest of the Channel coast on a platter. But Bradley had had to spend so much strength at Falaise that by the time he could get additional troops to the Seine crossings most of the German Army in Normandy had effected its belated escape.

Bradley's decision to co-operate with Montgomery in setting a trap which would be sprung at Falaise resulted in probably the single bitterest episode in Anglo-American relations on the field of battle in the entire war. It was a time of violent action, tense expectancy and short tempers. To spring the trap, the British forces had to pick themselves up from their dug-in positions and advance through hills which the Germans had had just as long as they to dig-in and organize defensively. In fairness to the British forces in the field, they were called on to organize an attack overnight, through the same kind of country, and on the same scale, as the initial attack at St. Lô, for which the Americans had spent weeks preparing and gathering their forces. The British were also attacking in territory which was of vital importance to the Germans. The Germans fought desperately to hold their escape route open.

The Anglo-American argument began because to fulfill their commitment to close the gap, the British had only thirty miles to go, whereas the Americans, striking from the south, had to traverse three-quarters of a circle, swinging wide in an arc one hundred and twenty to one hundred and fifty miles long, bringing their supplies along with them. On the record, the Americans got where they were supposed to get, driving hard into what had been the rear of the German defensive position—while the British attack ground to a standstill just north of Falaise. Just south of Falaise there is a town called Argentan. The international army boundary arbitrarily divided the British and American battlefields just beyond Argentan, on the Falaise side of it. Patton's troops, who thought they had the mission of closing the gap, took Argentan in their stride and crossed the international boundary without stopping. Montgomery, who was still nominally in charge of all ground forces, now chose to exercise his authority and ordered Patton back to his side of the international boundary line. After waiting what he thought was a reasonable length of time—it was two or three days as I remember it—Patton organized a provisional corps, put it under command of his Chief of Staff, Gaffey, and left it there at Argentan to guard the mouth of the gap, while he himself proceeded to direct his troops on to the Seine.

For all his flamboyance, Patton was a gifted commander with a flair for handling armor in open country. Many of his men thought of him as brutal and insensitive (actually he was thin-skinned and sentimental), but he saved their lives. He understood the shock effect of armored cavalry and with this knowledge he won battles with a few hundred casualties where other generals might have lost thousands. Patton's corps now ran amok in the rear of the beaten enemy, reaping rich rewards for daring.

For ten days, however, the beaten but still coherently organized German Army retreated through the Falaise gap and so lived to protect their crossing of the Seine and finally to make good their escape back to the concrete shelters beyond the German border.

Actually, the argument over the closing of the Falaise gap is almost an idle one,* for while the record is there, and the gap

* This is a minority opinion. Every senior officer concerned whom I have been able to talk to still feels that the failure to close the Falaise gap was

at all—and then everything would begin to move again. At the battalion CP all that would be known was that a call had come through and that they were to get going.

You could rarely follow a battle on any operations map closer than division, and mostly you had to go back to corps, where they wove together the threads of information from two or three divisions to learn what it was all about and how it was going. But at Army Group the symbols were always neat, and three lieutenant colonels followed one another on duty twenty-four hours a day, tidying the map up, keeping the non-essential information off it, seeing that it showed only what the Commanding General would need to see when he came in to catch up.

But wherever the line moved ahead, somewhere along this road or that, it met death and passed on. It passed on as the neat graveyards further back filled or as the corpses were overlooked and just simply rotted away.

In the surgical tents with the six operating tables all in line and the six surgical teams all working under the six identical and standard sets of floodlights run by the portable generator outside, they cut the legs and arms off. They packed the intestines back as well as they could. They sewed up the bodies and stitched the scars—and then they read the tag on the next body that was laid on the table in front of them, and the nurses sterilized the knives and the needles and the scissors and the forceps and laid them out again. And they carried what was left into the dim tents or, if it had a blanket over its face, they laid it in the lengthening row outside the tent so that it could be taken away and buried.

On the road, as you passed them, you could almost see the men who had not been hit yet grow more tired. You could almost see the sense go out of their faces, and their eyes seemed to grow bigger as their faces got dirtier and dirtier and whiter under the dirt.

That would be up near the front, near where the red and blue symbols met on the map. They grew tired in the rear areas, too, as the army went across France, but they were never wan with fatigue there.

By the time it had reached the Seine, the Army was altogether veteran. You could feel a kind of casual competence about the way all its different parts moved. Its vehicles were not worn out yet, and the enemy was on the run.

What followed the savage killing of Germans at the Falaise gap, the fall of Paris and the crossing of the Seine, was the great race for the borders of Germany. The British raced up the coast, hugging their lines of communication across the Channel. They were led across the Seine, taking over the crossings which the Americans had secured and turned over to them near Rouen. The Americans were past Paris, on each side of it. The First and Third Armies straightened out their boundaries, the First Army, under Hodges, taking the inside track to the north and the Third Army, under Patton, swinging wide on the south. Patton, as usual, trusted his flank to God, the Air Force and the Maquis.

I've written "inside and outside tracks" because the supply lines of both American armies were arc-shaped—they swung in wide, mileage-eating circles all the way around from the base of the Cherbourg peninsula, past Paris and across the Seine, to the east. The shape and length of these supply lines set the stage for the next act. If most of the action itself took place on the ground, that was because the Air Corps had already won its battle of France. The victory of the Allied air forces over the Luftwaffe was already so thorough that control of the air was something we all took for granted. Every once in a while, though, the wonder of those first days ashore would come back to us, those early days through which we expected to be bombed and strafed and harassed, as we so often were in the early days in Africa. But instead of German planes above us, there had only been—and you could look up at any hour from dawn to dusk—those slowly curving fours of Allied fighter planes, flowing gently back and forth across the sky, serene and sure of themselves.

On the ground we had begun to be frightened for the safety of our concentrations while still on the south shore of England; statistically we had written off so and so many thousands of troops, which we assumed would be sunk by enemy air action crossing the Channel. Next, we had known that we could not leave our landing craft to dry out between tides while we unloaded them, without a certain number of them being bombed and burned, as they had been at Salerno. We abandoned camouflage discipline when we put in the great supply dumps back of the beaches simply because we could not spare the time or the men to disperse and hide them. We were willing to take losses there, too, in order to gain time and volume by handling the supplies in the open. We took all these chances—and yet nothing that we had feared from the Luftwaffe ever materialized.

It was not because the Germans did not have planes and pilots. It was because the Allied air forces fought them out of the sky, burning their fields behind their lines. The Allied air forces did not win this victory with miracle weapons. The battles in the sky were not like the full-page advertisements in the American magazines, which showed a sky full of flaming German planes and the Allied fighters waving gaily to one another from their super-aircraft. The edge that the Allied aircraft had over the newer Messerschmitts and Focke-Wulfs was slight. Numbers we had on paper, and even in the air—but it doesn't do a squadron leader any good to have statistics on his side when his formation of sixteen planes is jumped by the sixty that the enemy happens to have at a given place at a given time. Victory in the air had to be won by nerve and skill—and had been paid for.

On the ground, the victory at St. Lô was possible because for nearly two months both the British and the American infantry had worn down the German divisions opposite them, caused them casualties faster than these could be replaced, slugged it out. In the air, too, the success of the whole invasion in Normandy was the result of months of slugging it out in the skies over France and Germany. That slugging match began long before D-day—the whole intricate process of harassing enemy aircraft production, of provoking, fighting, and winning mass dog fights, and of battering the outposts of the enemy's air empire until they were driven back to distances from which their aircraft could not compete with ours as equals. This whole process was dangerous, bloody business, and many of the men who won it were dead and burned to ashes long before we came to fight in France on foot.

We had not known whether the Germans would be able to

bring up new air forces to concentrate against us after we landed. Weeks before St. Lô, however, the returns were all in. Plans involving flying columns with only aircraft to protect their flanks could be made and successfully executed. By the time the race across France began, we did not even bother to mention enemy air action as a capability our commanders need worry about.

The Air Force would look after the Luftwaffe; and the Air Force did. And as they hit out beyond the beachhead, the Allied airmen not only accounted for the Luftwaffe but they also saw to it that the Germans' ability to move even on the ground was crippled by the need to re-lay railroad track, to fill in road craters, and to replace blasted bridges. So when *we* took the ground which had been behind the German lines, *we* learned firsthand a little of the Germans' difficulties in moving armies against such obstacles. From the Seine onward we inherited the chaos which our own air forces had created in the Continent's transportation system.

At Paris, our supply lines from the beach were already well over one-hundred-fifty miles long—and the nearest point on the German border lay two hundred road miles ahead. Supplies are moved over the ground by rail, by trucks and by pipeline. Pipe to carry gasoline can be laid at a rate of several miles a day—plus whatever time the pipe must wait for bridges to be rebuilt before it can cross broad rivers. Simple cuts in the rail line can be rapidly repaired, but only the strongest bridges can carry rail traffic across deep gorges or even small rivers. Roads can cross rivers on ponton bridges that take only a few hours to put up (when no one is shooting at you). But roads are the least efficient of the three sources of supply. They burn the very rubber and gasoline they haul to the front; they take enormous amounts of equipment and large numbers of men.

We were beyond Paris only twenty-two days after the breakthrough. Clearly, from Paris on, that lengthening supply line would become a major problem. It is doubtful if this could be seen from America, for on the map it must have looked as if at Paris we were almost as close to England as at Avranches—and we were to be even closer to England when we reached the Belgian border. But the Channel ports had been destroyed and not even the British Army, actually in the ports themselves, could use them.

It was back at the Normandy beaches that the dumps were—the hundreds of thousands of tons of supplies all unloaded and sorted out and catalogued and waiting. And it was back to the Normandy beaches that we had to go to get them.

From St. Lô to Avranches, to Paris, to the German border, it was back to the beach for anything from a thirty-three ton tank to a cigarette. For the British, whose beaches were just west of the Seine, it was a relatively straight haul along the coast—and even this route lengthened to over two hundred miles. But from the American beaches, the supply lanes had to circle inland skirting the British zone in order to avoid impossible traffic tangles. Only then could they begin to point towards Germany. The road miles stretched—one hundred, two hundred, finally a good four hundred miles. To supply sergeants, this became like getting into a truck in New York and running out to Buffalo, New York, to get your men breakfast.

At this juncture of the campaign the enemy is forgotten, for the enemy at the moment is interested only in getting the hell out of your reach. From August 24 (the day the Seine was crossed) to September 13 (the date of the first penetration of the West Wall) not the operational planners, the strategists and the tacticians, but the supply services took control of the front line and determined where it should be. Before they had done with their battle, they had reopened the whole problem of command and control of the Allied armies in Europe, put the Supreme Allied Commander, and the whole concept of his office, to their first real test on the Continent—and started a controversy about which historians will no doubt be arguing fifty years from now.

In the pursuit itself, from the Seine to Antwerp and the borders of Germany, there was only one historic incident. This was the cutting off of a part of the unused German army retreating from the Pas de Calais. The German High Command never recovered from its original preoccupation with the Pas de Calais area—and the possibility that the Allied landing in Normandy might, in the end, prove to be only a diversion. Throughout the Normandy campaign, the High Command had left the German Fifteenth Army near Calais to wait for the second coming there. As the battle of the beachhead worsened for them, the Germans began to rob their Pas de Calais army for reinforcements—but these were grudgingly spared and the main forces of the Germans' reserve army continued to look nervously across at the cliffs of Dover, and to rest on its arms.

When the American First Army broke eastward across the Seine, their progress threatened to cut off this reserve. It might have been thrown into a last-minute attempt to hold the Seine but in the end the German Commander-in-Chief in the West waited too long and had to order its hasty retreat. To date it had never fired a round.

The retreat route of the German Fifteenth Army led through the city of Mons, just over the borders of France into Belgium. Its formations took off for home in administrative march (rather than in formation prepared for combat) around the end of August, a few days after the fall of Paris. Its commanders did not know that an American armored division had gone through Mons and was already close to the German borders and that one American infantry division had been motorized and hurried north and east to the vicinity of Mons itself to protect the armored division's flank. There, twenty-five miles from the nearest friendly troops, the American 1st Infantry Division was spread out—a battalion in this village and another in the next, virtually grounded for lack of gasoline after its long trek. And there the German army retreating from Calais ran head on into the Americans.

An American infantry division at field strength is around fifteen thousand men. Actually, no more than a few thousand of the 1st Division's troops were ever engaged at Mons at any one time. These managed to kill or wound approximately six thousand Germans and take twenty-two thousand prisoners in a single forty-eight hours of action on the Belgian border. Column after column of Germans, their weapons and ammunition packed away for what they expected to be a peaceful journey, their field officers riding in limousines at the heads of the columns, ran into American road blocks and quickly fortified village strongpoints—and were slaughtered. No one had told them there were any Americans between Calais and Germany and they fell into ambushes some of the columns could have avoided altogether for a few miles' detour.

The American infantry had stopped at Mons mainly because they had no fuel to go further. They had literally only the gasoline in the tanks of their vehicles with which to maneuver them in battle. They were as surprised as their enemies when the battle began, for the German columns arrived from a direction they had thought was their rear. The Krauts which the VII Corps (of which the 1st Division was a part) had been chasing with the 3rd Armored's tanks had simply disappeared ahead of them across the Belgian plains. The whole action was one of these pieces of luck which are not luck at all.

It was pure luck that the American infantry sat astride the very roads the Germans had marked on their maps as safe for a retreat —and that the American division that the Germans hit was one which had fought through Africa and Sicily, and on the Continent from the dawn of D-day—a veteran division that knew how to handle such a situation, that protected its rear as a matter of course, and whose cooks and orderlies could fight as knowingly as most combat infantrymen in an untried division. But it was not luck at all but savvy and enterprise that the First Army had taken its most experienced divisions and raced them ahead to straddle the most commanding road centers on the Belgian border.

When the first German field officers who were captured at Mons came in they were sure the war was over. The first generals to be taken thought so, too. One colonel who commanded a regiment of artillery asked only that his captor take a letter to the colonel's wife in Berlin, saying, "You will be there within a week." The generals stated that the German Army had simply ceased to exist, that they had been without orders from higher headquarters for days and that they knew of no German plan except to retreat into the interior of the Reich. They informed us that the West Wall, while reasonably complete in pillboxes and other fortifications, was not manned—and they said they did not know of any reserves in Germany available to man it.

It was September 3. I was there at the battle of Mons. I spent the first day of it in a battalion strongpoint and the last looking over the twenty-two thousand prisoners which had been herded and packed into a big stone building which appeared to have once been a prison or a house of correction. I saw the German Army go to pieces with my own eyes. I thought surely the war would be over by Christmas. There was still the problem of supply—but I knew what was unknown to the Commander of the 1st Division, who was storming up and down and swearing because Army would send him neither gasoline nor ammunition—nor even one K-ration a day for him to feed his prisoners. I knew what he did not know, and that was that the bottleneck in transporting supplies up to the front had been foreseen before we passed Paris. Miracles were not only possible but probable when problems were foreseen. We were so rich in resources and ingenuity—and no problem ahead of us compared with the problems we had solved in the breakout beyond St. Lô, and in taking France back from the Germans in little more than a fortnight. Surely, the war would be over by Christmas.

But it wasn't.

In broad strokes, this was the situation in western Europe in the early fall of 1944:

Two American and one British armies (the Canadians hugged the Channel coast) were racing for the German West Wall against only scattered rear guard opposition. There existed no German Army in the West as such. There were simply the unco-ordinated elements of a beaten force. The German High Command—and this was a vital factor in the case—was still in an extreme state of demoralization as a result of the executions ordered by Hitler after the attempt on his life. The executions themselves only began the German officer's personal problem—the heart of it was that after the purging, no general felt he could trust his neighbor in the line, his seniors or his subordinates. Military and political authority were hopelessly tangled, with everyone spying on and accusing everyone else.

The first reports of the generals lucky enough to be captured were right; the Germans had only one military objective in the West: to get back out of France, but fast. It was true that the fortifications of the West Wall were there to get back to but it was equally true that these defenses had no regular garrisons, were in many places incomplete and that beyond the West Wall, Germany was wholly unorganized for defense.

On our side of the picture, the supply lines of the two American armies now stretched in a curve nearly four hundred miles long and on the first of September we were wholly dependent on motor transport beyond Paris and partially dependent on motor transport all the way from Paris back to the dumps at the beachhead. The famous pipeline on which the gasoline supply was based—miraculous as was the speed with which it was laid—had only just crossed the Seine.

This strained supply situation, as I have said, had been foreseen, and Bradley had called on Eisenhower's headquarters to get him up what he had to have, no matter how. Had the supply forces in France had a better organization, the subsequent problem might never have developed. This may seem paradoxical because supply on the Continent was well enough organized to have already performed two genuine first-class miracles. The first miracle was the supplying of four armies over the open beaches, which the OVERLORD planners predicted would be inadequate without the assistance of speedily captured ports. The second miracle was the supplying of two armies after the break-through at St. Lô. They were fed, fueled, and ammunitioned on the run, all the way around from St. Lô to past Paris. So the implication that there was something amiss in the organization of supply sounds extreme. But it is nevertheless true.

The supplying of the four armies over the open beach was, first, the result of six months of plans and preparations in England. The whole process of landing and unloading tonnage was part of what was known as the build-up. Supplies for the build-up came out of the great dumps which had been accumulated in England before the invasion began. They were moved across the Channel according to an intricate timetable which had been prepared, complete to the last detail, for a full six months after D-day. The feat of getting these supplies across the Channel was the joint accomplishment of the Royal and American Navies, with protection from the air, courtesy of the Anglo-American air forces.

The unloading on the beach, a physical effort comparable to building a whole city of pyramids, involved a competitive effort in which the British supply organization on its beach and the Americans on theirs strove to outdo one another. The British, with their great preconceived artificial harbors, and the Americans, amidst the tangled wreckage which the big June storm left, raced each other for tonnages landed, and week after week came out in almost a dead heat.

The second supply miracle resulted from the inspired efforts of every supply agency concerned, including the monumental efforts of the First and Third Armies themselves to keep their dumps in business.

It also included the first use of the big fleets of C-47 freight planes in Europe, to nourish columns on the ground. The use of air supply to fuel armored columns had been the dream of American planners since General Devers' regime in London, and undoubtedly before that. Air transport had done a terrific job to the beachheads during its first weeks and much of the Air Corps' own equipment had come over by air. After the break-through, shuttle planes could go in to German air fields as fast as the ground forces uncovered them and cleared a runway. General Marshall paid air supply people compliments in his official story of the break-through. But mostly the feat of keeping the columns streaming across France was the accomplishment of inspired ground forces, and the word inspired is used advisedly. There are few medicines as strong as sudden victory, and every headquarters seemed to rise to meet the occasion.

What was lacking, then, when the same people had a second occasion to rise to—the occasion of the enemy army disintegrating on the border?

The first answer lies in something dull known as an organization chart.

The way an army in the field is supplied is by the troops and facilities of a higher headquarters—specifically through means at the disposal of what's known in the American Army as the Communications Zone. The Communications Zone is the area just behind the armies' battle zone. In the textbooks, the Communications Zone runs the railways which bring up supplies to the railheads, from which the armies' trucks haul them forward. In France, the Communications Zone not only ran the railways but also laid the pipelines and had, in addition, a great reserve of approximately two hundred and fifty companies of Quartermaster trucks, fifty-six two-and-one-half-ton, six-by-six trucks to each company. The Communications Zone also had control of the air transports and freight carriers of the Air Transport Command. The Communications Zone had a separate headquarters but, like every other military organization in France, was ultimately responsible to the Supreme Allied Commander, whose headquarters directed its policy.

On the supply organization chart, then, under SHAEF came the Commanding General of the Communications Zone. The supply channel then went through Army Group Headquarters on paper only—that is, Army Group, as a tactical headquarters, had no supply facilities of its own but simply requisitioned supplies for its armies from the Communications Zone. The Communications Zone trucks themselves did not unload at Army Group but delivered their supplies direct to the dumps from which the two armies drew.

The Communications Zone itself consisted of not one but two headquarters and organizations—the Communications Zone proper and a sub-organization known as Advance Section Communications Zone. These were the famed COM Z and AD SEC whose identifying initials, on the bumpers of so many thousand vehicles, puzzled the German line crossers, trying to gather identifications of fighting units in the field. (Some of the poor little German spies we captured had their notebooks full of nothing but AD SEC and COM Z symbols and numbers, wholly useless to their bosses in making any identifications more perceptive than that there were a lot of Americans around.) AD SEC—Advance Section of the Communications Zone—was what its name implied: a headquarters charged with supply to the advanced areas of the Communications Zone. It had originally been created to solve the Communications Zone's problem of operating on both sides of the Channel; it remained in being, after everyone was over on the Continent and became a source of semi-duplication of directional effort.

The net result of all this organization on top of the supply system was that many people were bosses of parts of it and no one seemed in charge of the whole. Eisenhower himself could direct it through the supply section of his staff, his G-4—but his G-4 was and wasn't the senior Supply Officer. On paper, the senior Supply Officer would seem to be the Commanding General of the Communications Zone—Major-General John C. H. Lee, who had once had his own private train to ride across the open spaces of southern England. But not General Lee, but General Plank, who commanded AD SEC, bossed the Quartermaster truck companies and was in charge of repairing railways and laid the pipelines.

These three headquarters had the authority over the facilities but it was Bradley in the field, and his generals, Hodges and Patton, whose armies had to have the supplies. It was they who knew how many gallons and how many tons it would take to get where and do what. Bradley had the responsibility, but no authority whatever, back of his rearmost army boundaries. This flaw in army organization made Bradley helpless.

The top-heavy organization of three headquarters—SHAEF, COM Z, and AD SEC—would have been troublesome enough at any time but at the time we most needed the supplies in the field, it was made impossibly complicated by the addition of a geographical problem.

AD SEC, the first to land in France, had advanced daringly into a château near Isigny when it was still within sound of artillery fire. It had advanced daringly into the château near Isigny—and it stayed there long after the center of gravity of the supply system had moved hundreds of miles east.

SHAEF had waited until the pretty seaside town of Granville, just above Avranches on the Channel coast, had been liberated. Within a week after SHAEF got to Granville, the center of gravity of the flying American columns was almost beyond reach of telephone communication. SHAEF then pulled itself together and moved into Versailles when Bradley's main headquarters moved out in the wake of his flying armies. This was not too bad, with the airports which were part of the Germans' Paris defense system so close to the headquarters. Eisenhower chose to stay in Versailles rather than go on into Paris, much to the disgust of such junior officers of his command as did not have the staff cars and limousines to do the ten miles into town whenever they felt like it.

Lee's COM Z Headquarters, however, was not so modest and jumped direct from Grosvenor Square in London's Mayfair to the George V and the Majestic Hotels in Paris. Its arrival there was accompanied by such a soft, squashy sound of sinking into plush that Eisenhower ordered Lee to take his headquarters out of Paris immediately or (Second Thought Department) as soon as communication facilities elsewhere could be established. The wording of the order was very stern but Lee and his headquarters got safely through the Second Thought loophole for, patently, there was no other spot in France where its communication net would be as good as it was in Paris. They stayed put.

I came back to Paris for a day shortly after COM Z had moved in, and an old friend of mine who was a colonel showed me his suite in the George V. He said, "Now I know why the German Army was beaten in France. This place is too damn pleasant. The German officers just dug in here—and let us dig their boys out of the foxholes." He looked around, patted the silk cushions on the divan and added, "And as far as I'm concerned I can't see anything silly about fighting a war that way."

My friend in COM Z was making a joke that day but it was no joke that the beginning of the crisis in the supply system in France came at the very time COM Z was on the move from London into Paris. A great rear echelon headquarters, with its tons of files and thousands upon thousands of clerks, typists, guards—its statistical departments, its coding and decoding rooms, its huge telephone exchange and all the other complicated paraphernalia of big business, does not move from one capital city into another—and into one where they speak a strange language, too—without an enormous loss in time and efficiency.

Some of the hardest and most conscientious work of the war was put in in COM Z—the hardest, most conscientious, and also the most plodding and pedestrian. By its very nature, it was not an organization which could rise, like the command of a field army, to a sudden crisis. Devising brilliant plans, cutting its own red tape to save time, inspiring and driving the men under its command, these were not its stuff. To the American supply troops themselves, the most inspiring thing in Paris the first month after COM Z moved in—liquor and young ladies to one side—seemed to be the black market where if you knew the right cab driver you could make a fortune over a week-end selling the gasoline you were supposed to haul, or even if you knew no one you could stop and trade your rations on the Place de L'Etoile, under the pleasant little trees that surround the arch under which the Unknown Soldier from World War I lies dead and thoroughly buried.

As the coming crisis gathered, there was neither the leadership nor the inspiration in any one of the three headquarters to rise and make history—at best there were only reasonableness, hard work and worry. There was the hard work of one individual, the venality of another. The soft winds of late summer rustled the leaves in the garden of the château at Isigny, they blew gently through the marble halls at Versailles and they whispered down the Avenue Kléber, which the Americans had rechristened Avenue de Salute, past the white helmeted MP's who guarded the Hotel Majestic. The soft winds of fate whispered and whispered, and the moment passed. It was the first week in September and the opportunity for the supply agencies to be ready for the crisis that had arrived was gone.

Now it was up to the field forces to stop yelling for more and to be realistic about what could be done with what was available.

After St. Lô, Omar Bradley's headquarters had ducked through the hole in the German line and set itself up first in a little town near the coast just above Coutances. After Avranches, it went south past the battlefield of Mortain and came to rest at Laval, a road center of some size on the base line of the Brest peninsula. It looked as if that might be a spot from which operations in any direction could be handled. By then, the situation had developed so rapidly that Bradley split his headquarters into three sections. The rearmost echelon had already been left behind with the burial records and the court martials. Now the unwieldy main headquarters was left at Laval and Bradley set up a tactical headquarters for himself as close on the heels of his army as he could get and still stay on a main axis of communication.

The Signal Corps always said where headquarters might move,

for it was the Signal Corps that projected its map lines furthest ahead of the fighting troops and announced, "Along this route we can give you wire communication." They based these lines on the civilian facilities which they hoped the Germans would leave intact and on their plans for wire strung by their own Signal battalions. These were the specially trained and equipped battalions that wove France into a network of copper, shining in the sun—wire strung along poles neater and better placed than the poles along Route One from New York to Washington.

The code name for Bradley's 12th Army Group was EAGLE. While EAGLE Main was still camping in the grove the German airforce headquarters had used at Laval, EAGLE TAC (the tactical headquarters of the 12th Army Group) first parked its trailers in the fields outside Chartres, then passed through Versailles, skipped Paris, stopped once and came to rest in a muddy race-track on the outskirts of Verdun. EAGLE Main moved forward to the Trianon Palais Hotel just back of the palace itself at Versailles and waited for SHAEF to push it on up.

It was at Verdun that the sub-section of which I was a part moved up from EAGLE Main to EAGLE TAC and pitched its office tents a few feet from the trailer in which the operations map was. The first cold winds of fall had begun to blow and after a summer under canvas we moved into the fleasy little hotels of Verdun to sleep and eat, and put on our rubber boots to slosh through the mud which the race-track had become to get to work. Our hotel had been the one in which the German officers had kept their mistresses, and the chambermaids used to tell us about them and how they (the chambermaids) had leaned out the window and booed and catcalled when the Germans' women were loaded into trucks and taken away just before it was all over.

As late in the campaign as Verdun, Bradley's EAGLE TAC was still a headquarters almost aggressively simple and austere. Omar's own trailer stood in the mud a few yards away from the trailers in which his five principal generals worked—his chief of staff and the generals who were his four G's. There were two other trailers, one for the operations map where, day and night, twenty-four hours a day, the latest reports from the units ahead of us were posted. It was long and narrow, like a circus van. When

Eisenhower and the generals from AD SEC and COM Z came up to study the map, they all crowded in like sardines and pushed and shoved one another and looked over each other's shoulders while the briefing officer tried to sum up the information he thought the generals should know.

On the walls of the other trailer, the Intelligence maps were posted. There the running appraisal of the German strength was kept posted; and there the news that came back through our line-crossers, and the mental jigsaw puzzles which were the reports of interrogation of prisoners, were put together. Omar often held his conferences there. There was an operations map on the walls of his own trailer and both enemy and friendly situations were posted hourly on it. But the Intelligence trailer was even more private and even more secure and the walls definitely did not have ears, for sentries kept strollers well away. Verdun, an ugly professional garrison town, was suspected of being hostile at the time we arrived. Although the suspicions were unfounded, we all lived within great loops of barbed wire, up and down which sentries walked.

Because in our section we were concerned with filling in the outlines of the General's plans—and even had the right, through channels, to propose our own plans—we had access to the Intelligence trailer and we used to sit and gossip there after the General's briefing was over. In September, we sat and gossiped but mostly we sat and swore. It was still early in September when everyone knew what should be happening—and what wasn't.

It was just before we went on to Verdun that another officer and I had gone up to visit the First Army, and then had gone on to run into the battle of Mons. We came back with first-hand reports but our own G-2's were ahead of us. They knew everything we had heard from the German prisoners and they knew a lot more, too. The thing was breaking up across the border. We could look on the G-2 map and see the country ahead of the advance columns of both the First and Third Armies. There were gaps where there were no German troops at all—no troops identifiable as divisions—there was a battalion here and an officers' training camp there, but no divisions. There were big holes in the German line where we had no identifications of troops at all.

Germany was wide open. They were pulling back out of Luxembourg, they were streaking towards the border in long disorganized columns.

We talked one day with two American officers who had just put back on their uniforms after wandering around in the German rear dressed as workmen. The French behind the German lines spat on the Boche now and the Boche slunk away to his barracks and did not even mutter. The young SS Troopers were bad tempered and threw grenades in the windows of the houses as they left the towns where they had courted the girls and stole the silver. The show was breaking up back there. Men who walked through the West Wall beyond the Maginot Line came back and told us that the farmers had filled in the dragons' teeth to make roads across them, that the concrete wasn't even poured at some pillbox sites.

We looked at the aerial reconnaissance. There was some activity in the rail-yards along the Rhine but we could see no mass movement of troops coming from the eastern front. There was only the stillness of demoralization in central Germany.

Verdun was an important crossing of the Meuse. It was on the main route which the Germans must know we were following. The Luftwaffe did not even come by night to bomb at the bridges.

In the G-3 trailer the little blue rectangles that were American divisions drew high numbers in their game of parchesi. They skipped across the board, counting the miles in fives and tens. In the G-2 trailer the little red rectangles which were the German divisions seemed to grow fewer rather than more numerous. Division after German division was now listed in a lengthening column under the curt caption DESTROYED.

And in the Plans Section we knew that Bradley's plans were made to finish it in a month, in six weeks, in two months. And we knew that Eisenhower had Bradley's plans too, because we had seen Bradley off to take them to Eisenhower at Versailles, and later Eisenhower had come up to visit us, and our own officers had briefed him. The original draft had been written on August 24 and was called "Blueprint for Victory." It bet everything we had on Patton's Third Army—bet that if the Third Army could be kept moving it could crack the West Wall beyond Metz and split the whole German border defense. But the orders which might have put the Blueprint for Victory into operation had been written—rewritten—and rewritten again—and still we could not get them back marked "approved."

These were the awful weeks when The Great Opportunity passed us by in the field, as it had earlier passed the supply people by in Paris. To the staff officer, they were far and away the most awful in Europe. We had to watch the flying American columns grind to a halt, and one after another lose contact with the fleeing Germans for want of the gasoline to pursue them. We had to watch the war not get won.

There had been no time when September came to shed tears for what the supply services might or might not have been able to accomplish had they been better organized or more inspiringly led. Belatedly, they were doing an heroic best-they-could, marking one-way arterial routes to the front and reserving them for express truck traffic. These were the famous Red Ball highways which were cleared of all other traffic but the thundering convoys of the Quartermaster companies, running twenty-four hours a day with their lights on through the night. There was no time to cry over the fact that there was no more than enough tonnage reaching the front now to keep one Allied army moving—and three Allied armies were trying to get through to Germany— two American and one British—four, if you counted the Canadian, which was devoting itself to handling the German fortifications along the coast.

But there *was* time, as September began, to see what could be done with the single army that might be kept moving if *all* the supply facilities available were concentrated behind it. Bradley felt that now was the time to turn the whole West Wall position, quick, quick, quick, before the Germans could reorganize there. He felt that if he could drive an army far enough and fast enough into Germany in the midst of the Wehrmacht retreat from France, the whole German State would collapse. He felt the terrific urgency of the situation, in the sense that this was one of those fleeting moments when the whole course of history can be turned by a single decisive action. From the Commanding General, his staff caught the same sense. If he had the broad picture, we had all the details, small and large, that fitted into it and we saw that they were consistent. They added up in our minds to the certainty that it *could* be done.

It was not like before D-day, when there was the imponderable of the Channel between us and the Germans. St. Lô did not compare with it in certainty, because at St. Lô we had to bet on the superior co-ordination, teamwork and drive of whole armies, of corps and divisions, on troops that had never been through even maneuvers together. Here, as we approached the borders of Germany, we knew both our own troops and the enemy. The Luftwaffe, still moving its bases backward, was almost nonexistent as a military factor. All the situation called for was a coordinated push behind *one* army, giving it all the nourishment, all the rich red blood of supplies, that the arterial Red Ball highways could carry and then, after it had gone through into Germany, while the weather was still good in the early fall, it could be fed from the air, by driving the huge fleet of transport planes which had carried three airborne divisions into France on D-day and which could easily fly over a thousand missions a day from the Paris railheads into successive German airfields as they were captured. The morale of the American troops at the front was almost exuberant. This was the end of the chase, the kill—this was the quick way home.

All these things were in Bradley's mind—and had been worked out on paper in the plans and appreciations his staff wrote for him to submit to his superior. All these things, and the sense that if the Germans were ever allowed to catch their breath it would all be different. The retreating Germans would halt and pull themselves together. The West Wall was there, in depth; if they could get themselves set in it it would be ten times worse than even the Bocage country had been. It would mean weeks running into months of grueling infantry attack. It would mean dead, dead, dead. Behind the West Wall, the Germans could maneuver their reserves. They would have time to raise new divisions, to move troops from the Eastern Front. In back of all the German effort was that straining to perfect the secret weapons which would make ours obsolete—to fit the submarines with their new devices, to get the jet planes and the V-1's and V-2's in mass production.

Bradley could see all these things and plan for them but the wherewithal was not his to command. He was still the white-haired field commander, the man whose armies had done it—had broken out of the beachhead, liberated France and crossed the German border—but to be an unbeaten field commander wasn't enough; it was the allocation of the men and material behind the rear boundaries of his battle zone that counted now. And the paper said this was none of Bradley's business.

In this situation, history called for a Supreme Allied Commander—not necessarily a brilliant one, but a bold and forceful man, making at least good horse sense. Such a commander would have believed in his victorious armies and their field commander. He would himself have seen that a single army could have been driven into Germany through the military chaos that was the Reichswehr then—as a whole army had been driven through the hole in the German line at St. Lô—and that such an army now, rammed home, could in a fortnight wholly destroy the usefulness of both the West Wall and the Rhine as military obstacles and, capitalizing further on confusion, had at least an even chance of taking Berlin and forcing peace in another. Hitler's Nazi state was not merely brittle at the time; it was already cracked by the successive shocks of the attempt upon Hitler's life and the defeat in France.

Hitler's commanders on the Eastern Front had seemed paralyzed throughout the battle of France. Their morale was low. The Russians were beating them at a bloody chess game on a monster scale, striking first in the north and then in the far south. A majority of German generals in the High Command were not merely willing but anxious to make peace with the Western Allies, to "save some of Germany from the Russians," about whom they had a very bad conscience and of whom they were very much afraid.

The mythical Supreme Allied Commander who could have handled this situation would have had to have acted with great decisiveness and to have contributed an effective and inspirational leadership, at least to the supply troops under his command, to wring from them that extra 10 per cent in effort which was vital to a situation in which literally every five-gallon can of gasoline and every 75-mm. shell for the tank cannons counted. But no more than that was demanded of him; in the field he had a brilliant and successful commander in Bradley, and Bradley, in turn, had a savagely successful cavalry leader in Patton to carry out his plans.

Perhaps General Eisenhower himself will some day answer the question why he failed to rise to this situation. I can testify to the fact that the opportunity was there, that its development had been foreseen since before Paris, and that by the beginning of September it was being argued to Eisenhower with all of Bradley's honest sincerity—and occasionally with the assistance of Patton's profane rhetoric and Hodges' plodding persistence. But I can only give the objective picture of what happened in Supreme Allied Headquarters in September, as we saw it happen from the field.

The first thing was that the opportunity became so obvious that Montgomery saw it, too—and Montgomery's superiors—the British air marshals and generals at SHAEF and the British Chiefs of Staff in London. From Caen to the Belgian borders, the British had been without plan. They had been carried along by the sweep of Bradley's army; they simply moved along the coast of France and into Belgium on the left flank of the American First Army. Now, seeing the opportunity, Montgomery & Co. proposed their own plan for capitalizing on it—if Eisenhower would allocate *them* all the supplies. As early as mid-August, Montgomery argued in almost the same words Bradley used—for wherewithal to end the war. He wanted to drive on Berlin.

Just as it had been in the question of whether to invade or not to invade in 1943, both political and military considerations were involved. The conflict of political interests between the Allies—as to who should command the crushing blow—was basic and obvious. The military difference we will return to.

To understand the flavor of the Anglo-American differences at this moment, you must recall that the land and air supply facilities at stake were almost exclusively American. Despite their short supply line, the British had barely enough transport to keep themselves in the field. The huge reserves were all American: both the Quartermaster truck companies that had been supplying the

American armies over the Red Ball route, and (a new factor) the organic transportation—the transportation which is the standard equipment of a field unit—of the new divisions which were landing in France in August and September. These divisions could not be used at the front—they were just off the boat and needed time to collect themselves. And even if they could have been moved up, they would have simply added to the supply problem when they got there, being just that many more mouths and gasoline tanks to fill. Besides, the American divisions in the line, although many of them had been fighting since D-day, were adequate to the situation. The Germans had no troops that could stop them and with victory and the chance to get home thereafter right around the corner, the last thing they wanted was to be relieved and rested. They wanted to get on with it and to finish the job. So the newly landed divisions might safely be left on the Cherbourg peninsula and the transportation that they had brought with them could be added to the supply facilities of the pursuing army.

So enormous fleets of trucking were available. So were great fleets of transport aircraft.

In the air, the British had a huge fleet of American cargo planes which they used in their airborne operations—four hundred or more C-47s—and there were always the great fleets of Lancasters and Halifaxes which might be diverted to carry cargo, although they were, of course, under a different command and had their own work to do. But the really decisive fleet of cargo planes was the carriers which transported the two American airborne divisions already in France, with the third on the way—and the planes of the Air Transport Command. There were nearly a thousand of them. And when these facilities were exhausted, there was the fleet of Forts which by now outnumbered the British bombers.

To date, the airborne operations in France had been at one and the same time a political problem and a standing joke. The political problem arose in the organization of both British and American airborne resources into a single command known as the Allied Airborne Army. The standing joke was that every operation the Allied Airborne Army had planned since D-day had had its objectives overrun by the ground forces before the cavalry of the air could get off the ground to strike. They had promised to deliver Chartres, and Bradley had said that would be fine—but the First Army was sitting in Chartres while the Allied Airborne Army was still checking its equipment. They were going to get us crossings over the Seine—but we were over the other side of it before they had finished studying their aerial photographs of the terrain. All three of the drops back of the beaches on D-day— by the two American and the one British airborne divisions—had been relative successes, but they had been preceded by many months of planning and rehearsing, and no one in the airborne business seemed to have mastered a technique for mounting an offensive from the air fast enough to keep ahead of breakaway armor on the ground. Nevertheless the Allied Airborne Army Headquarters continued in business and the principal resources for striking and supplying from the air remained under its command. This fact made it a vitally important factor in any discussion of what to do next after the German borders had been reached.

All these were pieces of the politico-supply puzzle that was Eisenhower's to solve, knowing that wherever he threw the weight of supplies and airborne troops, national prestige would be involved. But even leaving such difficult imponderables out of the equation, there remained those honest differences of honest military opinions. The Supreme Commander had plenty to brood on.

The year before the invasion the British had argued for the Balkan route into Europe; the Americans believed in the direct assault on Europe across the Channel. A similar difference of opinion had even then begun taking shape on the question of how Germany should be invaded. The British wanted to invade through the lowlands of Holland and across the Hamburg plains, striking at Berlin. The Americans believed in what was known as the Frankfurt corridor. Curiously, the arguments with which the Americans supported their positions were the identical arguments which had led the OVERLORD planners to pass up the obvious landing at Calais for the five times longer crossing to the beaches of Normandy—while Calais was the more direct approach, Calais was where the Germans expected us; the long way round the dense fortifications there had proved the shortest way home.

Similarly, American planners now felt that the German defense would be at its strongest on the northern plains, which were cut by big rivers and thousands of tiny waterways and which, while wonderfully flat, were so low that the ground was rarely solid enough to support heavy armored vehicles off the roads.

In contrast, the Frankfurt gap was a rocky road, requiring the cracking of Metz, the crossing of the Moselle and the Saar, and a penetration of the West Wall at a place where it is densest. But to offset these obstacles, the southern route offered (1) the crossing of the Rhine where it was only half the width it attained near its mouth, (2) broad unfortified valleys for avenues (the Hamburg plains were packed with military installations, organized into training grounds for the German army), (3) firm footing for vehicles, which could leave the roads anywhere, (4) the strong possibility of surprise, since it was known that the Germans were vastly more apprehensive about the northern route which led so directly to their capital, and (5) at the far end of the Frankfurt corridor into Germany there were magnificent possibilities for strategic maneuver. An army breaking through there had the free choice of three directions in which to exploit—north, to Berlin; east, to join with the Russians; or south, into Bavaria and Austria.

The deeper one drove into the Hamburg plains, on the other hand, the more obvious one's intentions became and the more easily could the enemy concentrate against them.

The difference of military opinion over how to invade Germany did not stem from individual differences of individual commanders in the field—or at least they did not during the time I was familiar with them. They seemed rather to be broad general differences of opinion, with most British officers favoring the northern route and almost all American officers in the field favoring the southern.

Those of us who had fought through the differences that had preceded the invasion were certain that British objectives were not strictly military but included political objectives as well. They wanted Berlin and the north coast of Germany as insurance that in the event of the German collapse these should not fall into the hands of the Russians.

The two opposed points of view were well developed even before Normandy; by September the conflict was clear. Bradley asked specifically for the supplies to drive either of his armies into the Rhine plain beyond the West Wall, then over the Rhine in the neighborhood of Frankfurt and straight east from there—planning, if the Combined Chiefs of Staff so desired, to take Berlin from the south after reaching central Germany. Montgomery, acknowledging the same opportunity, argued that *he* be given first priority on all Allied supplies. He wanted this priority to strike a sudden lightning blow through Holland across the Maas and the Rhine near their mouths, and thence to invade the Hamburg plains.

I believe that in August of 1944, a Supreme Allied Commander with the qualifications set down above could have ended the war by Christmas by decisively backing *either* Montgomery or Bradley. But there was no such Supreme Allied Commander. There was no strong hand at the helm, no man in command. There was only a conference, presided over by a chairman—a shrewd, intelligent, tactful, careful chairman. This chairman had gotten his job as a result of a trade in which his chairmanship—with the title of Supreme Allied Commander thrown in—had been swapped for the real control of the situation by three Commanders-in-Chief (one each for land, for sea and for air) and for the effective domination of the planning by means of the foresighted packing of key staffs with carefully selected superior officers. The man on whose shoulders the title of Supreme Allied Commander rested had been especially selected for his ability to conciliate, to see both points of view, to be above national interests—and to be neither bold nor decisive, and neither a leader nor a general. The key to his original selection was the approval of Winston Churchill and the British Government. They selected Eisenhower by the simple process of being in a position to veto the selection of any man who they felt might not be sympathetic to their point of view. Eisenhower was sympathetic and he got the job.

The dressed-up histories will probably ascribe Eisenhower's hesitancy in August to "concern for his flanks"—fear lest one of the armies get out too far and be exposed to a flanking side-swipe. But Bradley had proved at St. Lô that Allied superiority in the air and Allied mobility on the ground (when fueled) were more than compensations for an exposed flank. Moreover, when Bradley broke Patton loose the Allies still had organized German armies to contend with—while after the Seine had been crossed, the Allies faced only remnants of fleeing enemy formations.

The situation could, however, be described with more sympathy for the Supreme Commander. It is not entirely fair to blame him for his failure in what was never meant to be his responsibility, i.e., field command. If Montgomery had won at Caen, or if the July plot against Hitler's life had been successful, Eisenhower's war would have been won for him without his being required to make any decisions at all affecting the field of battle. It was the sudden necessity of choosing between Montgomery's and Bradley's battle plans that was his trouble—and that necessity was thrust upon him unexpectedly by History.

All this had not been foreseen by the men who devised OVERLORD and OVERLORD's command set-up—and who picked Eisenhower for its Supreme Allied Commander. They had assumed that the field command would be adequate to such situations. *Their* trouble can be traced to their failure to realize how helpless is a field commander—whether he be a Montgomery or a Bradley—who has no control over his own supply facilities. Both Montgomery and Bradley were at Eisenhower's mercy in the matter of allocation of supplies from the beachhead and the United Kingdom.

Thus in the ultimate analysis, it was the OVERLORD planners who were to blame for the ineffectiveness of both the American and the British field commands in September of 1944. It was the OVERLORD planners, mixing political logic with military, who had put Allied supply facilities under a commander who by their own definition was not to make field decisions.

In the situation which confronted him in August, 1944, with the German armies disintegrating in France and nothing behind them, General Eisenhower reacted as consistently with his character as any chemically pure reagent acts in a chemical formula. His job was to be cautious and open-minded—and he remained cautious and open-minded on the subject of what to do next while Paris fell and we pushed on to the German border. Early in August, he had answered Montgomery's demands by diverting transportation from the American to the British zone. He diverted just enough to break Bradley's momentum without solving Montgomery's problem. By the end of August, the supply crisis had developed; after the military opportunity had passed, Eisenhower was at last convinced. He bet all the chips he had left—not on Bradley but on Montgomery, and too late.

All the chips Eisenhower had left to bet still made quite a pile.

Three new American divisions which had just been landed on the Cherbourg peninsula were turned into trucking organizations, their combat personnel grounded. These started American supplies rolling to Monty's men.

The United States was next committed by SHAEF to deliver five hundred tons of gasoline per day to the British dumps at Brussels. The truck route that carried this precious cargo into the British area was called the Red Lion—as a kind of opposite number to the Red Ball route. It took a minimum of eight truck companies, each of fifty-some two-and-a-half-ton six-by-six trucks, running twenty-four hours a day, to keep the Red Lion fed.

Incidentally, the original commitment on this particular deal was for fifteen days but procrastination and miscellaneous inefficiencies within the supply set-up stretched this out until almost double the original commitment was delivered.

But probably the most telling blow of all, to Bradley's American armies, was the diversion of facilities for their supply by air. The American advance had opened up a big field at Orléans and by the twenty-fifth of August this depot had a supply capacity of fifteen hundred tons of gasoline a day. As a factor in fueling the advancing armies, these dumps were of unique and extraordinary importance for two reasons:

The first reason was that the fifteen hundred tons a day of gas which the C-47's could fly into Orléans came direct from the dumps in England—and were therefore a net addition to the resources on the Continent. They were free and clear, and over and above, what the pipelines and the tank trucks could deliver.

The second reason was the location of Orléans—almost due south of Paris itself. Gasoline at Orléans was already well on its way to the front. It is over two hundred road miles from the Cherbourg beaches to Orléans—and all these gasoline, and tire, and equipment eating miles were cut out of the supply line there with a single slash.

It was Eisenhower's decision to take all the priceless fuel at Orléans away from Bradley and his armies and to give it to the Allied Airborne Army, which now in turn he gave to Montgomery.

The troops of the Allied Airborne Army—the American 101st and 82nd Airborne Divisions and the British 1st Airborne Division—went with the supply facilities and were now Monty's to command.

And finally, in addition, Montgomery got the full weight of the Allies' strategic air forces to support his operation.

Something like seven thousand tons a day were left for the supply of the two victorious American field armies—seven thousand tons a day to give them fuel, ammunition, rations and whatever else they needed, including winter clothes. This would have left Bradley poor enough, but Eisenhower and Montgomery were not through with him. SHAEF next proceeded to specify the allocation between Bradley's armies. The First Army, which was to protect the flank of Montgomery's coming operation, was given *five* of the seven thousand tons a day—to make sure The Master would be safe. The other two thousand tons Bradley was allowed to give to Georgie Patton.

Two thousand tons a day was barely enough to keep the Third Army in the field at all! The five hundred tons of fuel a day diverted to Brussels alone cost Patton the mobility of *three* divisions.

Gone was Bradley's freedom of action. Gone was any chance of air supply to support a break-through—if a break-through could be effected at all, anywhere, with the rounds per artillery piece per day now strictly limited and every unit using its organic transportation not to carry it forward but to bring up its supplies from the rear.

The troops of the newest American force—which were to become the Ninth Army *—were, of course, completely stranded, all

* Originally the American Eighth Army. The British asked us to change its name to avoid the possibility of its being confused with Montgomery's

their transportation having rolled away up the coast to our allies.

For Bradley's up-till-now victorious armies, the jig was up. The plans for the blitzing of the Frankfurt gap—the Blueprint for Victory—were laid away and Patton and Hodges had to content themselves with husbanding their supplies and concentrating on limited objective attacks by means of which Bradley still hoped to wedge the West Wall open before the tide of returning German strength set in too heavily against us.

Montgomery took what had been negotiated for him from General Eisenhower and made his plans to drop the airborne elements now under his command in a line stretching sixty miles in front of his then forwardmost elements. He hoped to secure river crossings which would lead him over the Maas and the Rhine into the lowlands of northern Germany before the winter rains fell. The idea was that the parachutists would secure ground on which other airborne units would be landed, by glider and plane, in the enemy's rear.

Montgomery's best armored divisions, now refitted and built up again, would strike overland, connecting up the areas taken by the airborne troops. The infantry would follow. To the two American airborne divisions, he assigned the capture of the Maas crossings. The British 1st Airborne would drop just beyond and secure the crossing of the Rhine itself at Arnhem. It was a daring plan and far and away the most ambitious airborne operation ever undertaken. The German capture of Crete from the air had been on a much smaller scale and while as many airborne troops had been used in Normandy on D-day, they had dropped only a few miles inland where they could be quickly rescued and supplied by the landing forces.

On September 17, Montgomery struck.

Montgomery lost the battle of Arnhem but he furnished British poets with material for yet another "Charge of the Light Brigade" —in the heroic stand of the British 1st Airborne Division, part of which was cut off on the far shore of the Rhine. These heroes did secure the bridgehead he sought but Montgomery was unable to drive reinforcements through to them in time. Lightly armed as

famous British Eighth Army, even though that army remained in the Mediterranean Theater throughout the war.

all airborne troops must be, with only food and ammunition for a few days, they fought brilliantly until they were overwhelmed. The armor that was on the way to rescue them was only a few miles away. There were three brigades. Some of two of them got away back to safety on the near shore of the river. The third remained on the far shore. Its officers and men were all killed or wounded, exhausted, and finally captured. Out of seventy-five hundred paratroopers in the operation, over five thousand were lost. It was a debacle.

Throughout the campaign, military Intelligence seemed the British Army's single most effective weapon. It is ironic that Montgomery's defeat at Arnhem was the result of British Intelligence's only real failure in Europe—if the burden of the Ardennes, which they were later to share with American Intelligence, is excepted. The heroic British Airborne Division dropped out of the air smack into the middle of a Panzer corps in bivouac— the one Panzer corps in the entire German Army of which British Intelligence had temporarily lost track. It overwhelmed the airborne troops who landed in its midst and successfully stood off the follow-up forces.

Thus the big fall show which might have ended the war was over before it had hardly been begun. It was a tragic anticlimax to the victories in France, and the supply resources it had tied up were irretrievably lost to the American situation. Neither the truck companies nor the airborne troops could be released to us until the opportunity to exploit our advantages was long past.

Despite their decisive defeat, however, Montgomery's forces gained fifty miles. The American links in the airborne chain had successfully held the Maas crossings and were able to consolidate their positions. The British press did what it could for Montgomery's reputation with these fifty miles and the true stories of how bravely Britons had died at Arnhem.

September became October, October became November. If you were a headline reader you will remember only stirring victories—Liége, Brussels, Aachen, Antwerp, Metz—all taken by victorious Allied arms. But in the field, we knew by mid-September that we were in for it. The momentum was gone. We knew by the first week in September, when Eisenhower took all the surplus ground transportation and the entire air lift away from the American armies, that the momentum *had* to go. Bradley had been licked—at the conference table. It was his first defeat.

General Omar did not resign himself to the situation. He fought stubbornly to battle his way through the command and control channels in his rear. He fought stubbornly, and not very well. What he sought was some way by which he could concentrate what was left to him of the American resources on the Continent, so that he might yet save the situation at the front. His advancing armies still had some ammunition—there would be no really heavy expenditures until they reached the fortifications of the West Wall itself. To some extent, the country could supplement their rations. But they *had* to have gasoline.

Bradley tried going to Paris and meeting "off the record" with the American supply officers who controlled the channels through which his tonnage came. Once he asked them to forget food and ammunition—and even the winter clothes that were in the holds of ships already in the port of Cherbourg—to forget them all, to cut the forecasts and the red tape, and to put every man and every truck to hauling gasoline. He said if he could get six thousand tons of gasoline a day for six days he'd have the war over in a week. He was ill advised and desperate as he saw the opportunity slipping away from him. It didn't work.

The American supply officers in COM Z rose to the occasion and sent him gasoline at the expense of tangling supply priorities all the way back to the United States. They sent gasoline up by road, but since Montgomery had all the surplus supply facilities, it became a rob-Peter-to-pay-Paul process. More petrol meant less other supplies. Less other supplies going up to the front meant dislocations in the intricate timetable. Finally, it meant ships left unloaded in the harbor of Cherbourg; some actually had to be sent back to England unloaded to make way for other ships.

Omar became worried and harassed. The staffs of both his armies were frustrated and enraged. Watching the iron cool, they tried to strike it any way. They tried to do too much with too little and the troops began to take it on the chin.

Behind the American Army, the railheads moved slowly up as

the bridges were repaired. The pipeline crept forward. Gradually—very gradually—the supply situation improved. But the trucks were beginning to wear out now and the weather was getting steadily worse. The figures for vehicles worn out and wrecked on the Red Ball route became fantastic.

After Montgomery had failed him sadly a second time, Eisenhower listened once more to Omar's plea to continue on the offensive. But it was already too late. Without enough supplies, and with their momentum gone, the two American armies put on an all-out attack in November. It took ground, it bit into the West Wall and actually pierced it in three places. But it failed to break through. It lacked either the brilliance of concept or the timing of St. Lô.

General Marshall, in his official report, credits the failure of the November offensive to bad weather. Bad weather wasn't the cause; later on, the American Army was to prove it could win through much worse weather. What caused the failure was that the whole swing and drive of the American armies had been killed when Eisenhower stopped them by taking away their only hope of keeping going—denied them the use of the surplus American truck companies and the huge air lift which went over at Arnhem. And Bradley himself had lost his grasp of the situation. He was trying to win by slugging now and that wasn't his specialty.

After the November offensive failed, the next issue was whether to consolidate on the German border for the winter or to try to keep going. Bradley still felt that to stop was to invite the Germans to repair the breaches in their Wall and to skyrocket the number of casualties it would cost us to work our way to the Rhine. If we waited, every pillbox taken would mean a battle. Grudgingly now, he got permission from Eisenhower to try to keep going.

Throughout the fall, Patton remained irrepressible and still talked of going on through the West Wall and across the Rhine at Frankfurt—without supplies and even if he had to push the vehicles by hand. Both Patton's victories and defeats were inevitably the result of his belief that, in a pinch, morale and daring could be substituted for solid weight and fire power. His first flying columns to approach the German border had pushed in amongst the fortresses of Metz, almost unopposed at the time. But, as at Brest, he found that there was a vast difference between an advance guard getting into a fortified city and his having that city solidly in hand. Without the gasoline to move his infantry up, he was driven back from Metz. When Patton finally gathered enough troops to make his first attack in force, he suffered a defeat which almost cost him his reputation—although there remains a question of whether the unsuccessful tactics were Patton's or one of his corps commanders interjecting some notions of his own.

At Metz there were three generations of fortifications piled one on top of the other. There were the medieval foundations, with masonry twenty feet thick—and on top of them, the heavy buttresses that had been built in 1870—and then came the fortifications that had been added after the last war. These proved Patton's pitfall when a brilliant German commander organized a group of officer candidate scholars into a field force to man them. They stopped the XX Corps of Third Army cold. Patton had neither the men nor the artillery to force them, and aerial bombs splattered against their heavy masonry with no more effect than raw eggs broken on an elephant's hide. It was not until late November that Patton was able to force the position. The real moral of all this action was that the original "Blueprint for Victory" plan that Bradley had tried to sell Eisenhower in August would have worked. For Metz, the key position in the area, had in the beginning been overrun virtually without opposition. The Germans at the time were in full retreat; they did not even feel themselves strong enough to man the great Metz forts. Only when Patton was allowed to run out of gas did the enemy regain his courage and return to put up a fight.

To the north, the plodding Hodges did better with his infantry-wise First Army. The 1st Infantry Division—which liked to think of itself as a one division army and had great 155-mm. rifles on tractor mounts which could be used for direct fire against pillboxes—took Aachen on October 21, with assistance from two other divisions on its flanks. Aachen was the first sizable German city to fall and a city not only smack in the middle of one of the most heavily fortified positions of the West Wall but also a fortress city which was under personal orders from Hitler to hold out at any cost. But after Aachen had fallen, Hodges had nothing left with which to capitalize on the victory.

The attempt to keep the all-out offensive going in November had failed. From one end to the other the whole American front began to stalemate and solidify—just as Omar Bradley had foretold it would if we ever let our drive come to a halt.

The morale of the American troops, which had been so high, began to drop; the men who had been buoyant and full of spirits on the march began to feel tired now. Cold winds came, and rain. There had been no time to prepare for winter warfare; the troops were not even clothed for it. Every yard taken in the West Wall meant casualties from the enemy; every night spent in German mud meant more casualties from frostbite and trenchfoot. Winter clothing became so urgent that we began to fly up what we could get of it.

No one had to have any inside information now to know that something had gone wrong with our plans. But no man knew just how wrong they had gone—for what we had yet to learn was that between September and December something had happened inside Germany—something important, and bad for us, had happened during the time which Hitler had been given to get his breath. We did not know then what it was, but the men in the line could sense it. As their morale dropped, they knew that the morale of the Germans opposite them had begun to rise. The Krauts were getting tough again.

9 God Presents the Bill for SHAEF

WHAT had happened in Germany in the fall of 1944 was that Hitler had recovered from the shock of the conspiracy against him and the attempt on his life. He had been surprised and frightened, but now he knew that enough of his senior commanders remained loyal to him to make it possible to stand. As a result of his purging of those whom he considered weak and uncertain in the German High Command, and as a result of the inevitable tightening of German morale and unity now that the enemy in the West was at the border—as a result of these things—and probably some kind of spiritual rebirth in Hitler himself, Der Fuehrer regained some of his old brilliance.

It was striking, during the months from June to November, how lethargic the German High Command was—how slowly it reacted. It was muddle-headed and indecisive. Individual German corps and armies fought ably—often with savage skill. When the German radio boasted of the brilliance of the disengaging actions, by and large it spoke not bunk but the truth. In tactical maneuvers, the German Army knew the book and practiced it. But the whole show had clearly been mismanaged. It had seemed to lack central control.

Because of these things, what happened in Germany in the fall of 1944 came as a distinct surprise to most of those who had been daily students of "most secret intelligence" about the enemy.

Within a few weeks the change could be felt: there was purpose now in the handling of the German armies in the West, a decisiveness which was new and startling. What Hitler did with the breathing spell which was given him in September can now be reconstructed in detail.

Hitler's last campaign called for the complete reorganization of his forces in the West, the raising of a whole new army, almost literally overnight. He had to bring the Allies' victorious armies to a halt and then mount an offensive capable of destroying them. In the decisiveness with which he went about accomplishing these things he lived up to the reputation for effectiveness he established when he began his conquest of Europe. These were the steps he took:

First he created the *Volkssturm*—a German version of the British Home Guard. As early as July, American Intelligence officers had tried to argue with their British opposite numbers that if the Germans chose to fight in their own country, we would be faced with a home guard. The British had said that this was poppycock, that we did not understand the German character: the Germans were incapable of creating a home guard. They made only mercenary soldiers. But Hitler did create one, in a matter of weeks, giving it armbands for uniforms and whatever weapons could be found. After combing out local storehouses, he even resorted to an order directing ground force personnel of the Luftwaffe to turn in their pistols and rifles to equip the new troops.

Into the bunkers of the West Wall went the home guard, where a handful of professional non-coms could organize the fire power of a regiment, safe within well-sited concrete gun emplacements.

At the same time, Hitler emptied his convalescent hospitals and threw together a very sizable force of what we would call 4-F's. The Germans called these units "Stomach Battalions"—because most of the soldiers in them suffered from stomach disorders. The Stomach Battalions even drew special convalescent diets from the Quartermaster Corps. Stomach Battalions backed up the *Volkssturm* in the West Wall.

When we fought in the West Wall, we lost on every casualty trade. When we attacked, our casualties were able-bodied young Americans, well armed, veteran and highly trained. The first waves were shot by men safe behind concrete and steel. When we took our losses and pressed on to blow up and capture these fortifications, we killed—or put into our prison cages—German farmers and cripples.

Thus Hitler solved the immediate problem of stabilizing his Western Front, of making our further advance expensive at the very time when, at the end of our strained supply lines, we could least afford a fight.

Immediately behind the fortified West Wall, backing up the home guards and the cripples, Hitler spread out his remaining field divisions—his line infantry divisions and his run-of-the-mill Panzer divisions. These divisions kept the cripples from making a free choice as to where they would die—they died in the West Wall, either facing us or facing the German Army if they turned tail. Even more important was the mobility these field units now achieved. The German road and rail net was relatively safe behind the West Wall. The effectiveness of the field units was thereby doubled because, spread out at regular intervals in the rear, they could be concentrated rapidly against any break-through we might effect. Thus we could not exploit our break-throughs and the *Volkssturm*—and the impressed local populations—were given time to throw up new fortifications before us.

General Bradley once estimated that by December the West Wall, thus defended, was worth the equivalent of *fifty* new divisions to the German Army. In a manner of speaking, these were SHAEF's Christmas present to the Reichswehr.

The German line divisions behind the West Wall were supported by another newly organized classification in the German Army, the *Volksgrenadiers*. This force was made up of men who had all had previous military training and had perhaps been invalided out of the Army for minor ailments or been deferred to an essential war industry, but who, as individuals, were not quite up to the standards of the regular German Army. Under the command of regular army officers, however, the *Volksgrenadier* divisions were pep-talked into a reasonable facsimile of good military morale, the principal theme being that they were the people's super-army, with the historic mission of defending the people's sacred soil, the sacred soil of the Fatherland.

Volkssturm, Volksgrenadier—and Stomach Battalions—all represented new enemy units on our battle map, net additions to the German order of battle. In aggregate, they constituted a very sizable force.

But Hitler had only begun to have fun. Next he took the new class that was coming up—the boys who had just reached seventeen—and instead of sending it immediately into battle as replacements, he let the line divisions take older men from the supply services to fill their needs, and he concentrated the youngsters on the plains outside Hamburg. He ordered that they be built into a brand new army. He gave this group AAA priority on equipment and supplies and a first-class cadre—a cadre is the skeleton force of experienced men around which a new unit is built.

By this move, Hitler created a new force composed exclusively of able-bodied young men, fanatic in morale and magnificently equipped. This new German army was 100 per cent mechanized with the latest and best gear that the Reich could provide. It was known as the Sixth SS Panzer Army—and it was this army which, on the sixteenth of December, was to spearhead the attack in the Ardennes. The Sixth SS Panzer Army—and the *Volksgrenadier* troops which supported it—were organized and put in the field between the middle of October and the middle of December, when they made their historic attack.

At the time Eisenhower was fumbling around with the decision as to whether to back Bradley or Montgomery, the Sixth SS Panzer Army did not exist, the *Volkssturm* and the *Volksgrenadiers* were home in their feather beds and the Stomach Battalions were minding their diets in convalescent hospitals. The Supreme Allied Commander's giving Hitler the chance to shuffle the reserve manpower of Germany, and to create the Sixth SS Panzer Army, was at least one excellent reason why we did not win the war by the Christmas of 1944.

But to tell the story of the Ardennes offensive, you cannot begin with the German troops that fought in it; you must start with—you must go back to—the port of Antwerp.

After the British defeat at Arnhem, there was nothing for it— from the point of view of the Supreme Command—but to begin gathering the men and matériel necessary to invade Germany in force. The opportunity to blitz—to conquer by shock, to complete the disintegration of the German State by concussion—the opportunity to do all this, using only the men and supplies already on hand, was past. Now it would take solid force, and solid military force can only be applied by solid military tonnage—by supplies.

Never forget that, for practical purposes, the entire campaign to date had been supplied from the original beaches, good old OMAHA, UTAH, and JUNO and GOLD. Cherbourg and half a dozen small Channel ports contributed trickles of supplies. Le Havre and Brest had both finally been taken, as the original OVERLORD planners wanted—but both were in such bad shape that one's contribution was severely limited and the other was so far away that it contributed nothing whatever. In the very first week in September, however, the British advance along the coast had overrun one priceless asset. In the confusion of their retreat, in their moment of extreme demoralization, the Germans had let the port of Antwerp fall into Allied hands absolutely undamaged—its twenty-five miles of docks, complete with rail and unloading facilities, remaining in perfect condition.

There had been no battle for Antwerp; the Germans had simply moved out. It was a present. There was, however, a catch to the gift. Antwerp lies at the inland end of a deep estuary—and the Germans still held the mouth of it. The entrance to Antwerp from the sea is stoppered by the island of Walcheren. Walcheren was heavily fortified, in German hands, and it stuck in the throat of the estuary like an apple in a pig's mouth.

In Antwerp, the port which no planner had seriously dreamt of capturing intact, there were sufficient facilities to supply practically the entire Allied armed forces on the Continent. Antwerp is the third largest port in all the world. Moreover, for the purposes of the campaign, it was ideally situated—not merely because of its short sea turn-around from England but also because of the perfect road and rail net which fanned out from it direct to the Allied lines, right where they lay nearest the heart of Germany.

As soon as it became evident that we had a real fight on our hands to get into Germany, it had to be Antwerp or else. Everyone knew the beaches would go out with the first real storm of fall.

When Antwerp was uncovered, Montgomery's eye was still on the quick road into the Hamburg plains. He had by-passed as many German coastal garrisons as he dared, leaving token forces to guard them, and hurried on. He had not bothered to clear the Schelde estuary which led to Antwerp. The Supreme Commander whose headquarters had allowed one historic supply crisis to develop could not afford to allow a second. After Arnhem, Eisenhower asked Montgomery to go get Walcheren Island, and clear the banks of the estuary. (General Marshall's history records the fact that General Eisenhower reported the imperative necessity of clearing the Schelde on September 9, six days after Montgomery had taken the port itself.) There was no difference of opinion amongst Eisenhower's British and American advisers over the fact that we had to make Antwerp workable, but the need for it had long since become predominantly an American one, simply because the American forces on the Continent were by now so very much larger than the British.

Eisenhower put the problem principally to Montgomery, as the Commander-in-Chief of the ground forces at the site, but he put it also to the Royal Navy and the Royal Air Force—because Walcheren was a place you could only reach by sea or by air, and it was deep in the British zone. The first answer that the British Commanders-in-Chief are said to have sent back was that Walcheren could not be taken, that it was impregnable—at least at that season of the year, with winter about to begin. But the success of the entire campaign in Europe had now begun to hang on Walcheren. It *had* to be taken.

It was Eisenhower's second test of leadership, the first having passed only a few weeks earlier when he had had to make up his mind about whether to throw the weight of American supplies behind Bradley or Montgomery. Too late he had backed Montgomery, and Montgomery had lost for him at Arnhem. The Supreme Commander must have begun to wonder whether he was being objectively advised by the British officers on his staff. Again he sent the problem of clearing Antwerp back to the three

British Commanders-in-Chief and this time they sent the Royal Air Force out to do the job.

In Bradley's headquarters, where Walcheren Island had become more important an obstacle than the great German West Wall itself, this sounded a little better. The American forces retained their respect for the aggressiveness of the Royal Air Force throughout the campaign. A year before D-day, the Royal Air Force had fought one conference battle to assimilate, or at least to control, the American Air Forces in Europe. It had lost. The air marshals then fought a second conference battle, seeking to dominate the tactics the Americans used—on that issue of night versus day bombing. The Royal Air Force had lost again. But the Americans felt that the air marshals had taken their lickings at the conference table and laid off, and no hard feelings resulted. Moreover, throughout the campaign, the Royal Air Force continued to fight the Luftwaffe. They were ingenious and aggressive. They did not sweat their losses as the ground forces seemed too often to do; when they were given a job to be done, they went out and took a shot at it.

Given Walcheren Island to handle, the Royal Air Force went over some of the densest flak in Europe and knocked out the island's sea dikes, thus flooding a large part of it. But even the great flood they created left enough solid ground for the Germans to defend—and in a way made the task of invasion even slightly more difficult by adding to the water hazards.

Time was running short and the weather was getting worse and worse. There was no more time either for conference or for further study. Eisenhower had no choice now but to *order* Montgomery to take Walcheren Island. History was breathing down the back of his neck.

Montgomery ignored Eisenhower's first order.

We sat on the sidelines and waited for our liaison officers to bring us news. Eisenhower ordered Montgomery a second time to take Walcheren and a second time nothing happened. The British Army was resting and refitting. Now the Supreme Allied Commander was in a real spot. The American War Department was asking how come? The British as well as the Americans on Eisenhower's staff were telling him that he *had* to have action. In the American zone, after the first fall attacks, Bradley was as short of supplies as ever. He had three armies in the field to feed now—the Ninth American Army having finally opened up shop in the line. So Eisenhower sent a written message to Montgomery the context of which was repeated to us as saying, "You are a soldier and you are under my command. It is my understanding that a soldier's first obligation is to obey orders. I have ordered you to take Walcheren Island, and I shall expect you to take Walcheren Island." Montgomery at last complied and after two further minor postponements the attack was begun.

Antwerp had fallen on September 3. A little over two months later—on November 9—Walcheren fell, unlocking it, and the Royal Navy moved in to clear the Schelde estuary of mines. The Royal Navy was on the job. They put on a spectacular show, removing one of the trickiest underwater mine fields in history. The story was that among the gadgets they used was one which got to be the fashion for sight-seeing officers to go down and ride. It was a tough little tug-like boat with ice-breaker hull and sheet after sheet of steel on the bottom. This boat simply ran over a mine—magnetic, moored or detonated by the vibration of its propeller—and let the mine explode under it, giving crew and passengers a great thrill. I have my fingers crossed on this tale but however they did it the British got the job done.*

On the twenty-seventh of November, nearly *three months* after the port itself had been overrun, the first supply ships sailed up the estuary and Antwerp was open. To get Bradley the tonnages he needed, American supply people took over the running of the port, even though it was in the middle of the British area.

The Germans immediately began a violent V-weapon campaign against the port, a campaign which never stopped until the flying

* However they did it, it was one up for the British Navy because the summer before the American Navy had had so much trouble with the port of Cherbourg that the ground forces considered the job a near scandal. Again and again, the Navy had given us a date on which the port would be available only to have to postpone it because they were unable to make good their promise to get the harbor cleared. The Germans had left many new types of mines behind them, the hardest to cope with being one which let the first few ships pass over it unharmed and then blew the next in a channel everyone thought safe.

bomb and rocket launching sites themselves were overrun. But despite daily casualties often running into the hundreds, the work of the port was never seriously interfered with. The heroism of the men who unloaded the ships in Antwerp under the steady succession of deadly concussions that went on for months—day and night without respite—is one of the unsung sagas of the war. Censorship had to deny the enemy any information it could on where the enemy's missiles were falling.

Within a week after the port of Antwerp had been opened, surpluses in supply began to pile up behind the troops at the front. The era of scarcity was over—but so was the fall. It was then that the issue of whether to continue through the winter got its last going over in high level argument. Montgomery made no bones whatever about the fact that he considered the invasion of Germany now impossible before the summer of 1945. But Bradley still proposed to go ahead, to use the newly available supplies to continue the attack without hesitation. Montgomery's delay at Walcheren, following hard on his defeat at Arnhem, had again lost the British general the Supreme Commander's sympathy. So Eisenhower let Bradley go ahead with his plans. It was the first of December.

Bradley immediately ordered both the First and the Third Armies to complete their preparations for breaking out beyond the West Wall as rapidly as possible—the Third Army would head for Bradley's cherished Frankfurt gap and the First Army would hit the thin place it had worn down in the German defenses at Aachen, opposite Cologne.

I have described the big November offensive as a failure. This it was, in the sense that it failed in its prime objective of getting a foothold beyond the West Wall before the Germans could man the fortifications. But it had taken ground and was in fact still moving forward, here and there, at the time Antwerp was opened. Actually, the whole American fall offensive had been a series of limited objective line bucks; the war of movement had ended when the gas tanks had run dry in September.

With his supplies at last assured, Bradley paused to do a quick regrouping before making the final effort. Preliminary attacks and last minute preparations for it were still being made and the ammunition and petrol dumps were still filling for the final push, when the Ardennes counteroffensive began.

The port of Antwerp also played an important part in Hitler's timing of the counteroffensive. On the one hand, Arnhem and delay at Antwerp had given him the time to prepare; on the other, the opening of Antwerp, which would make it possible for Bradley to continue his attacks through the winter, gave Hitler notice that he could not delay too long.

Here was his situation as the last month of 1944 opened:

He had made an amazing comeback from the sad month of September. After apparently having lost his entire army in the West, Hitler had succeeded in stabilizing the front from the Channel to the Alps—and he now had a brand new army almost ready to go into action. Potentially this army was the best under his command in the entire campaign—spectacularly well equipped, under selected field officers and with the pick of Nazi youth in its ranks. All it needed was a little more training.

Hitler's V-weapons had not worked as well as he had hoped, but neither had the Allies' countermeasures been able to stop them. The new and vastly improved submarine fleet was well on its way towards completion; it would be ready by the following spring. Five-hundred-mile-an-hour jet aircraft were at last in mass production; there were enough in the air already for his Luftwaffe to begin studying the tactics of their employment, so that although they were still relatively ineffective against the Forts, he confidently expected to be able to challenge Allied air superiority within six months. Meanwhile winter weather was partially offsetting the Allies' advantage in the air.

In back of it all were the new secret weapons which his brain trust was still promising Hitler.

There is no doubt now that Hitler's original plan, following the fall of France, called for feverish scientific effort, for production and for training through the winter of 1944-45 behind a stabilized front—followed by an all-out campaign to destroy the western Allies in the coming spring. This would be led on the ground by the young men he had begun to hoard in the Sixth SS Panzer

Army, in the air with the new fleets of jet fighters—the whole continental battle area being in the meantime isolated by intensified and more effective submarine warfare. And in any inning now, Hitler's scientists might step up to bat and knock the ball over the fence.

All the elements of this overall plan were known to us by December. We had plenty of captured generals to interrogate. We had watched the Sixth SS Panzer Army gathering and commencing its training on the Hamburg plains—seen them in aerial reconnaissance photographs and talked to captured relatives of its officers and men. We felt that any resignation to a stabilized front would play directly into Hitler's hands. This was the basis of Bradley's decision to fight on through the winter—and it was Bradley's decision that denied Hitler the opportunity to make good his last ambition.

Early in the fall, while the people of America were still confidently expecting the end of the war any day, at Bradley's headquarters we had been moved by a sense of almost dire urgency. The public, of course, knew nothing of Hitler's ambitious plans. Neither did the public know that after we had lost our momentum through lack of supplies, our November and early December attacks on the West Wall had been bitterly expensive in men and morale.

For instance: two first-class infantry divisions in succession had been literally broken on the battlefield in successive attacks in the woods south of Aachen. Each of these divisions in turn had to be taken out of the line. They were decimated and disheartened. The West Wall trade (of good young Americans for crippled Germans) was paying dividends—to the Germans.

It is hard for anyone who has not at least been near it to understand what too long exposure in combat does to even the best organization, even the most veteran and experienced. I remember what happened to young battalion commanders coming out of the Hurtgen Forest—professional officers still in their twenties and veterans of the Mediterranean Theater.

Battalion commanders do not fight in front lines; they usually direct the companies under their command by field telephones from dug-in CP's. If they are good battalion commanders, they are very precious to their men, who build fires to keep them warm and see to it that they have a dry place to sleep and plenty of hot food and coffee. Their coffee will be strong and their food will be good because the sergeants will forage for them and the best cooks in the outfit will work in their messes. It is true that, while in the line, battalion CO's will be in command twenty-four hours a day, seven days a week—but each has a staff of officers to help him and to stand by the telephone and the muddy map on the wall when he chooses to go to sleep. So the CO does not suffer physically, as the GI does, eating cold food and sleeping in cold mud; the CO's strain is purely psychological. Yet the young battalion commanders who came out of the Hurtgen Forest— whose CP's did not happen to get direct hits from artillery bar- rages—were as near gibbering idiots as men can get without being locked up for it.

From the 12th Army Group Headquarters we used to drive up a few miles to the line to pick up personal friends—Academy classmates of officers on our staff. We brought them back and gave them a hot bath and all they could drink. We tried to get them to tell us what it was like in the line now. One man said, "Well, it's not too bad until the doughs get so tired that when they are coming out of the line and there is a dead dough from their own outfit lying on his back, in their way, they are just too goddam tired to move their feet and they step on the stiff's face because what the hell . . ."

On four successive nights this battalion commander had had to order four successive young lieutenants, each just off the boat from America, to take out patrols on which he knew they would be killed. They were. He said, "I can't do it any more. They can shove it."

Most of the young battalion commanders did not talk; they just sat across the table or on the edge of your cot and looked at you very straight and unblinking with absolutely no expression whatever in their faces, which were neither tense nor relaxed but completely apathetic. They looked, unblinking, and I can see the color of their eyes now. I can also see the field hospitals and the cold tents just behind the line, and the corpses outside the surgical tents. You drive by the surgical tents in the morning, going up, and there are two or three stiffs there on the ground; you come back in the afternoon and there are thirty or forty. They are short-handed on the Graves Registration squad and the G-2's are too busy interrogating prisoners to spare PW's for a burial detail.

Everyone is short-handed now because in the West Wall all the previous statistics of the campaign are going to hell and the replacements that are coming up are not enough and on the morning reports of the outfits in the line the strength is dropping down, down, down—85 per cent strength, 65 per cent strength, 58 per cent strength. Now in this outfit there aren't enough riflemen and they're brushing up the boys they didn't think strong enough for combat. They're brushing them up on their infantry tactics and sending them in.

When the strength of an outfit in the line drops below a certain point, something very bad happens to it and its effectiveness falls away sharply. What happens to it is that there are not enough experienced men left in it to make the replacements—the reinforcements—savvy. I keep forgetting that in the middle of the campaign we got an order to stop calling them replacements and to refer to them as reinforcements. The majority of the casualties, on any given day, in any given outfit, are almost always among the reinforcements—the men who can't recognize the whip crack of an 88 or who put their foot in the wrong place and get it blown off by an anti-personnel mine. If the original reinforcement gets through the first forty-eight hours, his chances of survival go way up. His chances seem at their highest after he has been in the line—oh, perhaps a week. Then you know, sitting in a high head-quarters, like an actuary behind an insurance desk, that the odds on his survival drop slowly but steadily and with mathematical certainty always down, down, down. The odds drop for every day he remains under fire until, if he's there long enough, he is the lone number on a roulette wheel which hasn't come up in a whole evening of play. And he knows it too.

It was like that on the German border early in December—with the good outfits getting whittled down and the relatively new outfits—they had not shaken down in combat yet—not good enough, not smart and tenacious enough, to take the ground you knew had to be taken. Army and corps commanders kept having to use the reliable veteran outfits over and over again until they were dangerously close to being spent.

It was like that in the American Army. In the slugging match that was going on, it was also very much like that—only worse—in the ranks of the *Volkssturm* in the West Wall—and in the regular German Army line divisions that the defending commanders kept having to call out of tactical reserve to throw into the line against us to prevent a break-through. Even with our guns in the open, firing against their guns in fortified positions, we had the weight of fire power and we were grinding and cracking the bones of the West Wall. It was only a question of time—and very little time at that—before the last now brittle ribs of the West Wall would crack, and we would go through out onto the Rhine plain, where the armored divisions which waited, idle in the mud behind our lines, could operate again. And when the rail was finally really running, and we got our transport back from the British, and there were all those shiny new divisions back on the Cherbourg peninsula coming up, and Antwerp was open—we would be over the hump. *One* more push! The next attack we knew would work!

Getting back onto Hitler's side of the battle, he learned that the V-weapons had not stopped the supplies getting through from Antwerp. His Intelligence saw the American forces gathering opposite Aachen, and in the south threatening the Saar. He realized that the *Volkssturm*, the *Volksgrenadiers* and the remnants of the regular army in the West would not be enough to hold now; they would not give him that winter in peace to rearm in. Bradley's armies were beating them—and Bradley's armies were not going to stop. So, once again with the boldness that characterized his early days, Hitler did something about it.

Hitler did something precipitate, something forced on him before he was ready. He ordered the Sixth SS Panzer Army to strike at once, even though its training was not complete, in a surprise attack. Alongside it, he put another newly outfitted

Panzer army, the Fifth. He supported them with everything he had, building the whole attack force up to twenty-four divisions. He gave it the works.

The Germans had code names for their operations just as we. The heart of the German attack in the Ardennes had the code name of GREIF, which means GRAB. Its grand objective was to grab Antwerp back. Its ultimate ambition was to win a battle as decisive as the American victory at St. Lô.

It was a beautiful plan and, if Bradley had given Hitler and von Rundstedt even another month to prepare for its execution, it might have worked. But by the beginning of December we were so close to a breakout that the grab had to be made with several fingers of the hand missing. The training and equipment of two of the divisions of the Sixth SS Panzer Army were seriously incomplete. One of these divisions never even got to the battle. The balance of the new army was also just that many weeks short of training and when the grand assault broke into the thousands of tiny little actions which ultimately decide the fate of all grand assaults, that lack of training put just that much more handicap on the forces racing to capitalize on the brilliant start they made.

In plan, the objective of the German operation was to blitz through from what is known as the Eifel to the River Meuse, there to seize crossings. It was then to proceed through Liége, a key American center, to Antwerp. Arriving at Antwerp, the drive would have split the American and British forces. With the loss of Antwerp, both Allied forces would be deprived of what had become by now virtually their sole source of supplies.

Immediately after this victory, a second drive was to start from near the Channel coast to the north. This was to cut the cut-off British forces in two—and "force a second Dunkirk." From this second Dunkirk, the British were expected never to recover—and Hitler assured his commanders that after this campaign they would never have another British Army to face. So the Germans would be left with only the Americans on their minds—and the Americans would now be supplying themselves across the whole breadth of France, largely from small ports, the beaches having already been shut down for the winter.

Hitler confidently expected the Americans to have to retreat to west of the Seine. There he would deal with them in due time—in the spring, when the whole Reich, invigorated by victory, would rise to throw the mongrels from the West back into the sea.

The blitz battle which was to make all these things possible was to be launched—in order to achieve surprise—in the most unlikely sector. *Gott* seemed to smile on the plan, for the "most unlikely" sector was not only happily situated—in relation to the ultimate objective—but led to the very avenue through which German armies had advanced four years before to turn the Maginot Line and destroy the French Army as a fighting force in a matter of weeks. Would the over-extended American Army, in 1944, prove more formidable than the then great French Army had in 1940? The avenue that was thus to be twice used to strike France down consisted of the roads through the Ardennes Forest—which Western strategists always seemed to think so unlikely an avenue that it had not been fortified by the French after the last war and was lightly held by the Americans in this. There is such rugged terrain in the Ardennes that nature does not seem to need man's help.

In 1940, Hitler's armies had broken out of the Ardennes into the plains of central France to strike in several different directions simultaneously. In 1944, the particular value of a break-through from the Ardennes lay in the fact that Liége was only a few miles beyond and that the German Army, having taken Liége, would have the huge American dumps there with which to feed itself—it could capture the vehicles and the petrol necessary for the final plunge to Antwerp, only seventy-five miles beyond.

All this and heaven too!—there were still other advantages to the sector which the Germans had chosen for the attack. The line dividing the opposing armies ran along the border. The terrain on the German side, opposite the Ardennes, was ideal for Hitler's purpose. The Eifel is densely wooded country in which large forces can be hidden from the prying eyes of aerial cameras. An excellent rail net leads into it, over which troops can be brought up quickly by night.

The weather too was to play its part. In December, in the Eifel,

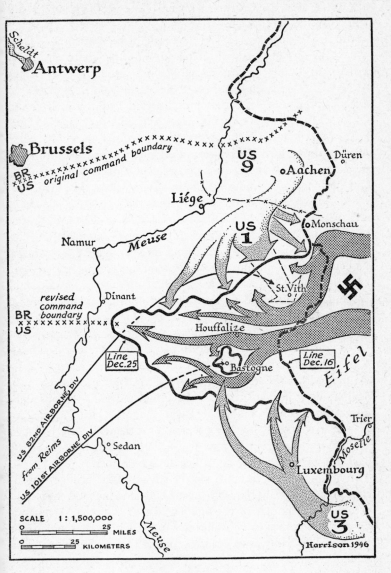

THE ARDENNES

one can count on cloudy weather. The Allies' air superiority would thus be neutralized.

And so the stage was set for the battle of the Ardennes—which Hitler was forced to launch prematurely on the sixteenth of December. In Bradley's headquarters, the possibility of an attack through the Ardennes had been discussed among the general officers several weeks earlier and Bradley had reasoned it out patiently. "We haven't enough troops to be strong everywhere. To stay on the offensive, to keep the Germans from recuperating, to break through to where we can use our armor again—to do all these things, we have no choice but to concentrate our forces. And that means thinning out the line somewhere. The Ardennes is still the safest place in which to thin the line. But, you point out, the enemy has the capability of attacking there? All right, let him come there if he wants to. We have got to destroy his army some place and if he comes out into the Ardennes, so much the better. We want him out of his hole."

Later on, Bradley was to use a military phrase to describe this reasoning. He referred to the thinning of the American line in the Ardennes as "taking a calculated risk." He meant that the odds were against the enemy's attacking there; they *might* come but it was worth taking the chance to play for the enormous advantages to be gained by staying on the offensive. And if we lost—and the enemy *did* attack—he could still be beaten there.

So Bradley decided to take the calculated risk—but it's only fair to the German commanders who mounted Hitler's battle to say that so skillfully did they prepare for it that not a single Allied Intelligence agency in Europe had even a suspicion of what the Germans were up to the night before they struck.

Montgomery, for instance, on the advice of the brilliant Oxonian, Brigadier Williams, who headed his Intelligence, had only just delivered himself of the opinion that the German Army was without any offensive capabilities whatever—that the only problem the Allies had was to get them out of their pillboxes and into a fight anywhere.

SHAEF, where they had time to pool British and American Intelligence sources and to study them at leisure, gave no inkling of suspicion in its regular weekly appreciation which was actually distributed, I seem to remember, just two days before the Ardennes offensive commenced.

At 12th Army Group, G-2 had been even more optimistic, feeling that the enemy's line troops were on the verge of cracking—which indeed was the very reason why Hitler chose that moment to attack. The G-2 Section had just written the strongest paper of the campaign, urging the most aggressive action in order to capitalize on the enormous casualties that we had inflicted on the German Army through November and December. Many German divisions in the line opposite us were known to be down to two or three thousand men.

We were first-hand students of the prospective battlefield too, at Group, for our headquarters were in Luxembourg, on the edge of the Ardennes itself, and the road we took riding back and forth to First Army Headquarters lay within anti-tank gun range of the German armies. We used to avoid it by night because now and then German raiding parties would come over and pick up a jeep or two. By the time the offensive was a week old we knew from captured documents that Luxembourg itself was a minor objective—to be taken to protect the southern flank of the main effort—and that the *Volksgrenadier* division in the line opposite us had actually practiced its crossing of the small river on the border, ten miles from where we worked, a week before the main attack jumped off.

When the attack came, it was a total and complete surprise, catching the first of the American relief divisions which had come up from Cherbourg on their very first night in the line. Two whole regiments were overrun and captured. Never had a battle in France gotten under way so auspiciously for either side. At St. Lô, the infantry had had to slug it out for whole days and nights before we were past the crust. In the Ardennes, the Germans went through our main line of defense at thirty miles an hour, without even stopping to shoot the prisoners they took—a luxury they reserved for some days later when they massacred several groups of Americans to save themselves the bother of marching them home.

The Germans seemed to have everything—surprise, speed, fire power and morale. When you looked at the map on the morning of December 17, it seemed impossible that they would ever be stopped—for they had torn a fifty mile gap in our lines and were pouring through it like water through a blown dam. And on every road ahead of them to the west there were Americans fleeing for their lives.

When the snow came in the Ardennes it was pretty but it made the roads very slippery. There was not really a lot of snow, as we measure snow in the northern states of America, although sometimes it drifted high enough to make walking through it hard. On the roads it packed down until it was ice-like. When a man was bleeding in an ambulance and the blood ran out under the tail gate doors, it splashed in the snow and left little dull red splotches by which you could have trailed the ambulance if you'd needed to.

The armor that came up slid badly on the icy roads and you would have thought an armored column had gone mad to watch its vehicles careening off trees, crashing through the corners of houses on turns. The thirty-three-ton tanks spun crazily on the gentlest slopes, sometimes turning completely around two or three times before they came to rest. In a day's move, an armored division might lose several hundred of its vehicles, wrecked, mired, overturned. The maintenance crews blew on their fingers and sweated with their gear as they came up behind and tried to find places to anchor their cables so that they could pull the casualties back onto something on which they could run.

I lived the whole battle on the fringes of the bulge, either in Luxembourg, where the headquarters were, or going on some errand or other. In the middle of it, I flew to London for a day and coming back we were grounded in Belgium. I had half a ton of aerial photographs of the German rear areas with me. I was bringing them back from where they had been printed in England. So I requisitioned a three-quarter-ton truck from an air field and took off across the point of the bulge. Just after dark it began to rain and the rain instantly froze on the roads. Twice we saved ourselves after spectacular skids and when, around ten o'clock, an MP stopped us to say we were coming into a blackout zone, I knew it was too much. We couldn't make it on sheet ice with no lights at all.

We stopped for the night in a village house where the MP detachment of four lived. They were great friends with the family, and we sat in the kitchen with a half a dozen relatives and drank coffee from the MP's rations. There were the crews of three other vehicles already stranded there—from an ammunition truck, a tank retriever and a convoy stray. All three vehicles had been wrecked one way or another; the crew of the tank retriever had been waiting six days for the member it had sent back for help to return. There were no Allied troops between where we were and the German advance guard except two detachments of French. The two detachments were rivals; one was a group of Maquis and the other was a company of the then embryo French regular army which had just been issued its uniforms and begun training near by. The Maquis were guarding the village where we were and spoke scornfully of the beardless ones who were out ahead—frightened of their own shadow, the Maquis said.

Back at Army Group we had never worried about the tip of the German salient; the military problem was to collapse its sides. As long as the Third Army was chewing into the base of the salient, we knew there was nothing the Germans dared or could do about deepening it. And we also knew—back at Army Group —that the tanks in the German spearhead were already out of gas and that the Germans' supply trucks were not able to get up to them. But it was one thing to know all this at Army Group and another to slither around on the ice on the tip of the salient. It was the next day, coming on into the headquarters, that we followed the ambulance that was splashing blood.

The snow and ice that bothered us was even worse for the Germans. At the beginning of the attack their radio had boasted that the terrible winter weather in the Ardennes was the friend of the heroic German warrior. It had been. But after the Panzers' first momentum had been stopped, the supply convoys which had to bring them gasoline and ammunition were going to pieces on the ice. And after the Third Army was beyond Bastogne, all the roads into the bulge were also under our artillery fire.

I had gone up to see the attack on Bastogne—it was launched an hour's creep over the ice from Luxembourg. It was a hard, stark thing. The wind swept through the broken trees along the roads and the armor in the field, even the tanks that had been hastily smeared with white paint, stood out in sharp relief, cold and naked. The troops built little fires of anything that would burn, even within sight of the enemy, to try to warm themselves. The infantry fought down one hill and up the next. The tanks were not much good then except as artillery. The dead lay frozen and stiff and when the men came to load them in trucks, they picked them up and put them in like big logs of wood. The frozen arms and legs got in their way when they were piling them. But everyone who had come through the summer before commented on how nice it was that the battlefield didn't stink.

After XII Corps' men got into Bastogne, I went there and the unusual thing about the ruins seemed to me how all the buildings were chipped by small caliber fire, and chipped high up, too. The wrecked town seemed to have been sandblasted with steel filings. This was from the strafing from the air, and probably from mortar fire too. On the edges of the town you could see, like a picture-story in a book, where the German columns had broken through the perimeter defense and come right up to the edge of the houses themselves. You could see this from the burned-out tanks the Germans had left behind. The Germans had come in and one by one their tanks had been shot through until, standing on a high place, the trail of them was almost like a snake cut into little pieces, winding across the hill on which Bastogne stands. Mixed in with the wrecks of tanks were the wrecks of the gliders that had brought the medics in when the garrison was surrounded—and here and there, black in the sun, were the little basketfuls of charred junk that is all that's left of an aircraft when it comes into the ground at three or four hundred miles an hour.

Out beyond Bastogne it was the same as this side of Bastogne— nothing but more snow, and more hills, and more woods. The trees along the road were blasted down about shoulder high by the demolition charges which dropped their trunks across the road to block it. The Germans had thus blown down miles of trees to protect their grudging retreat.

All through the woods around Bastogne, as you circled, it was strange to see the familiar little signs on trees and posts, with arrows pointing to this or that military installation, all in German.

Here the German army had been only the day before and had hastily tacked up its directions to its CP's and its ammunition dumps and this unit's or that's facilities.

Riding through the Ardennes, I wore woolen underwear, a woolen uniform, armored force combat overalls, a sweater, an armored force field jacket with elastic cuffs, a muffler, a heavy lined trenchcoat, two pairs of heavy woolen socks, and combat boots with galoshes over them—and I cannot remember ever being warm. Not that the temperature was so low, but there seemed a mean dampness in the air and the cutting wind never seemed to stop.

From the day after the battle began odd German planes came over whenever the ceiling lifted above the treetops. They were the first I had seen by day in France. They flew very low, following the roads, and burned a few vehicles. When I flew to London, I went with a planeful of German pilots who had bailed out or been forced down in damaged planes. They sat quietly on the bucket seats, and a big MP with a Tommy gun stood by the door to the plane and guarded them. Just after we had all gotten in, whistles began to blow around the edge of the field and then the machine guns started. Wiggling down to look out through the plane window, I saw there were four Focke-Wulfs weaving in over the field at about two thousand feet.

The field was guarded by several multiple machine gun assemblies on trucks—each a battery of four .50 calibers. They made a great racket but mostly I felt nervous about the MP. He stood stolidly, his Tommy gun pointed up the plane, and I thought that if the Krauts got anxious and started to try to get out, he would let them have it—and me too. I walked past the prisoners, who pulled their boots in respectfully to make way for me, and watched the show from the field.

The enemy aircraft went away and came back several times, as if trying to make up their minds whether or not to dive through the .50 calibers. There wasn't much bait on the field, just the transport we were in and a couple of Lightnings that had lost their way home and come down there. It was not an operating field, just the old German airport at Luxembourg which we were using as a landing strip for the headquarters. There were the wrecks of German planes all around, cripples the Krauts had burned themselves when they took off in a hurry. Finally the Focke-Wulfs went away and we took off ourselves.

The day after I got back from my trip there was a dogfight right over the main street of town, in and out of broken clouds. In the middle of the Battle of the Bulge, when that wonderful weather happened, there were only American fighters around and the mediums came over every day and sometimes twice a day and bombed at the bridges over the river just beyond us. The front line was very close, and the mediums were up high, so that we could see the whole show walking back from mess after lunch.

The big main street that runs through Luxembourg and over the high arched bridge was called the Boulevard de la Liberté (during the occupation it had been named after Adolf Hitler). All the Luxembourgers came out of their cafés and shops onto it to watch the bombings with us. There would be fifty or sixty planes in each formation. The different formations would come in from different points of the compass. Right overhead they dropped their baskets full of aluminum foil—"window"—to throw the enemy radar off the scent. Then all wheeled sharply at once, taking off on another course.

The aluminum foil would sparkle and shimmer in the sun as it fell, fluttering as aimlessly as a cloud of butterflies. Most days the planes themselves left long, even contrails which did not dissolve or blow away. After several flights had gone past, and their tracks had interwoven, there was so much contrail in the air that it was like a low cirrus cloud. When the planes got over the river you could see the ack-ack bursting, usually below and looking as if it was also behind them. They were too far away now for us to see the loads go, but the rolling thunder of them striking came very clear and distinct and made the Luxembourgers shake their heads and nod and whisper to one another. Up until we had come, the joke had been to refer to Luxembourg as "the last air-raid shelter in Europe." It had never been bombed by either the British or the American air forces. Ahead of the first American column, in September, however, our air force had blown the railway yards in the center of town apart.

From the German point of view, Luxembourg had not been an

occupied country—it had simply been "re-incorporated" into the Reich. Everyone there, of course, spoke German—and most of the local folk spoke French and English too, in addition to their own patois. The solid citizens of Luxembourg are not in the habit of concerning themselves with European wars and it annoyed them to have the Germans take over. The young girls—even the richest ones—had to work eight hours a day in a bank or some other dull place, and the young men had to be hidden out to keep them from being drafted. At that, many thousands of them were drafted and served in the German Army.

There were some Luxembourgers, however, who very much approved of the Germans. When we got there, these had been herded into a prison in the valley that cuts the town in two. We used to see little work gangs of them marched past every day, usually shepherded by a fellow-countryman on a bicycle with a rifle slung across his back. The prisoners always took off their hats and bowed their heads whenever they passed an American officer. They used to make me nervous with their obsequiousness.

When the Battle of the Bulge got serious, many of the Luxembourgers took in their Allied flags and they were very nervous. The leading Quisling amongst them had gotten away and was broadcasting nightly from Trier, which is only thirty-two miles away. He told them what he was going to do to people who had been nice to the Americans—and most of the people had been nice to us.

Despite the sophistication with which most of the Luxembourgers had taken the German occupation, there was a resistance movement there, recruited mainly from workers in the mills and little people from the villages. They had a lot of nerve. Armed only with rifles left behind by the Germans, and with only a tri-colored armband for a uniform, they scouted and went on patrols to keep track of the enemy.

The Luxembourg girls were not pretty—they were heavy-set and dressed badly—but they were the first girls the soldiers had met on the Continent who spoke English and they were very popular.

Whatever town we moved into became a headquarters town, because not only were there our own soldiers and officers but there were also the staff and trains of the Ninth Air Force Headquarters which always kept us in touch with our air support by moving in down the street or around the corner. In Luxembourg there were not only the 12th Army Group and the Ninth Air Force Headquarters but also, after the first week of the battle, there was Patton's Third Army Headquarters too, which came up and ran the offensive from some school buildings the other side of the big bridge from us. Until Patton's offensive got well under way, a daring break-through could have captured three of the most important headquarters in the American Army all within the radius of a few blocks—and they would have only had to come ten miles to get them; but I don't think the Germans ever knew this.

Because we had three headquarters there, and girls, and plenty of Luxembourg beer and champagne, and lots of nice warm buildings—we hauled our own coal from the Saar mines just south of us—we had several dances in Luxembourg and collected everyone's weekly ration and gave a big children's party on Christmas Eve. Our luxury rations consisted of a five-cent bar of milk chocolate, two bars of Baby Ruth or Oh Henry or some other concoction, a stick of candy Life Savers, a package of sweet biscuits, a razor blade and six packages of cigarettes. We kept the cigarettes and the razor blades, but there were barrels full of the rest of the stuff for the children.

To organize the party we had three or four pretty Red Cross girls who had come up to Luxembourg on leave to get a few days' rest just before the attack started and who stayed on because they wanted to and we liked to have them around and urged them.

At the last minute the Red Cross girls' children's party got itself a little snafu-ed, for through some mistake all the "nice" children in Luxembourg were already signed up for parties of their own. But the church saved the day and at the last moment the orphans from the local asylum were substituted for those who'd originally been asked. They came in twos, clutching each other's hands, and were so excited by the tree and the Santa Claus and everything that by the time they got the presents they were silent and bug-eyed.

The tree was not only home-grown but home-decorated. It was a local fir and it glistened with silver ornaments and snow made from the aluminum counter-radar foil the bombers dropped. The kids got their little bellies full, for there are more "nice" children in Luxembourg than there are orphans and the rations had been drawn for the greater number. So everyone had all that could be stuffed into her or him—ice cream and fine gooey pastry.

We never knew where the Luxembourgers got all their sugar from, for even the first week we came the pastry shops were full of goodies—and strings of sausage hung in their butcher shop windows. They seemed to lack only decent cigarettes. Being a re-incorporated part of the Reich was quite evidently something different from being an occupied country like France or Belgium. In France, beyond Paris, there had been not even a drop of wine, unless it had come out of an odd bottle buried for a special occasion. But beer and wine flowed freely in Luxembourg and the citizens' cheeks were round and red.

All through the Battle of the Bulge the Luxembourgers had a front row seat in the bandstand from which to watch the American Army parade by. Division after division and special unit after special unit of the Third Army sent its MP's ahead to mark the way and came shivering up from the South. Sometimes, on the busy corner behind the bridge there were the MP's of four or five outfits standing together to pick the vehicles of their units from the steady stream that came north and direct them out one road or the other. After a few days of watching it all, the Luxembourg-ers felt much better. Until two whole corps of the Third Army moved through, the most Americans they had seen had been the advance guard which had taken the town—the Germans had not stopped to shoot back much—and the guards and office personnel of our big headquarters.

After Patton's attack got cracking beyond Bastogne only supply convoys came through town and not too many of them, because the main railhead was north and west of us. When you took a jeep ride up to the front, everything looked neat and orderly again, with the batteries camouflaged and nice fat piles of ammunition handy. The men had made huts out of ammunition boxes and many of them slept under cover in vacated farmhouses. You could feel the strong pulse beat of the army once more. It had begun to move forward again now.

The Krauts had been feeling very cocky when they began the attack in the Ardennes. They couldn't lose. Yet in a matter of days they knew they had lost—and when the Germans lost the battle of the Ardennes, it can soundly be said that they lost the war for good and all. After the Ardennes, they were finished just as surely as the Confederate Army was finished after Gettysburg. It just took a little time—and a great many lives—to prove it. Here is the cause and effect sequence by which Hitler's defeat in the Ardennes finished him:

Between December 16 and January 15, the Germans lost the Fifth and Sixth Panzer Armies and thousands of supporting troops in the Ardennes, without gaining a single major objective. The blitz neither took Liége nor even crossed the Meuse. The assaulting armored divisions were not totally destroyed, but were so very seriously mauled, and took such appalling casualties, and lost such enormous numbers of vehicles, that they never fought again as a single cohesive striking force. This armored force was the last free piece on Hitler's chessboard.

By mid-January the great Russian offensive over the Vistula was launched. In scale, this offensive was the greatest single assault in all of World War II. It was a break-away success and within little more than two weeks it had crossed the German border on a three-hundred-mile front—two hundred and fifty miles beyond its starting point on the Vistula. There, across the German border, the Russian supply lines were for a brief moment impossibly stretched. The Russian Army was at its most vulnerable. But in the Ardennes the Americans had defeated and enmeshed the only mobile force in the Reich with which Hitler could have struck back in the East. The two-front war which Hitler had always feared had caught up to him.

With no reserve army with which to strike back at the Russians, Hitler had to reverse his entire strategy overnight. We know now that he did just that.

When the Russians consolidated their position on the banks of the Oder, Hitler switched priority from the Western to the Eastern Front. Throughout 1944, the Western Front had had the pick of German men and matériel—first choice. When the Russians reached the Oder, Hitler called in his commanders on the Western Front and told them that from then on they would have to fight the Anglo-Americans with what they had. They would get neither new weapons nor new divisions, but only enough replacements to keep them up to reasonable strength. They would not even be allowed to keep *all* the troops they had—they must extricate the remnants of the Fifth and Sixth Panzer Armies and release them, along with certain other units—to stabilize the intolerable situation in the East until something more could be done about it.

With this switch in priority from west to east, coming at the end of the frustration of the Ardennes offensive, the third act curtain went up.

On the Western Front it was now only a matter of time before the Americans, still being continuously reinforced, would be able to hack their way through the West Wall.

Once on the Rhine plain, it was equally only a matter of time before the Americans would succeed in crossing the last natural barrier to central Germany, the Rhine itself. I recall the later words of a German sergeant PW to his lieutenant in one of our cages: "But, Lieutenant, Sir," he said, "you told us not to worry because the Americans could not cross the Roer, but I told you then that it seemed curious to me that if the Americans could cross the Atlantic they could not also cross a little river." The Roer is a small river on the German border; the Rhine is just a little bigger river than the Roer.

We now have evidence that after the Russian break-through on the Eastern Front, Hitler planned a GRAB operation on a monster scale against the Soviet forces. But the sand was running out now. The Russian GRAB was to have been mounted in Pomerania and to have struck south from the Baltic into the base of the Russian wedge. The Russians were expected to leave themselves open for this drive by pressing on across the Oder to Berlin. But the Russian generals had been outplaying the German generals at military chess for two years. They continued to outplay them. While the Russians let the world press throw imflammable printer's ink on the notion that the Soviet armies were about to storm Berlin, the Russian high command turned two whole groups of armies north and simply took the Pomeranian counterattack base away from the Germans—in a single week's blitz.

Meanwhile, on the southern flank of their drive, the Russian conquest of Silesia had jammed the whole German production machine—for from Silesia came most of the steel for the new submarines which were being built on the Baltic, and much of the material for the new jet aircraft.

When, having crossed the Rhine, Bradley chose the Thuringian Forest in central Germany instead of Berlin for his final objective —and then sent Patton further south into Austria—the jig was up for even a last stand. What was left of Germany's industry had been dispersed through the Thuringian Forest, and Austria was the retreat route to what we then called the Redoubt. The Redoubt was the fortress area around Berchtesgaden where the Nazi party was supposed to have planned to hold out until they could get their underground organized for a counterattack on the peace.

10   Bradley vs. Montgomery

IF the defeat of Sixth SS Panzer and Co. in the Ardennes was the beginning of the end, nevertheless many interesting things happened between December 16, 1944, and May 8, 1945—history was written on the battlefield, and in the struggle for command and control of the Allied armies.

The German penetration in the Ardennes was a terrific shock to world morale. The military situation in Europe had obviously not been understood—and it could not be explained in the middle of the battle. Even such news as *was* released was harmful. German tank commanders, out of communication with their own headquarters after their break-through, and ignorant of where either their troops or ours were, came to rely on the British Broadcasting Company—BBC—for their day-to-day Intelligence.

The story of the battle of the Ardennes is dramatic itself. The main German effort was thirty or forty miles to the north of Luxembourg—over the border in Belgium. It consisted of two spearheads, each headed by a corps of two Panzer divisions. As the tanks of these spearheads drove through, infantry followed rapidly to consolidate the positions and to strike north and south to broaden the shoulders of the salient. The driving armor was headed due west and was to turn north to capture the Meuse River crossings. The Meuse circles the Ardennes Forest and beyond it the rest of Belgium and northern France lie flat and inviting.

The first hitch that developed in the attack went almost unnoticed at the time, so spectacular were some of the enemy's first day's gains. This was when the northernmost of the two attacking corps ran head-on into a local American infantry attack back of a town called Monschau and was stopped in its tracks, with heavy casualties from artillery fire. The southernmost of the two principal attacks, however, hit what amounted to a training sector of the American line and overran the infantry division which had just come up the day before. It surged over and through this division and its corps' artillery, and swept on, chewing into service areas.

Within forty-eight hours, a clean break-through had been achieved. In one place it was twenty miles deep and there was absolutely nothing between the Germans and the Meuse except isolated MP detachments which did not even have automatic weapons with which to challenge the tanks.

Adjusting themselves rapidly to capitalize on the gap they had made, the Germans swung the attack which had stalled at Monschau to the south and drove it in alongside the column that had made the penetration. Then the whole business was turned to the north in an attempt to roll up the broken line of the American First Army.

All this was accompanied by spectacular diversions in the rear of the American troops, along the road to Liége. These consisted of a daring parachute drop, from a low altitude and in high wind, and what amounted to a mass infiltration of American lines by specially trained German soldiers in American uniforms. The real parachute drop was accompanied by a succession of dummy parachute drops to add to the confusion.

From the first Germans captured in American uniforms we learned that they hoped also to assassinate the principal Allied commanders, beginning with Eisenhower and Bradley. The German boys all spoke American, of course, and had studied for their parts by mingling with the GI prisoners in the German stockades. Throughout the battle of the Ardennes one got about behind the American lines by passing such improvised tests as "What's the name of the Vice President?" "What's the island the Statue of Liberty stands on?" These word games were thought up by sentries on the spot to help them separate the sheep from the goats.

But the main concern was not such fireworks, but the pounding armored columns which every hour were reported further to the west. The weather played its part obediently and a solid blanket of clouds hung low over the hills, treetop high, protecting the Germans from observation or interference from the air. Occasionally a daring P-51 pilot would take his squadron down through and racing along the valleys at three hundred miles an hour would do what he could with his wing bombs and his machine guns. But for practical purposes the Allied armies might as well not have had an air force.

Under such circumstances, it was amazing the speed with which G-2 was able to put together a picture of German strength and capabilities. Probably this is because in any break-through some columns take the wrong road, others get cut off—and maps and first hand instructions to commanders are speedily available from the captured officers.

Presently our suspicion of what the Germans were up to was confirmed by the pace and direction of the drive. Posted on the war room map, the northern boundary of the initial penetration ran east to west just south of a road center called St. Vith; the southern boundary moved west towards a town on a hill called Bastogne and a few days later was seen to break around Bastogne, leaving it encircled.

All this we watched at Headquarters while we sandwiched the thermite grenades in amongst the most secret of our papers, to be ready to destroy them if we saw any gray uniforms across the hills. There were a few hours when the advance patrols of a third-rate German division were five miles down the road with nothing between them and us but a guard detachment and a few engineers. The German division didn't choose to fight but up north it was a different story.

Bradley's conduct of the battle was magnificent. While the reports were still suggesting that the German attack might yet prove to be only a local diversion, he had sensed that it was the real thing and moved to meet it with everything he had. Even a few hours' delay—to ponder and appraise and wait for more exact information from the cloudy battlefield—might have cost the battle itself. Instead of waiting, he acted at once and on a heroic scale.

He swung the major part of Patton's army out of the line to the south of Luxembourg and sent it north to relieve Bastogne almost before Bastogne was cut off. The snow had begun to fall and the motorized divisions passed through us in Luxembourg and went by under our war room window, half frozen in the snow and sleet.

Bradley saw Bastogne and St. Vith as the keys to the battle within twenty-four hours of the assault. The only wholly free reserves in France were the two airborne divisions which were resting in the vicinity of Reims, fifty miles west of the Meuse. Technically, they were waiting for employment at some unknown future date by the Allied Airborne Army and were taking orders not from the 12th Army Group but from the SHAEF Headquarters itself. Bradley got them back from Eisenhower quickly and put the 101st Airborne in Bastogne and the 82nd back of St. Vith. Moving even faster than the Germans, he got them into place before the Panzers reached either road center. He had already put a whole Combat Command (one-third) of the 10th Armored Division in Bastogne, to hold the fort until the infantry arrived.

On the hill at Bastogne, the 101st collected a miscellany of artillery and engineer units retreating before the Germans, turned them around and organized them. General McAuliffe, who was commanding the 101st at the time, was now all set for a fight. When the Germans came he was ready for them. Presently he was cut off and surrounded—but he was also killing German tanks as fast as they broke through his cordon. When the German commander asked his surrender he answered with a single word "Nuts," and left it to German linguists to figure out what he meant.

The 82nd Airborne reached a river line back of St. Vith, with the 7th Armored Division still out in front of it, and reported itself ready to take on all comers.

Like the 82nd and 101st Airborne, the 1st Infantry Division was also resting, but in the immediate rear of the First Army's line.

The 1st was moved up without its junior officers knowing what was in front of them. It took on the spearhead of the northernmost break-through and bent it southward and away from Liége.

Bradley then ordered Hodges to peel off the divisions he had around Aachen and wheel them back, through a ninety-degree arc, to hold the northern shoulder of the German attack. Hodges set up an east-west line through the Ardennes hills and his troops ran it out faster than the German attack could follow. The Krauts were never quite able to catch up to a free road which would lead them around the corner to turn the American lines.

Simultaneously, Hodges was ordered to set up a free corps under General Collins, the man who commanded the St. Lô breakthrough, to the immediate rear of this newly formed line. This corps was to be prepared to counterattack southward as soon as the German drive had extended itself and begun to lose its momentum.

With these moves made, Bradley felt he had the battle under control. With St. Vith and Bastogne holding, the Germans had but one trunk road west—the road running midway between the two towns through the little town of Houffalize. With only one road to supply it, the depth and strength of the German penetration were automatically limited—and Bradley had Patton already on his way to strike the first counterblow. Patton was coming up on the south, with a whole army, and Hodges was preparing Collins to strike down to meet it—the whole operation constituting a counteroffensive pincers to bite off whatever part of the German Army tried to drive on past the Houffalize bottleneck.

And right in the middle of the battle, with the major decisions all made and the German neck well into the noose that Bradley was preparing, Eisenhower lost his nerve. He did not lose it all by himself. He lost it when his British advisers lost their nerve and when Montgomery panicked.

The first reaction that came to our headquarters from Montgomery's—by liaison officer—was that the British would get up out of their foxholes and put on an attack in the north, where the Hun had had to thin his line to gather the forces for the Ardennes offensive. But within twenty-four hours after this had been reported to us, we learned that the entire British Army was in retreat.

Leaving only a skeleton force in the line, and with remarkable agility for a man who was often so cautious, Montgomery moved the bulk of the British Second and the Canadian First Armies back from Holland to a defensive semicircle around Antwerp, prepared for the last ditch battle he apparently thought he would have to fight there. Simultaneously, he screamed—to Churchill in London and to the Deputy Supreme Allied Commander, Air Chief Marshal Tedder, and to the Supreme Commander himself in Paris —for command of the American armies which were fighting between him and the Germans. These American armies were the new Ninth Army, under Simpson (not in a sector under attack), and the First Army, which was in the middle of the fight.

While Montgomery was yelling, the American War Department, to whom Eisenhower had been sending soundly optimistic reports, was also screaming—with words to the effect of "What the hell's going on over there?" It was up to Eisenhower again. As soon as Montgomery yelled for help, the Ardennes defense developed an international aspect and Eisenhower had no choice but to take a position, one way or the other.

Eisenhower asked Bradley if he could stop the Germans, and Bradley said yes. But Montgomery's counter to this was that the Germans were coming *his* way—towards Antwerp—and that he would not be responsible for what might happen unless he were given command of *all* the forces between Antwerp and the enemy.

Montgomery also advanced the curious argument that the German attack, having split the line, had broken the Ardennes into two battlefields and that each should be under its own commander; let Bradley stay in command in the south, he said, and I, Montgomery, will take over the northern flank. The word curious is used because, from a purely military point of view, the fact of the split in the line made it not less but more imperative that the defending forces remain under one command. A prime objective of the whole German offensive, in fact, had been to split the American from the British forces. It is a classic military pattern to strike where a boundary separates allied armies. There, co-ordination is weakest. What Montgomery was advocating, then, was giving the Germans their first objective—the splitting of the Allied command—on a silver platter.

In his dilemma, Eisenhower was surrounded by British advisers, and Montgomery was backed by the British Prime Minister himself. Under the pressure, the Supreme Commander gave way.

Without waiting to study Bradley's situation further, he took the First and Ninth American Armies away from the American general and turned them over to Montgomery.

The clearest case I have heard made for General Eisenhower is based on the fact that when he made his decision he was grievously misinformed as to the situation at the front. An officer who was present with him in the map room at the time reports that he was briefed by British Intelligence officers. The panorama painted was a nightmare of German spearheads. They were depicted as capturing the great supply dumps at Liége, refueling, and continuing on to the sea. If this picture had been true the battle would indeed have been divided into two equal parts. The capability of the enemy being stopped was ignored by the British Intelligence officers. It was ignored, my eye-witness concludes, because if the British admitted that the enemy could be contained—as in fact they already had been—the destruction of the counteroffensive was patently a one-man job of co-ordinating the efforts on both flanks. On the basis of the picture as presented to him, however, Ike felt there was only one decision to take—to divide authority between Montgomery and Bradley.

Even giving this story its full weight, what I cannot understand is why the Supreme Commander was so content to make such a momentous decision, risking the whole battle, on one-sided information. He was in telephone communication with General Bradley, and had been told the true situation but for reasons of his own chose to take the word of British Intelligence against the word of the American Commanding General.

To us in Bradley's headquarters, splitting the command was an absolutely appalling thing to do. The only argument for it that had validity was based on the fact that wire communications between our headquarters and First Army Headquarters had been cut. This was perfectly true, but there was nothing the matter with radio communications which were, of course, excellent and instantaneous. And while the direct roads were cut, liaison officers traveled back and forth throughout the battle by taking the long way around the bulge. The two American armies, to the north and south respectively, could each have been personally directed from a central location on the Meuse. Moreover, the plans on which the battle was being fought had already been made anyway, and the orders given to Hodges and Patton.

The split in command made no sense to us. Now the battle had been arbitrarily broken in two and the Germans had a windfall opportunity to defeat the two Allied forces in detail, one at a time. We had been sure that by striking simultaneously with both the Third *and* the First Armies, we could break the enemy's offensive. We were not at all sure it could be done now that we were cut in two.

As far as I know, in all history there is no exception to the rule that military allies mistrust each other's motives and criticize each other's performance. British criticism of Eisenhower, Bradley, Bradley's generals—and the performance of the American troops under them—all of whom together were blamed for having permitted the German counterattack to develop—was openly expressed in British staff meetings. Eventually, it was even to break into print in London. If we were appalled at Eisenhower's decision to turn two of our armies over to Montgomery in the middle of the battle, I'm sure our feelings were matched on Montgomery's staff when they first saw the American line ripped open on their battle map, and then observed the German army streaming through.

In France, the British had always regarded Bradley as too bold. Patton's recklessness seemed to them to endanger the whole Allied cause. Had he not run wild after St. Lô, careless of his flanks, heedless of supplies? Being human beings, the fact that Patton had gotten away with it only seemed to confirm, in the minds of his British critics, their deep suspicion that this crazy American was militarily unsound and had succeeded only because of fantastic and unreasonable luck.

The drive and impatience, the optimism and confidence of the Americans, their unwillingness to admit the validity of arguments based on the assumption that the impossible could not be done— I am certain that all these things worried the British High Command. They must have wondered, sometimes, whether history had not committed them to an alliance, at worst with madmen and at best with congenital optimists, the cornerstones of whose faith were ignorance and vanity.

This attitude was national and independent of personalities; it simply manifested itself in different forms in the guarded Oxonian of the Imperial General Staff and the high, rasping yelp of Montgomery. It had split every planning conference since Africa; it had been clear in the British reaction to the Johnnies-Come-Lately, so foolishly anxious to get their feet wet and their heads blown off on the shores of France. High level and low, the British had been literally terrified by our scatter-brained exploitation of the victory at St. Lô, when we had showered our armor over northern France, apparently regardless of either the possibility or the possible consequences of having it cut off by enemy counter-measures. Bloody lucky chaps, the Americans, who simply did not know what risks they were taking.

When, at long last, the "calculated risks" about which the American generals talked so glibly, caught up with them in the Ardennes, the grim smiles on the British faces clearly said, I told you so. There is no doubt whatever that their first reactions to the Ardennes break-through were that we had it coming to us, that it was a direct result of our own incompetence in battle. They may really have felt that it was up to them to save the day; the whole adventure of the Continent was at stake. At least nothing else seems to explain Montgomery's precipitous retreat to Antwerp or the almost desperate insistence of the British Government that Eisenhower turn over the American armies to Montgomery so that the Field Marshal might at least save something from the catastrophe.

If the British point of view seems prejudiced, so, of course, was the American reaction to it. Long before the Ardennes, Bradley and his generals, and their staffs, almost to a man, had concluded that, whatever the motives, British ground forces were timidly directed, by men who were over-conscious of the risks of battle. The British seemed too respectful of an enemy who, it had been demonstrated, could be had. They were too sensitive to risks—nothing ventured nothing gained—and too ready to resign themselves to obstacles and limitations which could be removed by ingenuity and greater effort.

"Whatever the motives"—no two Americans agreed exactly in their interpretation of what British motives in battle might be.

Some felt that British caution was innate in British character, some that it represented a rational solution to problems peculiarly British (the British *had* to be cautious because their resources were so much more limited than ours). One school felt that British reaction was part of a more devious policy, aimed at taking advantage of us—enabling them to fight the war with our weapons and our men and still claim the credit and the prestige for the victories.

The Germans, who also had British military policy on their minds, inclined to favor the opinion that British timidity was a weakness rooted in reason but favored by the soil of national character in which it grew. In their high level appreciations, their analyses of British intentions were as shrewd and knowing as their estimates of American capabilities were ignorant and sometimes childish—as when they misread the timidity of American infantry in the first battles in Normandy as indicating a national unwillingness to take chances, and thus found themselves as bewildered as the British by the dramatic exploitation of the victory at St. Lô. They felt more at home figuring out the British and one German expert wrote:

"Although even before the war basic British principles of command were taken largely verbatim from German models, and despite an earnest analysis of the experiences of the war and imitation of German command principles, British command has still not arrived at a point free from its hampering methodical form and resulting ponderosity. Improvisation, made possible by a modern, agile command, has scarcely been attained.

"Impressed by the rising losses suffered by the British Army, the British command has gone over in recent times to an even more cautious leadership in battle. Complete planning, detailed often boresome preparations for even the smallest part of the operation, superiority in weapons and munitions and air superiority in the attack zone are the conditions for a British attack. The striving to save English blood has been very clearly evident in the most recent battles. Bold undertakings, which carry greater risks, are avoided. Favorable opportunities remain often unused, for the command does not adapt itself quickly enough to the new situation. This cumbersomeness carries forward manyfold in the transmission to lower formations of orders which are all inclusive and detailed down to every last minute point.

"The preparations for an operation are generally excellently concealed. British reconnaissance and intelligence contribute much to these preparations with topnotch personnel."

These words are from a captured German War Department appreciation of command in the British Army.

General Bradley's personal reaction to having two of his armies taken away from him was to waste no time in arguments or recriminations but to redouble his efforts to bring the German drive to a halt by striking with what forces he had left. In the struggle for command and control, Bradley could not see beyond Montgomery, whom he regarded as the personal inspiration of all his troubles. Bradley's enemies in the field never troubled him; only his friends had the capacity to hurt or disturb him emotionally. He had long since acquired a distaste for the little man with the beret and the bark, and he had no longer any confidence in him as a general. He had seen Montgomery fail at Caen, when he was stronger than the enemy he faced, and he had not liked his counsel since.

Omar Bradley is by nature a gentle man and a temperate man, reasonable, patient and self-effacing. His whole technique of command is to build up the importance of the men who serve him and to play himself down. Even if they had had no issue between them, Bradley would not have liked Montgomery's personal arrogance.

When Bradley got the news that Montgomery was on top again, he felt that at least now Montgomery would contribute some of his own troops to his own battle. From the first day of the break-through, Bradley had wanted the loan of British troops to watch the mouth of the German funnel while he collapsed the sides. He hoped that Montgomery would use British troops to guard the Meuse, thus allowing the American First Army to concentrate everything it had for the counter counteroffensive.

The British troops which eventually joined in the battle of the Ardennes turned out to be a single brigade (a British brigade is smaller than an American regiment). This brigade skirmished with the German advance guard which had run out of petrol near the tip of the salient. The subsequent attempt of the British press to dramatize these skirmishes into important battles was so flagrant a distortion of the truth that Churchill himself had to make a personal disclaimer of them in the speech he made the middle of January when he reminded the British that, Montgomery or no Montgomery, the Ardennes was an American, not an Anglo-American, battle.

I can make no apology for having viewed the battle of Ardennes through American eyes and from American Headquarters. Field Marshal Sir Bernard will inevitably give his own version one day—but this is how it looked to us while the windows of our headquarters in Luxembourg shook with the concussions of the 155s that fired past us onto the roads where the Germans were.*

Montgomery took over the north flank on D plus 4 of the German attack. His contribution to the battle was a plan that almost lost it. His first reaction to the reports from the flood of liaison officers and observers which he let loose among the harassed divisions of the American First Army was that the American troops "had been so badly over-fought (by Bradley and Hodges) that the whole First Army should be taken out of the line and rested as soon as possible"—and he added that he thought the Americans would not be ready for offensive action again before May. This comment was his reaction to the plan he had inherited from Bradley, the plan for simultaneous attacks on the northern and southern shoulders to pinch off the salient.

Montgomery now abandoned all idea of attacking from his side of the salient, and the Germans were allowed to defend themselves from Bradley's and Patton's subsequent offensive, secure in the knowledge that the Allied troops on the northern flank had gone on the defensive and were digging in.

Having abandoned the offensive, Montgomery's next action was to plumber even Bradley's *de*fensive strategy. Bastogne and St. Vith were the road centers the Germans had to have to support

* The Germans fired back with a long-range railway gun and short-range rocket-boosted missiles—managing finally to nick the steeple on the church across the square from Bradley's headquarters and scoring at least one direct hit on Patton's.

any drive strong enough to carry them across the Meuse. The story of the holding of Bastogne by the 101st Airborne Division, and its subsequent relief by Patton's armies, is the history every newspaper reader knows.

What newspapers *did not* tell was what happened back of St. Vith.

On the day that Montgomery took over, remember, the American 82nd Airborne Division was drawn up along a river line back of the road center of St. Vith—and had the 7th Armored Division out in front of it. Thus it had cut, and completely controlled, one of the only two roads which led deep into the Ardennes. Both the armored division and the airborne division were being attacked with great energy by the Germans and were doing every bit as spectacular a job of containing these attacks as the troops at Bastogne. Upwards of one hundred German tanks a day were being destroyed by anti-tank and artillery fire.

Montgomery's first action in the Ardennes was to pull back the American armor which was in front of the 82nd's line. Looking on from across the bulge, this made some sense to us—even though it meant giving up the road center of St. Vith itself. It was on the conservative side, but it made some sense, because it bought insurance for the defense of the all-important road itself, which the 82nd still straddled. Moreover, the whole American position along the river line, now reinforced, was getting stronger every hour. And then, out of a clear sky, Montgomery ordered the entire position abandoned and a retreat into the hills begun.

In Bradley's headquarters, we thought—and it was a terrible feeling—that Montgomery had lost the battle for us and might perhaps have succeeded in prolonging the war a year.

Montgomery took the 82nd out of the line with a graceful little speech telling them they were "brave lads" and had done their share. He had made the Germans a present of the second road into the Ardennes and thus enabled them to double the depth of their whole penetration.

The defensive positions to which Montgomery ordered the American First Army to retreat were sound positions, and large numbers of Germans were killed from them. But from then on the north flank of the Ardennes ceased to be a factor in the battle.

As the attack which Bradley and Patton drove through from the south grew in strength, and overran Bastogne, and pressed on North beyond it, the Germans—as a direct result of Montgomery's over-caution—were able to move division after division direct from the north flank across the salient to meet Patton in the South.

Patton's comments, when he realized that the First Army had actually been put on the defensive—and the information had to be picked up by watching the action on the battle map because Montgomery's headquarters never bothered to tell us—was "to hell with Montgomery. We'll take the whole expurgated German Army and jam it up his expurgated!"

As had happened before, Georgie Patton never quite made good his boast but he ended Hitler's hope for victory with his brilliant execution of what was left of Bradley's plan. He struck so savagely and unexpectedly that the Germans were never able to exploit the road net that had been handed them on a tray with Sir Bernard's coat of arms on it. Instead of tooling triumphantly through the gap, Von Rundstedt had to turn his main effort *away* from his objective—Liége—to hold the Third Army at all, even though his defense was aided by terrain deep in ice and snow.

By the time Von Rundstedt succeeded in bringing one Third Army attack to a halt, a second—and later a third and fourth—had been mounted and were buffeting the Germans, crawling from hill to hill, crossing swollen rivers, fighting house to house through village after village. The whole timetable of the German attack went by the board. Instead of getting rich on captured supplies, the Germans were writing off fifty, one hundred, one hundred and fifty tanks a day, and losing men by the thousands.

When Georgie made his personal call on God and got the Air Force four successive days of perfect weather at Christmas time, the show was over. Georgie paid his call on God shortly after he had lost his temper at the weather. His losing his temper was unreasonable, for the weather was exactly what it should have been at that time of year. But Patton decided to do something about it anyway and called in his chaplain. He said to his chaplain that the time had come to pray and would the chaplain please prepare the appropriate sentiments. The chaplain is reported to have hesitated, expressing a doubt as to the propriety of asking divine intercession so directly. Patton is popularly credited with replying, "Who in hell do you work for anyway? Are you an officer in the Third Army or aren't you?" Maybe there's nothing in this story but we all believed it.

However the prayer originated, a few days later these words were set in type:

"ALMIGHTY and most merciful Father, we humbly beseech Thee, of Thy great goodness, to restrain these immoderate rains with which we have had to contend. Grant us fair weather for battle. Graciously hearken to us as soldiers who call upon Thee that armed with Thy power, we may advance from victory to victory, and crush the oppression and wickedness of our enemies, and establish Thy justice among men and nations. Amen."

These sentiments were printed and distributed to all commands and even as they were being read, the clouds broke apart, the sun shone and the American fighters came down by the hundreds and distributed their death and destruction along every road from Bastogne all the way back to the Rhine. The Germans had been losing vehicles by scores, to artillery and anti-tank fire. Their losses now went from hundreds to thousands of vehicles per day, day after day.

The battle of the Ardennes was over.

As Winston Churchill said, the battle of the Ardennes was an American battle, the greatest that American armies had up to that time fought in their entire history—the greatest in the number of troops engaged at any one time, the greatest in bloodshed and casualties sustained and, if the German ambitions are acknowledged, perhaps the greatest in its effect on the course of history. If I have written of the victory in the Ardennes as a victory secured by the counteroffensive of the Third Army, it's because, as in football, it's the backfield star, running with the ball, that gets the headlines.

Such scorn as I have expressed for the defensive tactics on the opposite side of the bulge is for a high level decision which deprived the American First Army of an opportunity to take the offensive, and which stalemated the Ninth Army, too. It is scorn for a caution so great that, in our turn, we felt our Allies were reckless—in relinquishing a road which might have let the enemy over the Meuse, and in giving it up simply to gain a few hours to prepare a few hills for defense.

I would not like this scorn to obscure the achievements of half a dozen American divisions in what turned out to be a toe-to-toe slugging match with the best troops the Germans had. It lasted day and night without pause or hesitation for over a week. The élite divisions of the Fifth and Sixth Panzer Armies bucked and bucked into the First Army's shoulder, now a few miles north of St. Vith. They fought with fanatical abandon. As they were stopped on one road, they turned to break through the next. Every division on the shoulder has its own saga to tell.

The stories of the individual actions are almost unbelievable— I know of one battalion command post, defended by two small anti-tank guns, a light tank, and a half-track and twenty or thirty battalion headquarters personnel, who together took the full impact of a spearhead of German tanks. They defended themselves in a two-story building until first its top story and then its ground floor were blown down on their heads. They fought in the ruins until every gun bigger than a rifle was out of action and then continued to hold off the tanks with bazookas. Finally, the Germans concluded that they had met more than their weight in opposition and withdrew (minus half a dozen tanks) to reform and try another avenue.

The best accounts of these individual actions subsequently appeared in *The Stars and Stripes,* which for weeks was packed with first hand accounts of individual actions so dramatic that a moving picture director would have rejected them as too implausible for a sequence of "The Perils of Pauline."

One GI machine gunner in the path of the German attack had arrived at the front the day before. He was a replacement, straight from the boat. His gun was sighted on the crest of a hill. Every other man of his platoon was killed by an artillery barrage that preceded a German infantry attack up its slope. All by himself, he halted the attack. All night long, singlehanded and alone, he killed Germans from on top of that hill, most of the night weeping so bitterly from terror and rage that he could hardly see his sights. When another American outfit came up in the morning they found him still there with literally hundreds of German dead and wounded on the field out in front of him—and still weeping. He couldn't stand the moaning of the Germans he had shot down in the night.

Most of the killing, though, was done by artillery. The Americans fought with their backs to huge concentrations of ammunition which had been gathered for the offensive that was being mounted when the Germans struck. They fired out into the German columns, often blind in the fog; when the fog lifted, one battery found it had destroyed a whole German column without having known it had been there—it had had ammunition enough simply to fire on a road where there "might be" Germans.

Some of the effectiveness of this fire came from the fact that many of the shells in these dumps were equipped with the "secret weapon" radio fuse. These were the shells with miniature radio sending sets in their noses. They exploded themselves high in the air over the Germans. Their invisible antennae reached down, felt the ground and told the explosive charge in the shell, "Now let them have it." The Navy had been using this secret fuse in the Pacific against enemy aircraft, over water into which the shells could drop and keep the secret of their construction if any proved to be duds. On the Continent we had just gotten permission to employ radio fuses against the Germans and our ammo dumps had been filling up with them. In Headquarters we thought we would have been willing to do without the advantages of the radio fuse—on balance—in exchange for postponing the Germans' knowledge of it a little longer, for the first thing the Germans captured in the Ardennes was a complete dump of the secret artillery ammunition. As far as we know, however, they made no use of their discovery. Either they did not know that they had captured something unusual or the scientists in their ordnance department were busy on other things.

By the time Bradley's attack beyond Bastogne had ended the German threat, the First Army, on the opposite shoulder, had administered such a beating to the attacking Panzer corps that not only were their offensive capabilities ended but the armies that Hitler had driven into the Ardennes had been so mauled that they were barely able to extricate themselves.

Even with his tanks slithering over the ice and his infantry-men's teeth chattering in the snow, Patton still dreamed of driving all the way north to St. Vith itself, trapping the Germans still facing the First Army. Again, Bradley himself had no such flamboyant hopes. After the spectacular four days of sunshine, the weather shut down again. Moreover, the Germans had now been in the Ardennes long enough to dig into its hills. Rapid advances, even with the relatively fresh troops which Third Army kept throwing into the battle, were impossible. So when Montgomery went on the defensive in the north, Bradley cut his maximum objective down to squeezing the Germans out of the Ardennes and inflicting such heavy casualties that the two Panzer armies would not bother him again. In these objectives, Bradley completely succeeded.

He completely succeeded on the battlefield—and almost suffered total defeat at the conference table. What happened at the conference table was that the British leapt into the troubled waters of the Ardennes to pull out the fish they had lost in the earlier angling: the prize politico-military fish of control of the war in Europe. However good or bad their case for the military necessity of Montgomery's taking over the American First and Ninth Armies, their exploitation of subsequent developments seemed to have chiefly politics for motivation.

Within an hour after the command of the American First and Ninth Armies had been put under Montgomery's temporary command, the British press was howling in headlines and arguing in editorials for the appointment of Montgomery as "Ground Force Commander"—over all Allied forces on the Continent, permanently.*

* This was not the first time the proposition had come up. As early as September, the Field Marshal had begun proposing to his superior that he, Montgomery, take over all Allied ground forces. There is no doubt but that he had the Prime Minister's backing in this notion. It was the logical reaction of the British Government to Eisenhower's indecisiveness in August —the British Chiefs' way out of the dilemma they found themselves in when they realized that the Statesman's Headquarters they had created in SHAEF was now being called on to function on the battlefield.

Eisenhower declined the offer but it is an interesting side-light on the position of the Supreme Commander at that time that in doing so he felt called upon to launch into what amounted to a lengthy apology to the Field

The last hand in the command and control game was being dealt. It was obviously very close to a showdown. To build up Montgomery as the "inevitable" ground force commander, the British had to tear down the man they had been so long building up, Eisenhower himself. Without scruples, they did exactly that. The British press turned on the Supreme Commander. They paid Eisenhower easy compliments as an administrator, called him no general and said that he was in obvious need—witness "the near-defeat in the Ardennes"—of a strong field commander to integrate the actions of all the Allied armies. All the arguments that had been advanced by British officers privately were now spread for everyone to read in the lay press.

The assignment of the First and Ninth Armies to Montgomery had been specifically defined by Eisenhower as a *temporary measure* to meet a "crisis in communication" across the Ardennes break-through. In the original order, it was stated that the First and Ninth Armies would revert to American command as soon as these communications had been re-established. Now, in the British press, it was publicly assumed that the First and Ninth Armies had been put *permanently* under Montgomery's command. The argument was then advanced that since Montgomery already had so much of the American Army under his direction, why should he not have all of it?

We did not know, in Luxembourg, what were Eisenhower's personal reactions to this British knife in the back. In the midst of the press campaign, Montgomery gave it official recognition by issuing a supercilious public statement that he personally re-

Marshal for not having done better on the continent. The Supreme Commander forgot about Montgomery's failure at Caen and instead of reminding him of it he reproached his British subordinate for having been so ungracious as to bring the matter up, calling attention to the American victory at St. Lô, the heavy casualties inflicted on the enemy, and so on, to prove that things weren't going as badly as maybe they looked.

It is also an interesting commentary that the British commander did not himself visit Eisenhower but simply sent his Chief of Staff, de Guingand, with his proposal. It was about this time that Montgomery was promoted to Field Marshal, thus outranking the Supreme Commander until the latter finally got his fifth star near the end of the war. As long as he ranked the Supreme Commander, Montgomery made a point of refusing to visit Eisenhower's headquarters, always insisting that Eisenhower come to him. And Eisenhower almost always came.

sented the public criticism of General Eisenhower, whom he said he had always found a charming fellow and with whom he had never had any difficulty in getting along. He thus inferred that he would be quite willing to let Eisenhower keep his title of Supreme Allied Commander so long as complete military authority in the field were delegated to Montgomery.

At this juncture, the Montgomery-for-president movement was close to a stampede. In senior headquarters everyone knew by then that the Germans had been defeated in the Ardennes, but the delayed effect of the German penetration was still evident in the world press—and the repercussions were still being felt in high places in London and Washington. The American Secretary of War sent Eisenhower a personal cable asking bluntly that he name the man responsible for our being surprised in the Ardennes, and directing that that man be removed from his position "regardless of his rank or responsibilities." * The whole Allied world which had been so complacent was scared now—and mad. It was open season for goat hunting.

In the confusion, the British almost won back command on the Continent by default, for want of anyone on the American high level team calm enough to investigate the facts. Those who stood against the British arguments were easily made to appear prejudiced or nationalistic or given to special pleading. Even the American press, from what we could learn of it in Europe, seemed to have been on the wrong scent.

At the last moment Montgomery, being Montgomery, overplayed his hand. He called in the press again and gave an unauthorized but on-the-record interview. In this interview he explained how he personally had won the battle of the Ardennes. His statements were strong enough; his inferences—that he had salvaged a battle that the Americans had lost before he came on

---

* In the book, the following were technically responsible, in this order: first, Eisenhower as Supreme Commander; next, Bradley as Army Group Commander; next, Hodges as Army Commander; and finally Middleton, who commanded the Corps sector in which the break occurred. None of these were relieved. No other officers were chargeable, since only officers in the chain of command can be held responsible for failure in the field. Staff officers advise but cannot make, or be held responsible for, command decisions.

the field—were even stronger. Something sparked in the German propaganda service which had, to date, been heavy-handed and ineffective in its attempts to stir up trouble between the Americans and the British. Some bright young man in Berlin took Montgomery's interview, changed no more than a few words—for his purposes, he could have left the text unaltered—and put it out over the Allied air on a British Broadcasting Company frequency.

To understand the consequences, it must be realized that BBC was a prime source of information on the Continent, not only to the Germans but also to us—and that practically every American headquarters from battalion to army group listened to it more or less faithfully. The American Army swallowed the German lure, hook, line and sinker, and a howl went up from Holland to the Vosges. BBC spotted the fake and hastened to disclaim it. But the damage was done.* The attention of the whole American Army had been focused on Montgomery's interview.

When the transcription of this broadcast reached General Bradley's desk, the gentle Omar—for the first, last and only time in the campaign—got all-out, right-down-to-his-toes mad. He regarded Montgomery's statement, even before the Germans tinkered with it, as deliberate misinterpretation. He felt that it reflected on every commander in the American Army and undermined the confidence and morale of American troops, and of the people at home. Until that date—it was the eighth of January—Bradley had not only refused to make direct statements to the press but had not even allowed a press camp at his tactical headquarters. The Public Relations Officer, who comes with the table of organization of every senior headquarters, Bradley had, until now, left at his main headquarters—which were always fifty miles or more behind the tactical headquarters from which he ran the campaign.

Bradley's whole technique of command, as I've said, is to efface himself and to build up—in their own eyes, in the eyes of their troops and in the eyes of the public—his subordinate commanders. That is one reason why the world knows a lot about Patton and not much about Bradley. It is not that Patton ran away with

---

* You will find American officers who still believe that this famous broadcast actually originated in the BBC studios. They are certain that BBC blamed it on the Germans only after it had become too hot to handle.

Omar's publicity. Patton was a ham, in the theatrical sense, but he adored Bradley and was utterly loyal to him. It is that Bradley encouraged Patton's getting publicity during the campaign because he knew publicity was food and drink to Patton and to Patton's GI's, who, like all good Americans, are just as happy to see their names in print as the brass. Bradley believed in his soldiers getting publicity and constantly enraged and frustrated his Intelligence officers by authorizing publicity for troops in the field even though the enemy might indirectly benefit. "Because soldiers like to see their names in the paper—and it's good for them," he said. But, for himself, Bradley went to great lengths to avoid publicity.

In campaigning for Montgomery's elevation, the British understood Bradley and were counting on his silence. They were confident that he was not the kind of a man who would or could defend himself from a friendly knife in the back. Certainly, he'd never been able to before. If Montgomery had not given out his unauthorized interview—and Goebbels had not played the spotlight on it—they might have succeeded. But when Bradley got mad he broke his own rules and let Montgomery have it back in the press. Even so, it took him a whole day to make up his mind to do it.

What convinced Bradley was recognition of the fact that the whole weight of the British Government and press was behind the drive to make Montgomery ground force commander. If the facts were not set straight, the least that could come out of all this was a seriously shaken confidence in American arms. And Montgomery would surely retain at least the command of two American armies. Discounting his personal distaste for the British commander, the hard fact remained that in Bradley's judgment, Montgomery was not a capable commander. It would be on his conscience if he turned two whole armies of American soldiers over to Montgomery without even an attempt to get the truth on record.

Feeling as he did, Bradley faced the fact that if he were put under Montgomery he would have no choice but to resign his own command. And he knew that Patton would resign with him. They had an understanding on that. Both men felt that they could not serve their country or their troops effectively under Montgomery's command. Bradley did not believe in Montgomery either as a general or as a man. He would be betraying his trust to the American Army and the American people if he pretended he did—or seemed to acquiesce by silence.

Painfully and laboriously, for he does not do these things well, he sweated out a statement to the press, trying to find the words which would convey the facts and yet not sound like special pleading. On the ninth of January he asked the reporters to drive up to Luxembourg and gave them a personal release.*

Buried in a description of the battle was one sentence which jammed a stubborn toe in the door the British were trying to slam in his face. It was the flat statement that Montgomery's command of the First and Ninth Armies was temporary, not permanent—and that this command would revert as soon as physical contact had been made between the First and Third Armies across the Bulge. This public statement put Montgomery and the British press in the position of having to call Bradley a liar if they were to continue to write that Montgomery's command was permanent—and Bradley could not be called a liar, for the temporary nature of the transfer of command was in writing in the orders that he had from the Supreme Commander.

Bradley's statement also called respectful attention to the inescapable fact that Montgomery *could not* have won the battle of the Ardennes because (a) he played no part in it until the basic strategy of the defense had been decided upon and (b) even then, he commanded only the northern half of a battle which had been decided, as all the world now knew, at Bastogne.

It did the job. The release caught the Montgomery press in London off balance and, instead of rolling with the punch, for once they tipped their hand. They screamed with rage and called Bradley names. He was accused of having "insulted Montgomery."

With the facts now getting themselves straightened out, this was too much for either Washington or Paris (where Eisenhower's headquarters still were)—and even 10 Downing Street

* After this instance, Bradley opened his own press camp and gave frequent and characteristically frank briefings to the correspondents.

saw the game was over. When Bradley's interview was published, Churchill telephoned Eisenhower personally to ask him to relay his apologies to Bradley for the handling of the Ardennes story in the British press. Confidentially, Churchill now said, all this pother came from a small group of Montgomery's friends, whom he described as "an embarrassment to the British Government."

To Bradley's staff this seemed the old trick of the private apology for the public insult. But Bradley himself believed in its sincerity. Whatever Churchill's motives, it remained a fact that not until Bradley had defended himself was the return of the First Army to American control assured. It took place when the First and Third Armies met near Houffalize.

But not all the damage—and it seemed real damage to us—could be undone. The First Army came back to Bradley but the Ninth Army remained under Montgomery's control.

The allocation of the Ninth Army to the British has a history which antedates the Ardennes. As usual in positions taken by the British, down underneath the politics and personalities there was a foundation of logic which, if you did not agree with it, had at least to be met in argument. The logic underneath the British desire for American troops and supplies to command was that, on their record in the war, they were entitled to a 50-50 partnership but could only contribute 20 to 25 per cent of the actual effort. Thus, they reasoned, it was up to the Americans to give them the additional forces to bring about a 50-50 balance and to allow them to get 50-50 billing for 50-50 victories. Montgomery, their commander in the field, could not keep up his end unless he were allocated the wherewithal from American sources.

By the end of 1944, the British Army on the Continent was so far past its peak strength that to stay in the field at all, and to provide the replacements necessary to keep its line divisions up to strength, it had begun its planned resort to cannibalizing. Eating one's own units means breaking up divisions to furnish officers and men to keep the rest of the army a going concern. The British Army was, therefore, dwindling in size and would have to continue to dwindle—so long as the British Government persisted in its policy of maintaining large garrisons in the Mediterranean and other outposts of the Empire, safeguarding their political future abroad instead of their military present in Belgium. From the minute they landed, onwards, the Americans could plan bigger and bigger attacks, using larger and larger forces. But Montgomery had been able to keep up his end only as far as Caen. To fight at Arnhem, for example, he had had to borrow two American divisions and vast fleets of air and land transport.

The British Chiefs of Staff were arguing that when the spring came the Allied main effort should be in the north under Montgomery. But if Montgomery was to put on any offensive in the north, even though he delayed it until the coming spring—or, rather, particularly *because* he planned to delay it until the coming spring—he had to have more troops to build up his shrinking army. These forces the British had succeeded in negotiating out of Marshall or Eisenhower during the fall of 1944, before the Ardennes. Hardly had its troops begun to land before the Ninth Army was earmarked for the British.*

While Bradley had argued that he both needed and wanted the Ninth, once General Simpson's forces had been traded away his attitude was that American objectives in the south could still be taken, provided we got enough replacements for the divisions we had, and provided enough supplies were allocated to us.

The Ninth Army was a relatively unimportant chesspiece in the Ardennes game. Holding a section of Belgium that the Germans had practically denuded of troops, poor Simpson cried plaintively to Montgomery for permission to attack. The Field Marshal would not even receive him to listen to his plans.

Following Montgomery's historic Ardennes interview, Bradley told Eisenhower on the telephone that he felt American prestige had been so hurt that he thought Eisenhower should now give him back the Ninth as well as the First Armies. Eisenhower never refused. He said he thought Bradley might be right. He now had plenty to think about on the subject of prestige himself. But he did nothing further about it and Simpson's Ninth Army was to

* When Bradley saw it was inevitable that Montgomery would get his northernmost army, he arranged to put the Ninth there—as a sacrifice play to save the veteran First. It had previously been planned to put the Ninth into the center section of the line—incidentally, at the exact spot hit by the Ardennes counteroffensive.

stay under the Field Marshal's command until after the crossing of the Rhine.

On the field and at the conference table, then, the battle of the Ardennes, fought in harsh climate and over hilly terrain, ended in a victory for the American command. But the conference victory was grudgingly conceded, incomplete and hedged with qualifications.

It was not until the Russians struck on January 15 that Bradley was really in a position to capitalize on both victories. When he did, the road was clear to the Germans' destruction.

On the rocky road of Anglo-American military relations, the Ardennes was a milestone. Until the Ardennes, Bradley and his officers had made an honest attempt to deal fairly and frankly with the British, to work together in open covenants openly arrived at. After the Ardennes, no one was ever frank with anyone. Fair, there was a scrupulous effort to be—almost a doubling over backwards; but frank, never. Bradley—and Patton, Hodges and Simpson under Bradley's direction—proceeded to make and carry out their plans without the assistance of official command channels, on a new basis openly discussed only among themselves. This basis squarely faced the facts that in order to defeat the enemy, by direct attack and in the shortest possible time, they had (1) to conceal their plans from the British, and (2) almost literally to outwit Eisenhower's Supreme Headquarters, half of which was British and the other half of which was beyond their power to influence by argument. They completely succeeded in both objectives and won the war.

11   Despite Hell and High Levels

At the time the Germans were forced to give the Eastern Front their principal attention, they felt reasonably sure they had nothing immediate to fear from the Anglo-Americans. Hitler still had nearly three months of winter on his side and he counted on its bad weather to offset Allied air superiority and to bog down even any limited offensive that might be mounted on the ground. Serious threats he discounted entirely. He was confident that the Americans would take at least until spring to recover from the dislocation of their plans in the Ardennes. The British, he accurately foresaw, would have to wait for long days of sunny weather to dry the marshes along the north coast. But when the big scale withdrawal began, and the roads from the Ardennes back to the Rhine were clogged with vehicles elbowing their way to the entraining points where they would be loaded and shipped East, the Allied hounds smelt the coming kill. Overnight the Ardennes depression lifted and a wave of optimism swept every Allied headquarters in Europe. The inside dope was: "The next big offensive really will be the last."

Now the issue of where the main Allied effort would be made became the focal point of all high level argument. Would the Allied armies concentrate against Hamburg in the north or against Frankfurt in the south?

Eisenhower was no sooner out of the hot water of the decision he had made in the Ardennes than he was back into it again, trying to conciliate and appease the arguments of the two groups.

Once again he found himself unable to make a clean-cut decision. But this time his failure to commit himself played into the Americans' hands—for we had no doubt the cards were stacked against the idea of the main effort being made in the American zone, and the longer the showdown was postponed, and supplies were *not* shut off from us, the more time we had to prepare to go anyway.

In January, 1945, the Supreme Commander had particular reasons for hesitation. The Malta Conference was about to take place, and here his plans would be subject to review by the President and the Prime Minister, the Combined Chiefs of Staff and his own personal boss, General Marshall. All correspondence between Marshall and Eisenhower reflect the latter's almost boyish attitude towards the American who first proposed him for his job. He was nervous about Marshall's approval, anxious always to find an approach that would please him. And at this particular time he was more than ever concerned with Marshall's good favor after having had his first real taste of censure from the British during the battle for the Ardennes.

It was at the Malta Conference (immediately preceding the meeting in the Crimea) that the Hamburg plains versus the Frankfurt gap came completely out in the open and was debated to a showdown. The British were unequivocally for the Hamburg route. Having been painstakingly setting up their argument for a year, they had the visiting American Chief of Staff on their side—on a short-route-over-the-flat versus a long-route-through-the-hills line of reasoning. The British chiefs had begun selling the Americans this bill of goods from way back in Freddie (COSSAC) Morgan's day. Eisenhower must have been immensely relieved. Perhaps there would be no conflict after all. But he still felt a little uneasy because Bradley's arguments for the southern route were still unanswered and he no longer trusted the British as thoroughly as he had six months before.

The American Chiefs of Staff endorsed the idea of a main effort in the north but were somewhat taken aback when the British came up with the opinion that they could only support the operations of twenty-five divisions on the far shore of the Rhine. Marshall did not consider this a strong enough force to complete the defeat of Germany. So the Americans arbitrarily increased the Hamburg plains effort from twenty-five to thirty-five divisions—and said OK. Bradley, of course, was in the field and could not speak for himself.

The American planners from Washington now reminded Ike that even after allocating this large force to the British zone there were plenty of troops left over for a secondary effort through the Frankfurt gap. Why not make it? Eisenhower was immediately responsive. Here was a way to please everyone. He threw himself into the argument, but the British continued to stand by their guns and insist that there be no secondary effort because even a sideshow might detract from the main effort.

The British lost this argument at Malta—blocked by their own admission of the supply limitations across the Rhine near its mouth. The secondary effort through the Frankfurt gap was approved—and Ike was ordered to make it, in addition to the northern thrust.

The extraordinary part about this story is that, despite this formal and unequivocal approval of at least a secondary effort through the Frankfurt gap, the conference at Malta had hardly broken up before the Supreme Commander, as we shall presently see, nullified it completely. In 12th Army Group Headquarters we did not know all the ramifications of the Malta debate but in quick succession we were told, first, that Montgomery was to put on the grand finale, with the Ninth Army remaining under his command, second, that the role of the First Army was to be so limited and prescribed that it was as if it too were under Montgomery's operational direction. And, finally, we learned that the Third Army, already chewing into the West Wall on its way to the Frankfurt gap, was to be halted in its tracks.

What happened between the decision of the Chiefs of Staff Conference and General of the Army Eisenhower's decision to let the agreed-upon secondary effort go by the board? Again, one day, the General may tell us himself but the odds are that it was nothing more mysterious than an organized campaign on the part of his own staff to persuade him that a secondary effort was impossible with the resources at hand and that, therefore, he had no choice but to stop Bradley and flag Montgomery through.

The reflection of this shows in the score of cables that passed through 12th Army Group, all illuminating a picture of dire British need for more troops, more specialized equipment, more supplies. The British put Ike under pressure and kept him there.

It is fair to General Eisenhower to add that the extent of the Russian victory, begun in mid-January, was still imperfectly appraised. There was no organized liaison with the Russians and the only authentic information that reached the Western Allies came from Stalin himself. Stalin had sent word that he would attack over the Vistula on or about the fifteenth of January, but he placed so much emphasis on a warning that he could not continue the offensive after the spring thaws set in that both the British and the American Intelligence agencies discounted the whole show in advance.

I am told that in Washington the War Department thought so little of the Russian prospects of victory that it was considered almost an even-money bet as to whether the Russians would break through the German line or quit cold and make peace with Hitler. In hindsight, this seems fantastic, but it is a logical successor to the military opinion in June, 1941, that the Russians wouldn't last six weeks.

Thus on the highest strategical levels in Washington and London no plans had ever been seriously discussed for how to take advantage of a sensational Russian victory on the Eastern Front—and when that victory materialized everyone concerned was wholly unprepared for it.

Eisenhower was so thoroughly in the dark as to the true nature of the German military situation after the Russian break-through that his only other contribution to the Malta Conference was a cautious case for clearing the Rhine plains in toto before attempting to storm the far shore. Here the Washington planners disagreed with him on the need, but not strongly enough to give him any orders to press on over the big river.

To the uninitiated in the American headquarters, Eisenhower's orders in the winter of 1945 meant the end of our active participation in the war. The First Army was hobbled and the Third Army was to dig in along the German borders, to dig in and turn the problem of the troops' morale over to the Special Service officers and the Red Cross. But long before the order to cease fire came from the Supreme Headquarters, insiders knew that plans had been completed for cracking the German Army opposite us, despite Hell and High Levels.

With the cards all down on the table, and the command game lost, all of Bradley's indecision over how he should handle the high politics of the campaign vanished. Once he had resigned himself to the fact that he had to outwit Eisenhower's headquarters and the British Government in order to get at the Germans, he was a new man, buoyant and relaxed.

Bradley still had his two armies, under Hodges and Patton, and both of them had been hoarding and hiding supplies for months. As left to his own devices, a GI will see to it that he has plenty of food and ammunition, no matter how the supply sergeant treats him, so two whole American armies had begun early in January to see to it that no one could ever again starve them for supplies. Now they already had what they needed, hidden in the woods and much of it off the books.

It began way down on the battalion level, when they commenced to call for ammunition to replace ammunition they had never fired—and to overload every vehicle with it. Five-gallon Jerricans of gasoline got written off the books as lost in action but reappeared miraculously as extra cans strapped on vehicles— by the thousands. The American Army had felt what it was like to be without supplies in September. They needed little urging to be persuaded that no individual should be caught short a second time. Every division looked after itself. Corps conspired to get the stuff for them from Army, and the G-4's at Army looked sad, talked poor and quoted endless statistics suggesting that supplies were melting away. COM Z let the stuff come up. Bradley's coffers swelled.

Looking over the enemy situation in front of him, Bradley liked what he saw. Now, for the first time, he faced a constant force— all new German divisions were going eastward. He faced a new general, Kesselring, who had been brought up from his defensive victories in Italy—but Bradley felt Kesselring had come too late, and Omar already had the measure of every German army and corps commander who served under Kesselring. The American Army Group Commander had the supplies, he had the troops, he had the plans and he had the enemy's measure. So he went to war, against orders.

Actually the play began a little earlier, when Bradley had managed to argue the one word "aggressive" into the stop-where-you-are order that Eisenhower had issued. So altered, the order read "you will undertake an aggressive defense"—as a feint, to attract troops to the American front, to keep them out of the way of the great British offensive. The one word "aggressive" was all that Bradley and Patton needed. They put their heads together and conspired like schoolboys.

Patton's army, having finished straightening out the Ardennes bulge, was drawn up along a little river on the German border. Obviously it was consistent with an "aggressive defense" that they send a few patrols to the far bank of the river, just to stir up trouble. The patrols turned out to be battalions, making assault crossings—in midwinter, across raging mountain streams that tore the pontons loose and swept the assault craft downstream. When they got across, they stuck there. Obviously it was consistent with an "aggressive defense" to consolidate such positions on the far shore. Patton ordered them consolidated, and heavy bridges were put in to take tanks across. But on the far shore there were hills overlooking these positions. So, still being consistent with the idea of an "aggressive defense," Patton sent his troops up over the hills, simply to protect the crossing site from enemy fire. And beyond these hills there was another valley, with another stream, which you had first to go down to the edge of, and then to cross, and then to protect by getting to the next ridge line beyond. Literally, so help me, in this way and no other, Patton put his Third Army through the impenetrable forests of the Eifel, the hilly woods from which the Germans had launched their Ardennes offensive. He took the one road into Germany that even the most apprehensive German staff officer could not have worried about.

As bait to lure Germans out of Monty's way, the aggressive defense of the American Army was an immense success. At one time the center of the American line had attracted no less than

60 per cent of the German divisions on the whole Western Front! And still the Germans there had to fall back!

Meanwhile, Bradley's orders to stay put had been modified so far as the northern end of his line was concerned. He was now told that, to protect the southern flank of Montgomery's attack, he should push on through the West Wall just beyond Aachen. After that he was to proceed out onto the Rhine plain, just far enough, but no farther than was necessary, to protect Montgomery from being side-swiped from the south.

These, and no more orders, gave Bradley and Hodges sufficient excuse to prepare the plans and mount the attack which was to carry them not simply ten miles beyond Aachen but actually across the Rhine and half way around the impregnable Ruhr area, to complete its encirclement. Here the reasoning was equally straight-faced: obviously it would be consistent with orders which directed the protection of a man's flank to proceed on out in front, even if one had to win the whole battle for him to do it.

While the preparations for all this were going on, Montgomery and the British press were hard at work heralding the coming all-Montgomery crossing of the Rhine.

It was to be second only, in historic significance, to the trans-Channel invasion itself.

The most elaborate plans imaginable were made to ensure Montgomery's successful crossing with the American Ninth Army and the British Second. Through the winter of 1945 whole divisions were taken out of the line and specially trained for the job. The newsreels showed them practicing their charges across the Meuse. The Royal and American Navies were called in to advise. All manner of amphibian apparatus clogged the roads, moving up to the forward dumps. The stage was being set. All would be well after all. With Montgomery in command, the Rhine would be stormed and the enemy beaten on British terms, with graceful bows to the contributions of the Americans and the Canadians. The battle for prestige at arms, which had been lost at Caen and lost again at Arnhem—and which had eluded Montgomery a third time when he tried to get credit for the Ardennes—was at last to be his, was to be the British Empire's!

It was in the bag—only when the opening night came on March

23, Hodges' First American Army had been on the far side of the Rhine for over two weeks, having crossed on the Remagen bridge, and Patton had gone over below Frankfurt, standing up—after the whole German Army Group B had been captured or routed on the near side of the Rhine plain. It was in the bag for the British—only within a scant two weeks after crossing under Montgomery's command, the American Ninth Army was literally to run away from Montgomery's control and to justify its insubordination beyond criticism by forming the northern pincer of the most brilliant encirclement action won by either side during entire World War II—and probably in all military history. And while Montgomery's tanks, as prophesied, bogged down in the mud of the plains just beyond the Rhine, Hodges and Patton together were to pass through the Frankfurt gap—fulfilling the promise they had made a year before at the conference table—and on the far side of the Frankfurt gap they were to lay all of Germany wide open and end the war.

As for the Supreme Allied Commander Eisenhower, he spent the spring legalizing victories won in battles he didn't know were going to be fought. Bradley was always conscientious about reporting *after* the fate of the battle had been decided. When the Remagen bridge, for instance, had been taken despite the fact that SHAEF had given specific orders to clean the near banks of the Rhine before crossing anywhere, Omar telephoned Ike at once—just as soon as he was sure Hodges' men were safely over on the far side of the river. And Omar was quite happy to let Ike report these victories to London and Washington as his own—after all it was his right, as the Supreme Commander—so long as he didn't report them until after Omar was ready to throw his next punch at the Krauts. And Omar kept on throwing them, one after another.

It was mid-February when the weather first broke. We just woke up one morning and there it was spring—balmy, warm. We thought maybe it was just for a freak day or two, but it went on and on. Winter just went away and never came back.

Within two weeks the roads went away too. We'd moved our

headquarters from Luxembourg to Namur in Belgium to be nearer the center of the Army Group, and when we drove back to Paris we found the long straight roads, some of which I suppose had been built by the Romans, had buckled and heaved until you couldn't even get through the bad parts with a jeep. The macadam surfaces split in the middle and up-ended a foot or two into the air and the foundations disintegrated completely, making mud ruts several feet deep. They put thousands of PW's to work on the road, dumping stone into the mud holes, and whole villages turned out to help.

Some trunk supply roads had to be closed entirely and others had twenty-miles-per-hour speed limits on them. It took the whole countryside a long time to dry out but it was worth it to have good weather for the air to work in and it stopped the worst of the suffering from weather in the line. There was still plenty of trench foot, however, from cold mud.

The offensive that broke out onto the Rhine plains had to be supplied over remnants of roads. Through the West Wall they were so bad that it was an adventure to travel even a few miles in a jeep. When we got past the hilly country on the border, the Rhine plain was heaven. The roads weren't really much stronger there but they had not had a winter's pounding under thirty and sixty ton American military loads, the way the Belgian and French roads had. If you could stick on the crest of them, you could go like hell.

We thought we'd seen some towns destroyed in Normandy— no one who had been there could forget St. Lô which seemed to have been taken apart brick by brick and cobblestone by cobblestone—but the first cities to catch it on the Rhine plain were really pulverized. After St. Lô, Aachen had been a compensating sight with its miles of burned-out buildings, but Jülich and Düren were really absolutely flat. The only useful thing in them were the streets, which could be cleared with bulldozers so that they were able to carry traffic. Along the sides of these excavations in the rubble ran heavy tangles of field telephone wire.

Beyond the dramatic ruins of Jülich and Düren, the German villages were just as dramatically unscratched. After the breakthrough, the armor raced on, apparently without firing a shot.

The thing we noted after France was not how much but how little equipment the Germans left behind them. We thought that they had been able to take it with them, but it's more likely that by then they simply had less to lose.

The villages on the Rhine plain were the first "normal" villages that we had met in Europe. There are loads of French towns that are unscratched but most we had seen had had at least a few buildings blown down, if not in our campaign then by the Germans when they'd come through in 1940. Having complete control of the air then, the Luftwaffe had seen to it that every village got at least one bomb to keep its inhabitants in their place. And even the French villages that had suffered no damage from explosives were grim and tired looking, and dusty and ill repaired. In contrast, the little German villages were neat and spruce looking. The French had been tired and hungry and, in the winter, wan and cold. The Germans were conspicuously healthy. You could see with your own eyes that they had sucked the blood of Europe and grown fat on it.

On the Rhine plains they were quite friendly to the Americans. Word of mouth intelligence that the Americans were not the savages that German propaganda had pictured them seemed to have spread ahead of us, and the villagers reported that retreating soldiers had told them not to pay any attention to the Party people's orders to resist. Nazi morale on the Rhine plains had become low anyway. Apparently for a long time when German boys came home on leave from the Eastern Front they had been encouraged by their families to go over the hill. They had been hidden out when the Wehrmacht came to look for them.

Our own operations seemed wonderfully confused in the field. The flying columns that had cut into the Rhine plains looked messy enough, even on the scrubbed and tidied Army Group war map. Out there on the flat, with the spires of Cologne sticking up on the horizon, you didn't see how even a division commander could even keep track of where his own troops were. All American military vehicles are identified by neat numbers and letters on their front and rear bumpers. Going down any given road, you'd pass vehicles from half a dozen units. The center of gravity of some was one hundred miles away.

It was all happening so fast that no one knew where anybody was, least of all the MP's who scratched their heads at the crossroads and tried to pronounce the names of places and to figure which road went where. I went up the day before we got into Cologne. The CP of one infantry division had moved three times the same day. The division was my good old 1st Infantry, and when I caught up with its headquarters it had just gotten orders to confine its attack to the southern edge of the city. The 1st Division was a little bitter about this. It thought it ought to be allowed to pick such an easy plum as Cologne was turning out to be. But instead, the part of the city assigned to it was principally featured by the sewage disposal plant. The 1st Division swore that when it got there it was going to reverse the pumps and counterflush all the toilets in town. Later on the city was spared this revenge when the 1st was allowed to go into the city itself after all.

Everyone was feeling very high at the successes of the past week, and I rode on out to a battalion that was already at the suburbs of Cologne. The German artillery on the far shore of the Rhine had plenty of ammunition and was doing its best to interdict the roads and catch the Americans taking cover in villages. But it was like trying to stop the holes in a sieve by sticking pins into it; the American troops were leaking through the gap in the West Wall and flowing across the Rhine plain in a thousand rivulets. Driving over the plain, even along the edge of the Rhine, you could easily miss the German fire by watching it fall. When you saw one town getting hit you simply took a road to one side or the other of it. There were no obstacles and visibility was fine.

When I got to Battalion they were having a very intimate little battle with a German major whose name I think was Mueller. They knew all about Mueller at Battalion; they had captured many of his officers and men soon after these had left him. Mueller was in a house in the suburbs of Cologne, running the Germans' war all by himself. He was out of touch with higher headquarters, but had just enough stout hearts left from whatever his outfit had been to help him round up the stragglers that were retreating back across the plains into Cologne. These he turned around, shoving guns into their hands, and sending them back into the fight. He had lots of guns and plenty of ammunition and he had some anti-aircraft cannon that were part of the Cologne defense with which to support them. The 1st Division's boys would surround one of his positions, plaster it with bazookas, and throw a lot of light machine-gun fire into it, and after a while out would come twenty or thirty prisoners with their hands up. But by the time they were rounded up and the place searched cautiously for booby traps, Mueller had another platoon in place in another group of buildings and it had to be done all over again. Mueller was described as having plenty of brandy and cigarettes and enjoying himself. That evening he must have run out of either brandy or stragglers for he suddenly disappeared and the American infantry went on into the town.

After I left the infantry at Cologne, I drove on down the Rhine plain, cutting across the columns of armor and infantry that were streaking south and east. One of them was the column which was to end its race on the far side of the Rhine over the Remagen bridge. For the first time since right after the break-through at Avranches, the boys seemed to be having a good time. There were new sights to see, and neither speed limits nor MP's, and everything was all hell bent for election. Now and then you'd hear a burst of fire in the distance or feel the thud of a shell come over from beyond the Rhine. But it was a comic opera war compared with the winter on the border. It made one feel very good to be riding along in the spring sunshine, neither tired nor frightened nor worried. When I got back to the hills where the West Wall had been forced, long supply convoys of gasoline and ammunition were already winding through. The engineers were putting up wooden bridges in place of the ponton crossings over the rivers that had been taken by storm the week before. They had even begun clearing the rail lines. All day long the bombers and the fighters came and went overhead and only once did I see the contrails twist themselves into complicated pretzels the way they do in a dog fight.

Victory had been a long time coming, but now it was bursting out all over.

There is a certain monotonous similarity to all military campaigns that makes them poor reading to a layman. But if the reader can stand a good old-fashioned "how-the-battle-was-fought" dinner table job, complete (figuratively) with knives, forks and spoons to represent corps and divisions, and tumblers and plates upside down to show the mountains and valleys—I offer the campaign which took the Americans across the Rhine to the Elbe.

In the long struggle over who made the most sense in running the battle on the Continent, this campaign was the final pay-off. There was a kind of homespun quality about the timing and action which should renew people's faith in the old American virtues: honesty and hard headedness, with a little Yankee slyness and wit thrown in for flavor. Bradley's conduct of himself, all through this last campaign, reminded me of Benjamin Franklin's at the Court of France—he combined shrewdness and subtlety of mind with simplicity and straightforwardness of character. He saw through the maze of conflicting passions and interests in higher headquarters—and mastered the highly complex fabric of the campaign itself—and never for an instant lost his sense of proportion. He remained wholly and wonderfully American and never once lost sight of the shape of his own country or of the problems with which he dealt.

The big campaign which ended the war was a three-ring circus. From March until May, acts were going on simultaneously in all three of the rings.

The northern ring was Montgomery's show—the much heralded, the brilliantly press-agented, Grand Crossing of the Rhine. But by the time the act went on—and it was put on well and was successful—no one was watching it, so exciting were the trapeze acts in the other rings—the First Army's ring in the center and the Third Army's ring in the south.

As throughout most of the campaign, there was also a sideshow running—the sideshow that was Devers' American 6th Army Group which had landed on August 15 in southern France, come up the Rhône and taken its place in the line opposite Germany on the south. The 6th Army Group was made up of the American Seventh Army and the French First Army. It was Some Sideshow—and many of the most heroic stories of the war will come out of the Franco-American campaign. The 6th Army Group liberated a lot of France, killed a great many Germans and captured some hundreds of thousands. It performed a valuable and important function. But it remained, from the day it landed on the Riviera until its final serio-comic squabble with the French Government over who would have the honor (and convenience) of occupying Stuttgart, a sideshow in history's circus.

The war on the Continent could not have been won without the 6th Army Group; but the 6th Army Group did not win the war. It remained a "me too" organization until it ended its fighting career without even getting the glory and the gratification of receiving the surrender of the major German army it had fought— a reward which went to Field Marshal Alexander and General Mark Clark at the end of the campaign which the troops of the 6th Army Group had begun before they came to France. This campaign, from which the 6th Army Group units had been diverted into southern France, was probably the bitterest, bloodiest, toughest, dullest, nastiest and least satisfying in the entire war, the Pacific Theater included; it was the campaign against Kesselring in Italy, fought all the way from the toe of the boot to the Alps through twenty heartbreaking months.

What happened in the two American rings of the circus campaign that ended the war, briefly, were these things, ring by ring:

The Patton Ring: As we've seen, Patton began by eating his way half way through the dreaded Eifel on orders that he stay on the aggressive defense. After he had gotten half way through the Eifel, the joke was so broad that Eisenhower belatedly legalized the advance—told him he might be where he already was—and added permission to strike out with a single exploratory armored column, just to see what would happen. The column that Georgie sent out on the sixth of March was the famed 4th Armored. The 4th Armored sprinted the rest of the way, fifty miles, to the Rhine plain near Coblenz, in two days. It crossed country so impossible that the tanks had to tow even the mighty two-and-one-half-ton, six-by-six trucks which are the toughest vehicles ever built by man. The 4th Armored went through to the Rhine so fast that it passed by a retreating German parachute division which thereafter was not able even to keep up with it and so itself reached the Rhine only after the Americans had established themselves there.

In the Patton Ring, now, the Third Army had flown through the air with the greatest of ease and one outstretched arm, reaching ahead, had its fingers touching the Rhine trapeze. In the next ring, the famous Remagen bridge tightrope walking act was about to go on. What led up to the Remagen bridge stunt was this:

The Hodges Ring: In February, Bradley was being kept well in his place by Montgomery. Field Marshal Sir Bernard was once again issuing orders through Eisenhower, and Bradley was directed sternly to see to it that the southern flank of the coming British drive was protected. Montgomery took no chances and spelled this out for the Americans: Hodges' First Army was to cross the Roer River, which bounds the Rhine plain on the west, in the neighborhood of Aachen, and was then to advance *half way* to Cologne—to where a second river called the Erft cut the Rhine plain in a natural semicircle around Cologne and where the enemy had been observed from the air to be erecting elaborate field fortifications. The First Army was to consolidate its position there.

This limited advance was the most that Montgomery foresaw the First Army would be able to do and, probably for that reason, the orders that Eisenhower issued did not specify that it should go no further. They simply emphasized the point that, at all costs, the position on the Erft had to be made secure, to guarantee that Montgomery be free from enemy interference from the south.

What actually happened was that, when the time came, just after Washington's birthday, the First Army broke over the Roer River so fast that, reaching the Erft, they simply swept on, across the stream and through the enemy positions, and were, a few hours later, in the suburbs of Cologne itself.

Just as Bradley had told Patton how to interpret *his* orders to assume a position of "aggressive defense," he now advised Hodges that after he had fulfilled his obligations to Montgomery (i.e., gone as far as the Erft), he was on his own. He was on his own, Bradley told him, to take Cologne and to capture a bridge over the Rhine—if he could find one still intact. All this Bradley did against

Eisenhower's orders, which were strictly to stay on this side of the Rhine.

Within hours, the word went out that it was open season for capturing bridges over the Rhine. Every corps and division commander in the First Army made his own plans—and in turn every regimental and battalion commander. This was the way the Americans liked to fight—to get it over with, to go places and capture things. For six long months, with this exception and that, they had had nothing but "Stop," "Slow Down," "We haven't the supplies for you"—red lights and orange lights, but rarely green lights. Here on the Rhine plain, they got the green light to end all green lights—"Take off into Germany and keep going."

Bradley's estimate of the enemy's situation was brilliant. These orders—which, mind you, were not written orders but simply understandings between commanders and up and down the various chains of command—were precisely the medicine the situation demanded. Montgomery was screaming to Eisenhower that, even with all the priority he had, and the American Ninth Army thrown in, and the British and American Navies, and all the air power that could be put over a single spot in Europe, even with all these, he still had to have more and still more combat engineer battalions and this and that extra to meet the dreadful German Army at all. Eisenhower himself wanted the Rhine plain cleared before going anywhere. But Bradley was betting that the dreadful German Army was so nearly licked that he could turn his commanders loose and let the devil take the hindmost.

Bradley was spectacularly right. The break-away American columns caused utter confusion in the German Command. The situation on the Rhine plain got so rapidly out of control that within twenty-four hours after the attack began, it became obvious to the Germans that they could not fight there but must get back across the river and blow the big bridges behind them.

The capture of the Remagen bridge by a flying column of the American 9th Armored Division, which struck southeast from the break-through over the Roer, was not the fluke it may have seemed to newspaper readers—or even to professional military men three thousand miles away from the scene. The Rhine bridges are enormous and are not blown with firecrackers. Even after such bridges are prepared for demolition, during a retreat the decision of when to blow one is one of the most difficult decisions to make in the whole military handbook. *Some* rear-guard will have to be left to die on the far shore or surrender or try to paddle back—the Rhine is quite a river to swim.

At the time the attack over the Roer was launched, there were still a dozen eligible bridges intact over the Rhine. Every single one of them had been picked out by one—and most of them by two or three—individual American commanders as prizes which would cap their careers in the field. The race for the Rhine bridges was a wild homestaking kind of a race, in the tradition of the American plains. When the starting gun went off, it was an odds-on bet that somewhere, somehow, one of the American columns would knife through the mêlée and get over a bridge before the detonating switch could be thrown. The 9th Armored simply won the race.

It got a dog of a bridge—a bridge which had been declared unsafe for heavy traffic by the Germans themselves a month before we got there—it had been so damaged by our own bombing. But most of that month the Germans had spent trying to repair it themselves (for their possible retreat) so it was just barely crossable by tanks when we took it.

The Remagen bridge was also at the most unlikely place for a crossing on the entire Rhine. At its far end rise cliff-like hills which would be almost impossible to scale if properly defended. Because it was so unlikely a place, however, these hills were not fortified. The first surge across carried the Americans on to the nearest hilltops.

Even so, one American senior officer, instead of glory, got relieved of his command because he did not push his troops still further on during the first forty-eight hours. The bridge remained under German artillery fire for days.

Throwing us out of the Remagen bridgehead became Hitler's personal preoccupation; he began a bloody battle to annihilate it. We were all afraid, for a few days, that the business might end in disaster.

The Remagen bridge died of its wounds just ten days after we took it. But those ten days were enough. By the end of them, there were two ponton bridges across and the First Army was on the far shore of the Rhine to stay. Enraged and now fearful of a breakout from the Remagen bridgehead, the Germans began robbing the rest of the Rhine line to throw in troops against it. The local reserves that had been waiting for Montgomery packed up and went south to try to hold Hodges.

Back to the Patton Ring: It was almost a bitter pill to Georgie Patton that while it was his troops who had begun the offensive to the Rhine plains and who had broken the German defense system in the hills before the attack in the north had even begun, it was Hodges whose men had crossed the Rhine first. But for once Georgie stuck to minding his own business, and minded it brilliantly. His business was clearly to get on to the Frankfurt gap.

The German Army that Patton had beaten in the Eifel woods retreated, not across the Rhine, but southeast across the Moselle. The Moselle runs at right angles to the Rhine and cuts off a big chunk of rolling, hilly country, bounded by the Moselle, by the Saar and by the Rhine itself. This hunk is called the Palatinate, and Frankfurt is across the Rhine, opposite the northeast corner of it. Even though he had reached the Rhine, Patton had still another battle to fight before he could even start through his beloved gap.

As when he faced the Eifel, Patton had no orders to proceed further. Once again he was told to hold everything—on the Moselle—and once again Bradley found a way to get Patton around both SHAEF and the German Army.

The south side of the Palatinate runs along the German border. Against the West Wall in this section, Jakey Devers' 6th Army Group had come to a full stop. It was here that Himmler himself had taken command of German SS troops and had mounted a diversion during the Ardennes offensive—a diversion successful enough to cause the American Seventh Army to retire to the Maginot Line. This was only a few days before the Germans were forced by the Russian offensive to call off their own attack and had themselves presently retreated in the opposite direction from the Americans—back into the West Wall. All this had stung Devers and Patch (who commanded the Seventh Army) so sharply that they had persuaded Eisenhower to lend them some of

Patton's divisions—first to secure the southern flank of the American line and finally to lead an assault on the Palatinate itself. This assault constituted no competition to the British grandstand play in the north—it was even a help, because it both weakened Omar and drew the enemy to the south. So Montgomery let it go on.

The 6th Army Group attack on the Palatinate was to be a full-scale offensive on a very broad front, and was to sweep the Germans back across the Rhine. It had been planned for a month, but by the time it was ready to go, Patton had captured Trier, thus unhinging the West Wall to the south, and had moved into the Eifel, pocketing great numbers of Germans and pushing the rest across the Moselle.

To give Devers a fair field, Patton was asked simply to hold the Moselle line while the Seventh Army cleared the territory to the south. After lending some of his divisions to Devers, Patton was not considered to have enough strength left to make any material contribution to the Seventh Army attack.

The whole Palatinate adventure, in other words, was to be a 6th Army Group party—but Bradley's prestige had risen again to a point where he was able to persuade the Supreme Commander not to subdivide the battle area into army group zones but to leave it to him to co-ordinate the show with his neighbor, Devers. Devers was agreeable and the big attack jumped. Only at the last minute did Bradley let Patton put a few troops across the Moselle to divert the attention of the Germans.

For a second time, Georgie's aggressive diversion stole the show. Again he used the 4th Armored. He let an infantry division make an assault crossing of the Moselle near its mouth and the minute the infantry had a bridge in, he put the 4th Armored through. The 4th Armored went through all right—thirty-two miles in the first twenty-four hours. Once again, its columns came out on the Rhine plain, this time opposite Frankfurt, dead in the rear of two German armies which had not merely been facing Devers but which had already beaten back the Seventh Army's first attack.

Having rendered the German position in the Palatinate untenable, Patton put another and then still another armored division through the hills, without stopping. The enemy began to withdraw and then to run for the Rhine. American armored columns crossed and recrossed each other as they drove through the disorganized masses of retreating Germans, making hundreds of pockets and taking thousands upon thousands of prisoners. As the

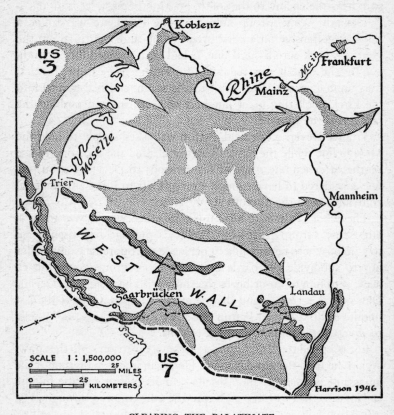

CLEARING THE PALATINATE

West Wall collapsed, the Seventh Army moved up to meet the Third and closed the final pocket near Landau.

Patton had pulled Devers on through the West Wall. He made him a present of the Palatinate and, again without stopping, turned his army around and crossed the Rhine below Frankfurt. He struck so boldly that there was hardly a shot fired at the first troops to land. The official date of the crossing is March 22. Actually, the Third Army had the crossing sites in hand some days earlier, having sent patrols over the river in force. But March 23 was the date that Montgomery had announced for his own crossing of the Rhine, and Georgie thought it would be fun to hold up the announcement of the Third Army's crossing until it would spoil Monty's headlines.

So it was that with an army that wasn't supposed to have enough troops left to make even a material contribution, Patton had done the whole of the 6th Army Group's job and made a joke of all Montgomery's elaborate preparations for the river crossing in the north. Moreover, at long last and by dint of Patton's efforts and his own backing of them, the Third Army was well along on Bradley's own cherished route into Germany—the route through the Frankfurt gap.

"*While in Montgomery's Ring* . . ." While all these fine things were happening in the center and south of the line, there was plenty going on in the north, too. Going way back to the beginning of the campaign, remember that to reach the Rhine for his big crossing, Montgomery had first to get through the remainder of the West Wall and then to drive the Germans off the plains beyond. To do this Montgomery planned a classic pincer attack with the Canadians scheduled to come down from the north along the curve of the Rhine and the American Ninth Army—now firmly under Montgomery's command—cutting first straight into the plain, north of Cologne, then turning north to meet the Canadians coming south. Thus the whole West Wall between Aachen and Arnhem would be pinched off and the Rhine itself cleared from Cologne all the way round to Arnhem. All this was to have been accomplished by a synchronized attack early in February. Once on the Rhine, Montgomery would regroup and wait for dry weather to cross.

The great crossing was to be known as PLUNDER; the Canadian push to clear the plains for it was called VERITABLE, and the American pincer of it GRENADE.

The jump-off date for VERITABLE was to be February 8— and for GRENADE, a day or two later. The staggering of the attacks was to throw the Germans off balance. As usual in British offensives, every detail had been studied and re-studied, checked and co-ordinated.

Despite this, things began to go wrong with operations VERI-TABLE and GRENADE before they had hardly begun. Things did not go at all as Montgomery expected, and this time through no fault of his own. In fact, if he talks to himself about the matter,

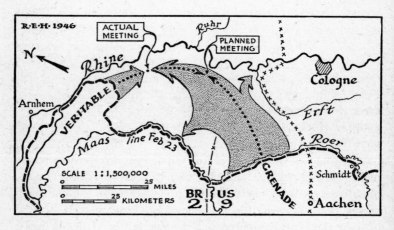

GRENADE OVER VERITABLE

Field Marshal Sir Bernard has a right to mumble that he may have missed the bus over the Rhine because of an American boner. The name of the American boner was the Roer Dams— and the boner had been pulled long before Montgomery took command of any American forces on the West Wall line.

The Roer water works are a series of dams in the hills south of Aachen. They had been spotted on the map by Army Group Headquarters several months before we got to them and diagnosed as a potential source of trouble. The Roer is a small river but it has flat banks and floods easily. The dams are there to control the floods, as well as to provide power for many small manufacturing communities near by. A study of them revealed that the Germans, by blowing these dams, could cause a flood which would make the Roer impassable for from several to six weeks—the length of time depending on the season, the state of the ground and the natural rainfall and run-off at the time of the flooding.

Army Group sent an Intelligence officer who specialized in terrain up to First Army, which was the army expected to be first to get to the Roer dams, to explain this possibility. First Army was in a bad mood that day and said: "We can read a map just as well as you. When we need any help from Army Group G-2, we'll let you know. In the meantime, you go on back to your high level nonsense and when you tell us to take those dams, we'll take them—probably the day before you get around to telling us to." That kind of thing happens in armies.

The trouble was that when, a long time later, the First Army had a chance to take the dams, there were a lot of other things going on at the same time. The dams are commanded by a road center known as the village of Schmidt. It was the 28th Infantry, under General Cota, which took Schmidt and sent a message back saying that, while it had the town, the going had been extremely tough and there were all the earmarks of a German counterattack in the intelligence that was coming in. If it materialized, Cota doubted if he could hold the town against this counterattack— and he asked for help. His casualties had been very high.

Since the First Army had not yet reached the Roer in force, and the dams and their significance had long since been forgotten, there seemed to be no reason for excitement over holding a town named Schmidt. Schmidt looked like any other German town on the map. Help was not readily available and Cota was told to do the best he could and if he could not hold Schmidt to fall back on some other nice German village. The counterattack came and the 28th Division, which had been fighting *hard* for weeks, took a shellacking and the Germans got Schmidt back.

The Germans knew how important Schmidt was. It was eleven long weeks later, after two other division-size, and finally two successive corps-size attacks had been mounted and beaten by the Germans that Schmidt and the dams were taken.

By the time the dams themselves could be seen from the American lines they had become a cause célèbre, and every staff engineer in the First Army and Army Group, and every officer in G-2 and

G-3, had his own opinions on how important they were or were not and on whether the Germans could or could not blow them up and, if they were blown, how long it would take them to empty and how great a flood the emptying could produce.

In this confusion of counsel, as soon as we had taken Schmidt and held the upper end of the lakes above the dams, the attack on the dams themselves was called off at the last moment—as unnecessary. A few days later, the Germans settled the argument by blowing the dams so skillfully that instead of their emptying in a single big flood of a few days' duration, the dams leaked out in small, continuous flooding which lasted for weeks.

All of which is a long way round the dams to the fact that on the morning of the eighth of February, when Montgomery's coordinated pincer attack on the lower Rhine plains was to jump, the Roer dams were still leaking. The Roer River, therefore, was still in flood. And its banks, for one hundred yards on each side, were quagmires too shallow to float assault boats and too deep, in water and mud, for infantry to walk through.

And when would the floods subside and the quagmire dry?

"Well," Colonel A said, "tomorrow."

And Colonel B said, "In three weeks."

General Q of the engineers said, "Hum" and "Ha."

So in the end, Montgomery, on the optimistic side this time, let go the Canadian attack VERITABLE in the north. The American attack GRENADE was not due to begin for twenty-four hours anyway; it would not throw things off too much if it were delayed an extra day. Actually it was delayed two weeks.

During these weeks the British attack was brought to a complete standstill. After an exciting forty-eight hours of success, the armor had started to go through the assault infantry. Immediately, it had run into that swampy ground which American planners had been telling Montgomery for over a year he would meet in the northern plains. Confined to roads, with the roads themselves often under water, Montgomery's tanks had been easy meat for the German parachutists whose job, fighting on foot, was to stop them. The Canadian infantry got through the West Wall all right, but ten miles further on they too bogged hopelessly down.

That was practically as far as VERITABLE ever got in the

battle for the Rhine plains. Instead of Montgomery's pincers closing in the middle as planned, the American Ninth Army, when it
finally jumped, took the lion's share of the plain, in addition to its
own objectives, in a few quick bites. Simpson's armor broke
away through München-Gladbach, where the footing was better,
and went on north to meet the British.

In their charge the American tanks performed what is recognized as one of the most difficult military maneuvers in allied war-
making: they successfully stormed and overran three successive
international army boundaries on the map. The fourth was too
much for them. Three times Montgomery had to move back the
boundary that separated the Ninth Army (American) from the
Second Army (British). Finally the line he drew slanted across the
Rhine plains only a few miles ahead of where the British offensive
was still trying to get going. There the Field Marshal stuck, and
Simpson's columns caromed off the imaginary line that divided
the battlefield to let the aristocratic Guards Armored Division
close the gap.

Thus it came about that the first victory in Montgomery's campaign, while spectacular enough, was, unfortunately for him,
spectacularly American. The crossing of the Roer and the taking
of the northern Rhine plain was the first offensive action directed
by General Simpson. Simpson's new Ninth Army did everything
right and won a champion's title in its first fight in the ring.

It is one of those arguments that should be reserved for a quiet
evening at the Army-Navy Club—and military comparisons are
even more odious than social comparisons—but a lot of us who
watched and directed their activities would put our money on the
Ninth Army Headquarters in any race in which the First, Third
and Ninth carried equal weights.

First Army was a complicated headquarters: ornery, cantanker-
ous and often unimaginative. It had the most veterans in it, from
the old II Corps staff in Africa. It got jobs done; you could count
on it. But, in football terms, you would have said that its plays
were too often directed between the tackles. It did not think in
terms of end runs or forward passes unless nudged by Coach
Omar himself—who personally thought out St. Lô, the exploita-

tion which took the Remagen bridge and the later encirclement of the Ruhr.

Patton's Third Army hated line bucks and wasn't very good at them. It was a touchdown play or nothing with the Third Army. When the Third Army did get a touchdown mission, its performance was breath-taking and its staff work was as hard-headed and responsible as its commanding general was debonair. Third Army staff work, in fact, was spectacularly sound just because its commanding general had a cavalier's approach to detail. Patton built up his officers by giving them responsibility, and all the authority they needed to carry it. The very fact that his demands were often unreasonable toughened his staff mentally and made it possible for them to deliver as they did in the Ardennes, when the slightest snafu in the planning or execution would have lost the battle.

Simpson's new Ninth Army seemed to us to combine the best features of both the First and Third. It was as steady and reliable as the First and after GRENADE we knew it could run and pass as brilliantly as the Third. It had just the right combination of respect for the experience of others and the cockiness which wins battles. And it was far and away the easiest of the three to deal with.

First Army was rarely frank and hated interference or advice from above or below. Third Army Headquarters had charm. A visit to it was always fun: it lived and dressed well, but you never knew, when Third Army claimed to have taken a town, whether it really had it or was just making with the publicity. Ninth Army talked straight and you knew that when it asked for ten thousand rounds of ammunition, it wanted them to shoot at the enemy—and not to hide away so that it might be able to surprise you by taking an unexpected objective at some later date.

The three Armies came to have very distinct personalities to the Army Group staff and I am sure we had our own quirks to amuse them.

Bradley's headquarters—at least his own field echelon, EAGLE TAC—was a pleasant place to work, casual and friendly. If Bradley kept his staff out of the plush châteaux—he liked to live simply and under canvas if possible—he more than made up for it, for my money at least, by letting his officers work and dress as they pleased, and come and go without formalities. There was no spit and polish at EAGLE TAC; we worked in field jackets and without ties—most officers fancied scarves made from old parachutes picked up in Normandy. We wore field boots because we were almost always in mud, and helmets, because Omar kept as close to the front as communications permitted.

Despite Omar's lack of demands on us, I do not know any general who was more conscientiously served. The very fact that he asked so little meant that everyone doubled his efforts to turn in a good performance. Even so, Bradley used his senior staff officers probably less than any other important general in Europe. He liked to deal personally with his army commanders and used to fly around visiting them in a tiny, two-seated, liaison plane with a sergeant-pilot. The Headquarters was reasonably busy keeping track of the situation and making the interminable studies which are required to keep a commanding general informed of what he should know, but one felt strongly that Bradley ran his show alone.

Looking back, Bradley seems to me to have been a lonely man, with the loneliness of one who has no intellectual equals in his immediate circle. As is the custom on high level staffs, the general officers who surround the commander are reluctant to let their subordinates deal directly with the boss. They liked to keep him to themselves. Bradley sometimes seemed to go out of his way to circumvent his generals and to talk with, and listen to, the juniors he came in contact with. In the Planning Section, we soon found that the easiest way to keep abreast of the General's thinking was to happen to be in the map room towards the end of a day, when he would stride in from the field and ask to be told what news had come in while he was away. Frequently he would discuss the battle with one of the young lieutenant colonels who posted the situation on the war room map. He would tell where he had been, what he had seen or what some general or other in the line felt about the situation—or he would comment on what he thought the enemy would do next and what we might be able to do about it.

The General was always alert and responsive—but very quiet. He spoke with a low voice, almost shyly. He seemed never to be disturbed deeply. During the most crucial times of the Ardennes counteroffensive, for instance, his judgment and the clarity of his analyses seemed wholly unaffected by the violence of the storm which raged about him. It was like a kind of a miracle, like seeing the flame of a candle burning absolutely still and straight in a room that is full of eddying winds.

To the young officers in the Headquarters, even to men who had never spoken a word with him, Bradley seemed like a father who would keep all harm away so long as he was there. When he was away from Headquarters, they were almost frightened; when he came back, even though they only saw him striding through the hall, everything was all right again. Father had come home. The break-through would be held and the Germans beaten. Omar would know what to do.

I never heard him say a harsh word to anyone.

If General Bradley was calm in the Ardennes, he was just as unmoved when he was running the circus on the Rhine plains. If there was a twinkle in his eye, you had to use your imagination to see it. Sometimes, as he watched the long fingers of the armored columns stretch out, breaking away across the map, he would quietly ask that their progress be rechecked—just to be sure. More often he just grinned or made such laconic comment as, "Doing all right, aren't they?"

But at the morning briefings, when the whole staff gathered in the big map room and successive officers summarized the news of each passing twenty-four hours, spirits were high, and the conversation was fast and excited each morning before the General came in.

The day after Patton crossed the Rhine, the little reserve officer lieutenant colonel who did the liaison with the Third Army, and who had driven up the night before with the details of the crossing, opened the morning show by announcing with a straight face:

"Without benefit of airborne drop, without benefit of the United States *or* the British Navy and *not* having laid down the greatest smoke-screen in the history of modern war, and without *either* a three months' build-up of supplies *or* a whole extra American army, and with no preliminary bombardment, and finally without even a code word, Lieutenant General Patton and the Third United States Army crossed the Rhine yesterday." The colonel from Montgomery's headquarters, who had not yet heard whether Montgomery's assault had been successful, grinned sheepishly and the whole room giggled.*

Montgomery's big show had gone on schedule. The British and American assault forces had crossed together after a terrific bombardment from land and air. It was a sledge-hammer blow on the head of an already mortally wounded bull. This time Montgomery had put down his airborne troops only a few miles beyond the river bank; they were speedily relieved by the ground forces. It could now be said that even the British were across the Rhine.

The script of the next act in Montgomery's Ring called for the Ninth Army to advance along the north edge of the highly industrialized Ruhr area and *sit*. Neither Montgomery nor Bradley felt that the built-up Ruhr areas should be frontally attacked. The two other sides of the Ruhr—we would now hold the northern side and the Rhine side—were to be cut off by air power only. Thus, according to plan, the Ninth Army's role was to be that of a defensive blocker, rather than that of an offensive ball carrier.

The First Army, under Bradley, was to protect Montgomery's flank as far as the Rhine; the Ninth Army, under Montgomery's own command, was to protect the right flank of the British Army on the far side of the Rhine—and on the north, the Canadian Army, which had crossed with the British, was to secure Montgomery's left flank.

The spectacular role in the campaign was reserved for the British Army itself, which would now be given the opportunity of breaking its armor loose and racing for Hamburg. Monty would out-Patton Patton. After Hamburg, Berlin would come next—presumably with the American armies still providing only flank protection on the south.

* Part of Patton's joke on Montgomery never got played. Montgomery had made so much of the importance of an airborne landing on the far shore of the Rhine that Patton decided to mimic him by organizing an airborne operation with cub planes—carrying capacity: one soldier per plane. He was going to use his artillery observation planes and the liaison planes attached to his own headquarters and so air-ferry a battalion of infantry over. Third Army never got around to it.

This was the way the Big Finale *was* to have been.

The only trouble was that the star actor went up on his lines. The break-away armor did not break away. Emphatically, this is not said in criticism of the individual British armored brigades and their supporting divisions. British armor had fought bravely at Caen and Arnhem and had been rested and refitted until now they were ready to fight again. They crossed the Rhine on a bridge

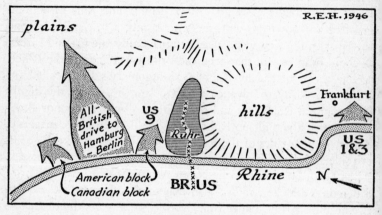

MONTGOMERY'S PLAN

that the Americans built for them and went out to do their job with dash and determination. But once again the terrain betrayed them. Off the soggy roads, their heavy Churchill tanks bogged down—and the roads themselves were one endless succession of blown bridges and road blockades where a few determined enemy paratroopers could hold up a brigade all day. Instead of dashing, the British armor had to creep out into the plains.

The acts in the northern and central Rings now joined—or, rather, the American act in Montgomery's show shot out of his Ring and landed in Hodges' and Bradley's center Ring. The joining was the strangest stunt, command-wise, in the whole war. The Ninth Army was under Montgomery's command on the north side of the industrialized Ruhr. The First Army, under Bradley's command, was breaking out from the Remagen bridgehead on the other, or south side of the Ruhr—that is, it was coming out on the *far* south side, through the Frankfurt gap, with a big hill mass sixty miles square between it and the Ruhr. Without prior plans (apparently) and with authorization only from God and history, Bradley suddenly took command of Simpson and his army—giving only the reason that it was, after all, an American army and he was using it only *beyond* the maximum objective Montgomery

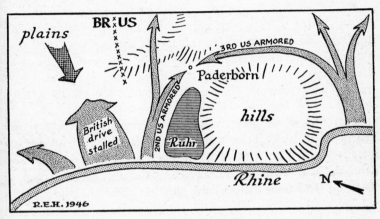

WHAT HAPPENED

had ordered it to take. Bradley did not issue written orders; he simply told Simpson what he wanted him to do, and Simpson did it.

What Simpson did was to turn the American 2nd Armored Division loose for a race to the back side of the great Ruhr area itself. Simultaneously, Bradley had Hodges take the wraps off the American 3rd Armored Division and run it one hundred and eighty miles around the southern side of the hill mass, and close the trap at a place called Paderborn. On April 1 the advance patrols of these armored divisions sighted each other west of Paderborn—in General Marshall's words, "cutting off the Ruhr and a large area to the south, in the largest pocket of envelopment in the history of warfare."

This was Bradley at his most brilliant—and slyest. On Bradley's advice, Simpson had literally run out from under Montgomery's command. There was nothing, however, that Field Marshal Sir Bernard, or the Supreme Allied Commander, or even the Prime Minister himself could say against it—first, because it worked and, second, because Simpson did not act until he had first doubled over backwards in fulfilling—and more than fulfilling—every possible requirement of his allies. He did all that the Field Marshal asked of him—first—and then encircled the Ruhr, too.

Where did Bradley get the supplies for his racing armies? The answer is that when a blitz comes off it uses very little matériel. It moves so fast that it hardly uses up the ammunition in the lead vehicles. And an armored column has the same ratio of gasoline consumption, on-the-loose to close-in-fighting, that a car has, cross-country driving compared to stalling around all day in traffic.

That this whole giant maneuver, although apparently spontaneous, had really been foreseen and planned in most careful detail—by Bradley with Simpson and Hodges—was easy to see from the battle map which showed how the 2nd and 3rd Armored Divisions had been maneuvered into just the right places from which each could take off for the encirclement.

The 2nd and 3rd Armored Divisions were each nearly 50 per cent stronger than the armored divisions which were activated after them. After the 2nd and 3rd Armored Divisions had been trained in the United States, the tables of organization for armored divisions were changed and all subsequent divisions were lighter by nearly five thousand men and much heavy equipment. The 2nd and 3rd Armored, then, with their extra gas trucks and additional heavy bridging equipment, were just the outfits for the big job they were called on to do. And it was no coincidence that they were in the right places when the time came for them to do it.

The argument by which Montgomery got the American Ninth Army under his command was his need for flank protection during his drive on Hamburg. After the encirclement of the Ruhr, this argument was too hollow for even the British at SHAEF to push, for Montgomery wasn't advancing fast enough to need any protection at all. So with the encirclement of the Ruhr, Omar Bradley not merely captured the single largest industrial asset the

Germans had left, and took over three hundred thousand prisoners, but he also got the Ninth Army back under his command —a fact which is a curious and conspicuous omission from General Marshall's official report.

More understandable is the former Chief of Staff's failure to emphasize the fact that the Russian's big offensive over the Vistula had taken the heat off the Western Front and allowed all these fine things to go on. He was writing about the home team. At Army Group it was a big day—in a quiet high level sort of way —when the Russian battle line edged on to the operations map on which we kept track of our own armies—and the two fronts became the two pincers in a single encircling movement. Now on a single wall map we could watch the interplay of the four great forces struggling for the Continent—the British and Americans, now under separate management; the Russians; and between them the Germans. They each seemed to us to reveal national characteristics—and it amused me to follow my own fantasy which was that nations made war very much the way they played games.

Certainly American tactics bore a close resemblance to a game of American football. We seemed always to be putting our head down and bulling our way into the center of the line—or executing some very fancy forward pass. Once the infantry had made a hole in the enemy's line, American armor seemed expert at broken field running.

In lots of ways the Americans' war was like football—it was a short month or two of training, a few plays worked out in advance, a hurried huddle to decide which to use, and then an unimaginative line buck or a tricky whirl around end to enjoy running in the open. It was a game played for cheers from the grandstand—or for a book in which to paste the clippings that have your name in them; a game in which people get hurt and a grim game which is taken seriously—but still a game.

On the other side of Europe we had watched the Russians for nearly a year. Surely the way they played was like chess. It was intellectual and it was ruthless. Chess is a game in which one sacrifices pawns and more important pieces—as part of a farsighted plan to gain an advantage. When a piece is taken, it is literally removed from the board. You could see the Russians' chess-like plans developing months ahead—and when they were a piece or two up on the Germans you knew, as in a chess game, that the end was inevitable—that the Russians would keep on pressing and trading pieces until their opponents had none left to trade.

Obviously the Russians regarded the battlefield as if it was a gigantic chessfield—they thought many moves ahead of the actual play, caused the Germans to shift constantly to meet their successively developing attacks, which ranged all over the board from the Baltic to the mouth of the Danube. The Germans never approached the Russians in understanding what was happening on the chessboard battlefield and appeared never to have had a really good comprehensive plan for the defeat of the Russians after the German generals ran out of their first pre-war staff studies.

The way the British on our left acted always made us think of cricket. Their game of war was interminable, characterized by feats of individual skill—and intermissions for tea.

The British played war as if it was cricket—in the right costumes and with good manners—and interminably.

The Germans? They lost the war because war wasn't a game of any kind to them. They took war *too* seriously.

So it sometimes seemed, looking at one end of the spectrum of war. I came to fewer positive conclusions, looking at the other end. About the viewpoint and attitude of the GI and the junior officers, in the whole campaign in Europe I never learned more than I knew in Africa. Certainly the average GI never learned what the war was all about from one end to the other, or really knew why he was fighting in Europe and for what. In his own mind, I think that to the end he fought simply to get it over with, and to get home. He fought to kill men who were trying to kill him. He also fought because he was told to fight—and because there was no respectable way out of fighting.

When he was at his best, the GI fought for a particular, individual officer whom he admired and loved, or for his friends, or for the group of which he was a member. The group he fought for most often was his squad or his platoon—less often his company or his battalion, sometimes even his division. He had a pride in the division of which he was a member but this was somewhat romantic and academic—he was rarely aware of who commanded the division he fought in, never knew where its headquarters were or what its other regiments or battalions were up to.

Commanding generals of divisions occasionally contributed some personal leadership to their men. Army commanders—even the much-dramatized Patton—directly influenced only the corps and division commanders who served under them. They were wholly mythical figures to the dough in the field.

Corps commanders, enormously important in any battle or campaign, were the forgotten leaders of the war. Neither the men they commanded nor the men who commanded them regarded corps commanders as permanent factors. The public never heard of them—and I would almost lay five dollars on the line for any city editor in the United States who could name me a single corps commander who fought in Europe, together with the vital statistics of his command—what army his corps served in when, and what divisions he commanded in what battles. Yet a corps commander, by his understanding and decisiveness, could make or break a battle. And so could how the doughs were feeling when they were called on to fight—whether they were tired and dispirited, or angry—usually at the Germans for some incident of purely local significance, such as an ambush baited with a white flag, or the shooting of prisoners of war by an SS outfit in the neighborhood.

All these things, from impersonal strategy to individual bad tempers, affected battles, and influenced the plot of them.

On the strategic high level, in the finale of the circus campaign, the plot was simply Bradley versus the Germans; in high level doings, Montgomery was licked.

But the British made good their reputation of never taking any licking as final. Throughout the winter and spring they continued to ask that Montgomery's appointment as ground force commander be considered, but just as continually they were turned down. They made one more effort to get control, but the effort rolled off the victorious American back like water off a duck's. The last British try came after Bradley, with the nicest timing of the war, had let go his drive to the east. He launched it at just the right moment to be sure that the encircled Germans in the Ruhr were worn down beyond power to hack their way out, and after just enough supplies had come up to the Americans' forward elements to make it certain that this time they could keep going until there was no more Germany.

It was at this juncture that Bradley made his most historic decision—perhaps his *only* really history-making decision. Until that moment, while he had won battles and even whole campaigns, Bradley had operated on a single strategic decision (to destroy the German Army) made by others and simply handed to him. In deciding, after the Ruhr, to join with the Russians on the upper Elbe rather than to drive for Berlin, Bradley made a decision, absolutely on his own, which the British, at least, believe was an historic decision which may yet leave its permanent mark on Europe.

Bradley was complete master of the situation again, in full command of the three armies that had now broken through the Rhine defenses and were free to exploit their victories. Analyzing the whole situation, Bradley felt that to take battered Berlin would be an empty military victory. (It was not known at the time that Hitler was to make his last stand there.) The German War Department had long since moved out, leaving only a rear echelon. The main body of the German War Department, including its priceless archives, had been transferred to the Thuringian Forest, and an advance echelon was already near Berchtesgaden to prepare for a possible last stand in the mountains. Berlin had been almost blown flat and was contributing practically nothing to the German war machine. The same Thuringian Forest that hid the German High Command was also known to be Hitler's secret factory area.

Moreover, Bradley felt that if he drove northeast from the Frankfurt gap to Berlin, he would be simply squeezing the German Army southward, forcing it to just where the Nazi party leaders might want it to be. In the south the German Army had ideal terrain for a last stand.

If, instead of staking all on Berlin, Bradley were to go due east, he knew he would meet the Russians on the Elbe somewhere between Magdeburg and Halle. With such a juncture, (1) Germany would be halved—sliced in two as decisively as Grant sliced the Confederate States when he sent Sherman through Georgia— and (2) by giving this job to the Ninth and First Armies, Bradley would still have the Third left to strike down through Austria, there to make a second joining with the Russians at Linz, thus isolating the Czechoslovakian stronghold.

Bradley was so completely the boss that Eisenhower had no choice but to approve—and forwarding Bradley's plan, he got approval back from Washington. I say Eisenhower "had no choice." This may be unfair. It is probable that Eisenhower not only agreed with Bradley's reasoning but was also by now emotionally disposed to back him. Eisenhower's sympathy for British arguments had never been quite the same since they had turned on him after the Ardennes. The Supreme Commander's principal American staff officers had become openly critical of Montgomery and, with the end of the war in sight, the big parades in New York and Washington were closer than they had been six months before.

This new attitude was reflected in a startling and, I am told, unsolicited cable which the Supreme Commander apparently felt the need to send to Marshall about this time. The staff in Washington was surprised by it because they were so unprepared for it and it was so violent. This message launched into a diatribe against Montgomery. It stated that the Field Marshal had been repeatedly and pointedly guilty of insubordination. Eisenhower stated flatly that he had several times given Montgomery more than enough to insure a victory and that, in each instance, Montgomery had failed him.

The Supreme Commander didn't stop with Montgomery. At long last he vented his feelings about Churchill and attacked Churchill for his direct dealings with Montgomery—his meddlesomeness and his continued interference outside of channels. For good measure, Eisenhower had then gone on the record that his Deputy Air Chief Marshal Tedder was useless to him except as an adviser on air matters. He said that a deputy who could pull his weight would have been a great help.

Either in this message or in another message to General Marshall, Eisenhower went off on another theme which also startled the generals who read it in Washington. In this message Eisenhower said that he was concerned about the verdict of history and wondered whether the right people would get the credit for the Allied victories in the field. He then plunged into extravagant praise of Omar Bradley, stating that in his opinion Bradley had the finest mind for strategy of any of the Allied leaders. This was "startling" because the emphasis was so thoroughly new for Eisenhower. Up until this message, the inference in the cables from Eisenhower had been that the strategy had been all his own. He had once actually said that the campaign was a group effort, indivisible into the efforts of individuals, and that no effort should be made to appraise the contribution of any one commander.

In this message Eisenhower did not stop with Bradley but continued by praising Hodges. He gave the Commanding General of the First Army credit for the aggressive exploitation which resulted in the seizure of the Remagen bridge. He did not mention that it had been against his own orders.

In ticking off Montgomery and patting Omar on the back, however, one gathered that Eisenhower was indeed concerned about the verdict of history and wished to write a few lines to set the record straight while he still had the pen in his fingers. Victory was now wholly assured and as the Supreme Commander, who was sure to get the elephant's share of the credit anyway, he could afford these gestures.

So with all these things in mind it *is* a little less than fair to say that when Bradley submitted his plan to cut Germany in two, rather than to race the Russians for Berlin, Eisenhower's approval was in any way forced. Bradley's plan gave him the opportunity to complete his gesture of self-assertion vis-à-vis the British and he promptly—and quite within his rights as the Supreme Commander —labeled the plan his own when he asked Washington's approval of it. And Washington did approve and the record in the Pentagon must certainly refer to the plan as the Supreme Commander's—

which I am sure suited Omar Bradley, for the fireworks it touched off were not the kind he felt at home handling.

Within twenty-four hours after Bradley's plan hit Washington and was read by the British representatives of the Combined Chiefs of Staff, the lid went right off Anglo-American relations. This time it blew off with such a bang that not even Montgomery's shrill voice could be heard in the din. The first roar came from the august British Chiefs of Staff in London. To hell with Montgomery—and to hell even with the Supreme Allied Commander! The blast went right over everybody's head in the field —right to the American Joint Chiefs of Staff in Washington.

The British blast was that Bradley had no right to drive due east to the Elbe but should join Montgomery to force the way to Berlin. The British Chiefs accused Marshall and the other American Chiefs of breaking a firm agreement to back Montgomery to take Berlin. The complaint charged the War Department and American Government with a specific act of bad faith.

The spirit of the reply which came boiling back from the American Joint Chiefs of Staff was in the idiom of General McAuliffe's famous "Nuts!" at Bastogne. The chapter and verse, spelled out, was that there had been no agreement, written, oral or implicit—and that there would be no change whatever in Bradley's plans, which promised the surest, quickest, most decisive total victory over the German State.

In general, both these papers, while sharp, were still in purely military language.

The next blast was neither pure nor military. Winston Churchill's hat sailed into the ring. He let go with a personal cable to Roosevelt in which the Prime Minister pulled out every stop. He recalled the days when England faced the Germans alone. He recited the debt the world owed England. He fought Dunkirk and the battle of London again. He changed his mood and accused Bradley of gambling with hundreds of thousands of British lives— presumably because Field Marshal Montgomery, still being held up by the remnants of the German paratroop army, needed more than flank protection to get to Berlin alone.

Mr. Churchill apparently said everything but the truth, which was that the military situation had nothing to do with it—Bradley being militarily one thousand per cent sound—but that, the quick defeat of Germany be damned, the British Empire wanted British troops in Berlin before the Russians got there and, en route, wanted British troops in Hamburg and Bremen, which it was feared the Russians might occupy and try to hold at the conference table.

President Roosevelt said NO—and the war and the President's life ended with very bad blood between the two great leaders of the Western powers. Roosevelt never forgave Churchill for his last message—and Churchill never forgave Roosevelt for turning it down.

Two American armies now raced for the Elbe. The Ninth Army beat the First Army to the river—and had its official heart broken when the Russians showed up later in the First Army's area for the historic meeting. There are wonderful stories about the meeting itself—and about the days that preceded it, when every officer who was not tied to his desk was roaming around in his jeep on the far side of the Elbe trying to find a Russian—and when there were so many American patrols over, also looking for the Ruskies, that our liaison planes kept mistaking their columns for Russian. It was a wonderful, gay, bollixed-up confusion.

Poor Georgie Patton! He never got to bathe in Brest; he had been cheated out of taking Paris by the Parisians; he had been beaten out of the first Rhine crossing by the Remagen bridge, and he had lost out on being first to meet the Russians—always a bridesmaid, but never a bride! Now he was ordered to turn his army around again, short even of the Elbe, and strike south across Austria. He did finally meet with the Russians at Linz, but by then the war was over.

In the advance to the south, one of Patton's tank commanders captured a bridge over the Danube intact. At that particular point the Danube was not too formidable a stream. The lieutenant colonel who took the bridge sent a telegram to the lieutenant colonel who had taken the Remagen bridge over the Rhine saying: "My bridge may not be as big as yours but the damn thing stands up."

Incidentally, this detachment's first official report to Third Army Headquarters was an object lesson on the thesis that whimsy and the military do not mix. The ciphered report read: "Have taken bridge over the Danube, and it's blue." At the Third Army message center a studious sergeant sniffed at the field commander's English and changed it, of course, to "Have taken a bridge over the Danube and it's blown." This message, in turn, was dutifully relayed back to Army Group Headquarters, and up on our map went the little red cross mark that meant the enemy had succeeded in destroying the first bridge Third Army reached on the Danube. Army Group engineers were still considering whether they should rush an extra bridge-building battalion to help the Third Army get over the Danube when the armored column was already fifty miles beyond it.

It was some time after the end of the war that British, American and Russian spheres of action in Germany were announced in the press. Actually they had been determined and formally agreed on at Yalta. They were posted on our Army Group maps. We had a special map just for their study, two months before the end of the war. The only uncertain lines were the borders of the French area, which was still under negotiation, France not having been represented at Yalta.

Bradley's plan, after striking through to the Elbe—which was deep in the territory which had been ceded to the Russians at the Yalta conference—was to retreat as soon as possible to within the American boundaries. Very practical considerations moved him. We had no sooner entered Germany than we began uncovering not thousands, but tens and finally hundreds of thousands of displaced persons and liberated prisoners of war, slave laborers and sufferers in concentration camps. An enormous percentage of them came from Russia and eastern Europe. These multitudes constituted a very grave problem to us. UNRRA's efforts were like a taxicab company's trying to move all of the commuters out of New York between five and seven. So Bradley ordered that all Russians, Poles and eastern Europeans migrate forward in the wake of the armies, planning to concentrate them in those Russian areas which he overran; then, drawing back, he would be able to give them back to the Russians without the expenditure of a gallon of gasoline or an hour's argument.

By the time Bradley reached the Elbe, Roosevelt was dead. One evening soon after Roosevelt's death, Churchill called Bradley personally, and going over Eisenhower's head asked him not to retreat from the Elbe—because he, Churchill, wished this area with which to bargain further with the Russians. Bradley said he thought that this might make trouble; it was sure to be misinterpreted, he felt, since the boundaries had already been formally agreed upon. Besides, it just didn't sound right. But by this time Bradley was through making decisions, one way or another, so he simply passed the problem back to the Supreme Allied Commander. Bradley felt that he was a military man and that Churchill's proposition was beyond his sphere.

At the time, Bradley had been given to understand that he was to remain in Europe after the surrender, to command the American occupation. Whether it was in any way related to this conversation with the Prime Minister is not known, but Eisenhower relieved Bradley of responsibility for the occupation shortly thereafter and the latter's career as a general in the field was over.

The actual end of the war could not have been more anti-climactic. As the three American armies broke the German State into pieces, the fragments surrendered. For the troops of the 12th Army Group, after the juncture on the Elbe, the show petered out. But one more story of the last days is worth telling, the story of the forcing of Czechoslovakia's Little Maginot Line which was once, before Munich, supposed to be stronger than its French prototype.

Czechoslovakia is ringed by such formidable mountains that, with the end in sight, Bradley hesitated to send troops against it. Patton's drive across the Danube into Austria by-passed Czechoslovakia, went south parallel to its borders. When Patton was well under way, troops of the neighboring First Army were moved down onto the Czechoslovakian border, not to attack but to protect Patton's flank and rear. There were still very strong German forces inside Fortress Czechoslovakia—thirty or forty divisions, as I remember it—and one full-strength Panzer division was known to be in the very hills Patton marched past. It was here, where the Germans were most formidable, that the Little Maginot Line was forced.

We saw the advance start as the daily reports from the American infantry there came in, and we watched the front lines inch up into the hills. Since no attack had been ordered, and our infantry seemed spread much too thinly to launch one, we were at a loss to understand the movement until some of our friends came back and reported what, they claimed, was happening up there. The infantry concerned had simply been in non-fraternizing country too long.

Czechoslovakia, by definition, was fraternizing country, and the sixty-five-dollar fines did not apply there. So, of a spring evening, the boys simply took off through the German lines to see whom they could find in the Czechoslovakian villages. This naturally involved some gun play, since the Germans on the road blocks and at the village strong points did not relish the competition. The whole thing was completely informal at first but after the GI's found that Czechoslovakia was okay, the younger officers began taking bigger and bigger patrols in.

If the commander of the German Panzer division had been a little less serious-minded, or been more sympathetic to spring, the American line might still have stayed reasonably in place. But when the first reports—that American patrols were reaching further and further into the fortified lines—got back to Panzer division headquarters, the Panzers lost their heads. They complained to high headquarters of the bold action of the Americans; it suggested that an attack in great force was imminent. The Panzers requested either heavy reinforcements or permission to retire to better positions. All this side of the picture we got later from captured documents.

By this time higher German headquarters were in no mood to fight; the Panzer division was told to fall back and the American front line patrols pulled their regiments and finally their divisions after them—and the first thing we knew, the whole front line was past the mountains and had debouched into the plains just this side of Prague. It was the Parisians who liberated Paris; you can credit the liberation of northwestern Czechoslovakia to the girls in the mountain towns, who were not only a lot prettier than the girls on the German side of the border but with whom it was also legal to hold hands.

At least that's how they told it to us.

The southward thrust of the Third Army was the last offensive directed by the 12th Army Group. After all the surrenders were in, Omar Bradley went back to Washington and was given the job of retrieving the Veterans' Administration's lost reputation. The officers who served with him worried about him in this job, because political in-fighting was not his kind of war and it looked as if he would be in for a lot of it.

Before V-J Day, there was a great deal of talk about which commanders would go to the Pacific. MacArthur picked Hodges, who was the gentlest of Bradley's army commanders. Many of Bradley's senior staff officers stayed abroad to study the military lessons learned in the campaign. The Headquarters itself went out of existence in August, almost a year to the day from the date it first took the field in command of troops.

The official surrender that ended the piecemeal surrenderings came on the seventh or eighth of May; we never knew quite which, even in Headquarters. So it had all happened in less than a year, in eleven months—the landings, the liberation of France, the storming first of the West Wall and then of the Rhine, and the disintegration of the Nazi State. In April and May, when we knew the end was close, we had time to look around in Germany and to take stock of what had been accomplished.

12 And Then There Was Peace

AFTER the Ruhr pocket had surrendered and the armies had begun their race for the Elbe, in the Plans Section of the 12th Army Group the war was over. There were four armies to be kept unscrambled and Patton's drive to the south to be directed, but the war was really over for us. Psychologically, it was like falling suddenly through a door against which one had been straining. Even though we had known the hinges were giving, we were quite unprepared for the collapse, and without an obstacle to press against everyone was off balance for a little while—and psychically confused.

In the first place, so intensely had everyone concentrated on the defeat of the enemy armies that for a long time it had seemed as if there had never been any other kind of life. In the second place, our kind of war-making had always had a kind of unreality about it. No matter how often we made trips into the field, or how close the war came to us, it tended to become an intellectual game, played against the German General Staff over there. On the staff level, one got to feel the enemy staff—its personalities and the way it thought and how it reacted—the way a doughboy in a foxhole gets to feel the Kraut infantrymen in the line opposite him and acquires a sense of intimacy in competition. My particular boss and I tried to get out in the field as often as possible to keep in touch with the realities of terrain and weather and the problems with which the troops had to contend. Some other officers in the Planning Section disapproved of even this. They felt it warped one's judgment to come too close to one part of the problem. It aroused emotions which you were better off without when you were playing military chess.

In the early beachhead days, when I had just come back to headquarters from a brief adventure in the line, the physical realities of war had been very close to me. But by the time we crossed the Rhine, the foxhole days were a long way behind me and, try as I would to feel the impact or remember the meaning of war, these things slipped away and the struggle became more and more a contest in wit and intelligence. So when the battle of wits was won, I remember feeling a sense of shock when I got out of the headquarters and looked around me—shock, really, just at finding the world still there—the world of people who suffered and were happy, who were hungry or were eating food, who were doing and feeling real things and were not just living with red and blue symbols on a map.

The soldier in the line, I think, felt the exact opposite of these emotions when the hostilities ceased. His world had been off balance on the physical side and he was amazed when he came up out of the foxhole to read in the newspapers that there had really been some sense to the whole business, some kind of plan, some purpose.

In headquarters we had lived for months in an intellectual world, concentrated on the intellectual side of war. We forgot—this is an overstatement, but qualitatively sound—the human side.

But the man who read the map and the man who crept through a field with his rifle at ready shared one thing: by the end of the war each had concentrated for so long on the immediate problems that confronted him that he had lost sight of the war, a war that was larger even than a theater in which a whole campaign was fought, the Big War that was a struggle to the death between two worlds. It was coming out of the map room and going out into that struggle that was the biggest shock of all at the end of the war.

After we had crossed the Rhine, EAGLE TAC Headquarters stopped at Wiesbaden, just north of Frankfurt, and then went on to Bad Wildungen, which is a morning's drive to the east. It was there that we ran out of plans to make and lifted our eyes from

the map and went out into the spring sunshine to see for ourselves. We were deep in Germany now and a great curiosity filled
me to see what it was like there. For years before the war, what it
was really like in Germany had been a preoccupation—something
to study and to worry about at first and, finally, to feel very
strongly about, but only academically because one hadn't been
there and one's information was second-hand information. What
was it really like in the State that had threatened civilization, that
was the cause of our being there at all?

Coming out of the unworldly preoccupation of the map room
and running head on into the realities of why we were at war at
all and what it was all about was a huge experience—for me, one
of the greatest of the whole war.

There is no substitute for having seen a concentration camp.
You may think you know how you feel about Fascist philosophy
or the Nazi party and its corruption of the German people but
unless you've seen a concentration camp you understand with
your mind or your heart but not with your whole soul. It isn't
enough to have seen where a concentration camp *was*—or to have
visited one after it has been cleaned up, or even when the bodies
are still there but after the huts and the rags have been burned and
the stench has blown away. You have really, I think, to have
come on one when it was alive and still had authority over the
men and women in it. After the guards are gone and the gates
opened, the authority of the system that created it hangs over it
for a little while like the stench; then it too goes and some of the
meaning of it is gone with it.

The guards had gone only the day before when I got to the
camp at Landsberg. The doughs had let the inmates beat one or
two stragglers to death with their bare hands but the rest had
gotten away.

The installations at Landsberg were a group of camps. Each was
a rectangular strip of ground about a city block in size, surrounded by a neat fence of barbed wire circled by two bands of
copper wire on heavy insulators. These carried high voltage
charges. These simple pens stood in fields of soft green grass and
lovely pine woods rose behind them. They were on the edge of
picturesque suburbs. Highways ran a few yards away and one of

the camps was near a crossroad beyond which the main track of a railway passed. There were no walls, no towers with armed guards, no machine guns. If you have seen even a corpse from Landsberg you will appreciate that these barriers to escape were unnecessary. The men and women who survived there could not normally have pushed over a five-year-old child.

Inside the wire in each camp there was only one building that rose above the ground. It was a shed, one story high, housing a kitchen. The inmates lived and died near by in shelter-like contrivances consisting of a gabled roof covering a ditch or trench. The trench ran the full length of the roof's fifty or sixty feet. The trench with the roof over it thus made a lightless corridor in which an average man could just stand, stooping. The ground on either side of the trench, stretching under the eaves, was covered with filthy straw. Here perhaps one hundred people lived—sleeping on the straw on the ground, under the eaves of the roof. The trench corridor between the two long continuous sleeping places thus made was three or four feet wide. This was the living quarters. Men and women sitting on the foot of their sleeping place could let their legs dangle into the trench. If they were strong enough they could sit upright there.

In these shelters they ate and slept and performed their bodily functions. The toilet facility consisted of a single large galvanized iron bucket about as big as a good-sized garbage pail. It stood at the end of the building by the structure's only entrance—a low door—the ground in front of which was scraped away so that one could get in and out. The roof was of boards covered with sod.

These structures looked very neat and symmetrical from a distance. Lanes of them were set in regular rows. The inhabitants climbed out and queued up by the kitchen to have their bowls filled with what food was given them and they took this food back to the dwelling places to eat it. After that, those who were able to walk were marshaled in the yard and marched out to putter at road work or some other civic improvement. There was nothing secret or hidden away about the camps at Landsberg and, of course, everyone who lived in Landsberg not only knew all about them but passed them daily on the roads and, if they were interested, stopped to watch the inhabitants working amongst them in the town.

The inhabitants of the concentration camp wore rough cotton pajamas with broad vertical stripes of a faded bluish purple. These costumes were all the clothes they had, and even these seemed in short supply, for many of the garments were so tattered and torn that the wearers were more naked than clothed. It was snowing the May morning we got there.

At the first camp we visited there were many corpses lying about—some with their heads bashed in, some with their throats cut with knives and some dead of neat bullet wounds. But on the majority of the bodies there were no signs of physical violence. The doorways to most of the huts were charred where there had been fire.

There were two or three hundred corpses in all. Most of them had been gathered that morning by some local Germans whom the infantry had rounded up, and these corpses were laid in rows just inside the wire beyond which the Germans had begun to dig a mass grave. Even with the fresh cold air with the snow in it, and the pine woods so close to filter it, the air hurt with the odor of the dwelling places. The corpses however did not smell at all. They did not bear the least resemblance to dead soldiers on a battlefield. There was no fat on them to decompose.

The memory of a concentration camp that is searing is not of the living conditions in them, or of the crematories—Landsberg, too, had its furnaces—or of gruesome things like the room in which they cracked the jaws and broke up the teeth of the dead to get the gold fillings. These things are so terrible that they are simply bizarre.

The searing memories are of the naked bodies—the bodies that are only bones with flesh drawn tight over them, and the indecency of the private parts of males and females in such settings. The bodies are such loathsome caricatures of human beings that if ever you have seen them you are repelled by the sight of your own leg, because in its shape it reminds you of one of those legs. It is a degenerating experience. It makes you hate human beings who are made of human flesh, when you have seen flesh like that. It makes you hate yourself and feel ashamed of your human body.

As we stood looking down at the naked corpses, soldiers coming by stopped and looked, peering through the wire. The stocky round-faced German men and women who lived in Landsberg, walking by on the road, did not pause. There was nothing new about these dead ones to them. These people were part of their lives.

We went from the first camp where everyone was dead to another where most of the inmates were still alive. The alive were infinitely more terrible, with their running sores and their coughs and the mad way some of them waggled their big bony heads on their scrawny necks. One boy ran up to us waving an arm over his head in a gesture of joy. He danced with joy and kept waving. Not a muscle in his face moved and his blue eyes were like marbles.

We found a cook who had almost enough flesh on him to be human. He spoke very good English which he said he had learned in Prague before the war; he had been planning to come to America. He told us about the last days of Landsberg. He said everyone in the concentration camp knew a lot about what was going on—not only in their own camp but all over Germany. As people were shifted from camp to camp, news circulated. When the word came that the Americans were near, the whole camp had been put to disposing of the dead. A great many people died there every day.

First the corpses were taken to a railway siding to be shipped to another camp where the facilities for burning them, apparently, were better. Then the Americans were reported still closer. The commandant ordered the camps themselves burned. Those who were out working were taken back in the middle of the day and told to go into their huts. Then the guards came and attempted to set fire to the straw so that all the inmates would be roasted.

There was no way out of each hut except through that one low door. The bodies we had seen clubbed, cut and shot were of the few with enough vitality and instinct to survive, to come through the flames and to try to escape. The burning of the huts had been only a partial success. The straw in the huts had been so soaked in filth and was so damp from the bodies that lay on it that it would not burn. But the straw near the doors, where it was a little drier, had smoldered enough to suffocate most.

The burning program was still incomplete when the Americans had reached the outskirts of the town. An occasional shot from a tank could now be heard. The commandant and all but a few of the guards left in haste. The ones who were beaten to death had stayed behind a little too long and the first soldiers had come to the gates and trapped them inside. Then the skeletons had risen to mob them. There was still a little anger and resentment left in the skeletons, even though almost every other emotion had been drained away.

In the camp where there were survivors, there was a hospital. It was a wooden barracks with two tiers of bunks with straw in them, and most of the bunks had two patients in them. In some, one of the two patients had already died. There was what was left of a doctor in charge, an inmate who had been preserved so that the suffering of his fellow inmates might be prolonged a little longer.

The men and women in the Landsberg camps could have been easily killed simply by not feeding them for a few days. They did not contribute to the wealth of the Reich, alive, because they were so feeble that the work they did was inconsequential. They actually cost the State money. Able-bodied guards had to look after them, and skilled electricians minded the high voltage lines, and someone had to collect the garbage they were fed. The thing that none of the Americans could get over was why all these thousands of people had been kept alive at all. It was not until you fitted them into the rest of Germany that you understood.

The really sinister phenomena in the Germany we found beyond the Rhine were not the concentration camps at all. These were like symptoms of a dreadful, obscene insanity. The sinister phenomenon was not the concentration camp but the labor battalion stockade.

In every little town beyond the Rhine—and near the factories on the Rhine itself as well—there were, according to the size and importance of the town and the factory, big or little fenced-off areas in which the men and women who ran the plants lived. They were not really guarded; there might have been a sentry or two, but no more. Sometimes the wire around them was not even barbed. They did not live in roofed-over ditches; they had frame shacks not unlike the worst of our war emergency structures. They lived comfortably in them, usually a whole room to a good-sized family. They had food for meals—with just the right amount of calories to get them through a day's work when they were herded into the plant, and to get them back again, still leaving them enough energy to sit about and talk in the evenings—enough even to breed.

Every little town had such stockades and in them there were the people of all the nationalities of Europe. They were peopled by a careful selection of the ignorant, the timid and the accommodating. There was enough human being to them to respond even to piece work incentives. For so much more work, they might be allowed to spend so much time outside the wire around their immediate dwelling, only being required to stay inside the wire that surrounded the whole settlement. They might even get more food, to give them more energy to do still better. These were the slave people—the millions upon millions upon millions who had been culled out of occupied Russia and Czechoslovakia and disintegrated Poland and Norway and Belgium and France and all the other enslaved countries.

As a vital piece of machinery in the creation and management of this slave state, the concentration camp played a vital part. The concentration camp fulfilled two functions. First: it was the place into which to drain away the educated, the intelligent and the potentially rebellious—the place to put away the ones who had too strong wills or too strong souls to make it possible for them to accommodate themselves to the new order. Second: to those who were borderline cases, it served as the "or else."

The inmates at Landsberg and all the other camps *had* to be kept alive, and the story of what had happened to them *had* to be circulated, so that the boy or girl, or the man or woman, who had contrary ideas about living and dying in the labor stockades would know what would happen to him if he tried to put his ideas into practice.

There are many millions in Europe, particularly in eastern Europe, who are only a few generations from a serfdom in which life-long labor in superstition and ignorance was the accepted order. On this base the Germans had built—displacing these from the villages, slums and ghettos of Europe, breaking what ties they had with soil or homeland. But first they had to root out the potential trouble-makers from amongst them—the too literate or the too vital—and those who were left became the great slave labor pool from which the factories drew their working hands and from which even the German housewife could get her kitchen maid and her cowherd.

The part that antisemitism played in this was also apparent after you'd been in Germany a little while. Antisemitism was a latent prejudice surviving from old antagonisms, which, when stirred up, operated as a kind of primer to the whole great operation. Since millions were to be enslaved, it was sound policy to start by enslaving the currently least popular. After all, the idea of enslavement had to be made acceptable to a people who had been "corrupted" by Christian doctrine. Having established the principle by enslaving Jews, the practice could then be expanded —until all Germans came to look on it as their right to have other human beings slaves to them.

Qualified sociologists can explain to you the process by which the moral degeneration of central Europe was achieved. Here I'm simply saying that when you got there you actually saw the process working, with your own eyes—as you can see the workings of the gears in the glassed-in model of an automobile engine at a motor show. The Jews, for instance, had long since ceased to be a factor in German life. They remained only as a horrible example, kept alive in concentration camps to show *you* what would happen if *you*—whatever your background, race, religion, or nationality—stepped out of line.

This quality of seeing how it had happened was striking, the first month inside Germany. Perhaps you can still see it there, but I expect it needs more perception now. When the American armies broke across the Rhine and the German State collapsed, and you went from town to town and city to city and saw how Germany worked, you really needed no perception at all. You needed simply to be curious. The system had been smugly successful for at least a short generation and it was not hidden but advertised.

It was advertised so vigorously, in fact, that it was all a little bewildering to an army of Americans who had by and large not the least idea why they were there except that there had been a big excitement and they had been drafted and everybody told them they were heroes now—Cinderella heroes who when the clock struck twelve, if they were still alive, would go back to their chores at home, and if they didn't go peacefully would be called malcontents and given apples to sell on the corner.

The tortured bodies in the concentration camps, the doltish faces that grinned from the labor stockades and the camps where the displaced hordes were gathered—these things seemed only to confuse most of the American soldiers, who couldn't digest the paradox of the good-looking young German soldier he met on the field (whom he admired because the German was good at his own trade of soldiering) and the German who looked just like him who guarded the concentration camp. To some of us, the saddest waste of the war seemed the waste of the opportunity the Americans had to learn what they had done in breaking the armed force of Fascism in central Europe.

Even thoughtful Americans had gone to war with only a secondhand or a presumptive case against the Fascist philosophy. Some journalists, a popular President, a few college professors and a politician or two had told them what Fascism meant—and which way the road led that began with antisemitism. But the evidence is that not many Americans *really* believed them. Certainly few really believed what they were told had happened to Germany after only ten years of Fascism—few put any real stock in the fact that the Germans had created a true slave state and were bent on molding the world in its image.

I recall a conversation when the 12th Army Group was in Bad Wildungen, which is in central southern Germany. There were a dozen of us sitting around the table after mess—all officers on General Bradley's staff. Two of the colonels were professional soldiers, the others of us had been lawyers, engineers, brokers—all college men, well educated and prosperous. It was the evening after several of us had visited a concentration camp. All of us had been in Germany a month or more. The first curious thing was that half the group still did not believe concentration camps really existed. They put the three who had just visited one on the stand, as it were, and cross-questioned them on detail after detail—were the young boys really castrated?—how?—did you see the scars yourself?

When they became finally convinced that concentration camps really happened, the talk passed on to the subject of labor camps —and the streams of the homeless whom we passed every day on the road. The almost unanimous opinion was that these men and women were no better than the tasks to which the Nazis had assigned them. Unmistakably, they were the stupid ones. The day before, we had watched a group of several thousand French. Everyone agreed they seemed a different breed from the French we had known in France itself.

It seemed to occur to no one, at first, that that's why they had been selected—because they were ignorant and tractable—and that you could not draw conclusions as to what Russians and Czechs and Poles, for instance, were like either—on the basis of observing the Russians, Poles and Czechs whom the Germans had chosen for their slaves. Then someone remarked on how much more intelligent the faces of people in the concentration camps seemed, even emaciated and tortured—how much more intelligent than the run of the mill displaced person. But no one, at first, seemed to put these two facts together.

The mood of depression I experienced then comes back to me as I write these things. I have no great conviction that we really learned the lesson we paid so much to learn. Yet the fact is that when we broke down the doors of Germany and overran the country, we saw the whole social political scheme for the degradation of man revealed, naked and unashamed. The suppositious second-hand case against Fascism that had been preached to the Americans in vain—when Fascism was enslaving Spain, for instance—was not merely "in general confirmed," it was specifically and dramatically documented. What we found testified chiefly to the inadequacy of words to describe it. The physical manifestations were all there and the moral degeneration was almost universal.

Any soldier in the field learns a little about this moral degeneration, as his standards change when he finds himself really cold and hungry, and really frightened. Yesterday he was kindly; now he would kill in fear. Yesterday food was only part of the background of his life; now he would steal it. Presently the soldier won't be frightened any more and the chow truck will come up and it will be like a bad dream. But in Germany fear and hunger were organized into permanence—and to impose them, greed and anger and pride were encouraged.

Perhaps the doughboy got more out of the experience of serving in Germany than the officers I knew. But I doubt it. Corruption can be contagious, and if I had to bet I'd bet that the doughs in the Army of Occupation absorbed more of German standards than the Germans did of ours. But only a few thousands are involved. The overwhelming majority of two million Americans who visited the Continent of Europe in the course of World War II were much too psychically bewildered, and homesick, and uncomfortable, to be impressed by anything. They simply came to dislike all foreigners—whether these foreigners were British, French or German. They hated foreigners the way all homesick people hate foreigners, I guess; foreigners and foreign ways.

It's a great pity that they got no more out of seeing Europe set free, if only because they were entitled to such a great satisfaction which was denied them by their lack of understanding. That satisfaction is to have been part of the army that broke the force that held the horrid Fascist State together—broke it bravely and brilliantly, and against what were in the beginning heavy odds. Amidst all this talk of "losing the peace" someone should tell the boys who fought the war that they won that much of it. They won a hell of a lot.

Someone should also tell them that there was a reason why they went to France, a reason really good enough to die for. The reason was the Fascist idea, which came so close to prevailing and would have prevailed—but for them. It was there complete in central Europe, and I'm sure also in Japan. If the Fascist states had prevailed—and but for the armed force of America, they would have—for without us the Chinese, the British and the Russians could not have stopped them—if the Fascists had beaten us, as surely as night follows day their corruption would have spread over the whole world.

Some people have asked me, in the dizziness of the early atom age, if after all we really won the war at all. The answer is "You're damn right we did." We broke a great and evil thing by force of righteous arms, even if very few of us knew what we were doing, even if most of the fighting was not for freedom but in a kind of P.S. 36 versus P.S. 37 spirit of competition for competition's sake. The American Army, with all the free people of the world its allies, did a great and truly glorious thing in breaking the Wehrmacht which stood guard over the labor stockades and the concentration camps and the system of which they were the blood and sinew. The Americans also earned for themselves a fine object lesson, if they will give it even five minutes' thought, in what it means to a people to abandon the fight for the dignity and independence of *all* men, and to substitute for the many, the interests of a few.

PART THREE

AND NOW WHAT'S THE SCORE?

13   Lessons Learned

WORLD WAR II was the first ever fought by Americans in really intimate association with an allied country. Our experience in World War I was too brief to count—we came into the war too near its conclusion and we renounced our alliances, backing away from the League of Nations, too soon thereafter. It was a tourist's adventure in working with other nations. Not until World War II were we to form a real partnership with another nation, an intimate association in which we actually met and solved at least our military problems as partners.

With our partners, we won the greatest war in history. The question now raised is how to prevail in peace. This time we cannot go off alone and sulk but must solve our problems in peace as in war, in intimate partnership with other nations.

What did we learn about handling an international partnership in war that is applicable to the problems of handling one in peace?

Our only really useful experience was with the British. Our alliance with the Russians was not a real partnership. It was, if you like, a conspiracy in the restraint of Germans. President Roosevelt met with the chief of the Russian State only twice during the war; we had no executive or administrative combined staff work with the Russians and, until it was all over, we were always separated from them physically by our common enemy. The Chinese, too, we dealt with at a distance—and the contributions to the war effort which the smaller allies or the larger occupied countries could make was not great enough to pose major problems in management. But our alliance with the British *did* involve large enough problems, and *was* intimate enough, to be accurately described as an international partnership—and as such it was the first into which we as a nation had ever entered.

The lesson we learned in fighting a war with the British for a partner was that they wanted their own way and were prepared to fight for it, using every means at their disposal to succeed.

We learned that even after we reached a nominal agreement with the British in an international conference, if this agreement did not please them—if they felt they had been forced into it against their will—they would do their level best to nullify it.

We learned a great deal about the way the British mind works —that the British always assume they are right, and will seek to arrange facts to prove it. We learned that they are persistent and stubborn about that—if they do not get the answer they want the first time, they will continue to gnaw at the problem of how to get their way.

We also learned that they believe in themselves so thoroughly —are so sure that wisdom and justice are on their side—that honorable men amongst them see nothing wrong in distorting the truth and in withholding information and otherwise conniving against us, in order that their national will shall prevail. They see nothing wrong in individually dishonest acts so long as these are committed in the name of patriotism—as a spy who steals a paper for his country is not a thief but a hero.

We learned that the British stick together, that in a crisis they will submerge their personal differences to present a common front.

We learned that they are farsighted, looking to their future welfare beyond the present.

What a lot we learned! After we came to understand their language and had mastered their idiom and gotten used to their foreignness, we learned, in brief, that they were like us.

The paragraphs above are "lessons learned"—a reasonably thoughtful selection of those elements of British character which most clearly and importantly influenced our wartime dealings with the British Empire. Try them on what you know of the

Russians—or the Chinese, or the French—and see if you do not begin to suspect that they would be equally applicable.

So the first lesson learned was that a nation—any nation—looks after its own interests first and sees nothing unethical in how it goes about it.

As to the little differences, there weren't many, when you knew all the facts. Take our difference over The Master, Field Marshal Sir Bernard Montgomery:

Montgomery was a general we did not like. We found him arrogant to the point of bumptiousness—bad mannered and ungracious. Let there be no doubt whatever about it: that's exactly the way the British found him too. In speaking of their leaders, the British are even freer with their criticism than we. They were outspoken critics of their military leaders and no man was personally more distasteful to them than Monty. There were scores of stories current in London about his bad manners—beginning with the snub the King was alleged to have given him. Monty is supposed to have been boasting to the King of the prowess of "my troops"; to which the King's answer was, "But I thought they were *mine*." (If this is not funny to you, remember it's a British joke; *they* think it's funny, and it puts Monty in his place.)

Monty got where he did—had the solid backing of every department of the British Government—simply because they felt that he was the only horse they could win with at the time. After a long record of uninterrupted defeats on land, Monty's name had become associated with their first victory—and a terribly important one—at El Alamein. Most informed Britishers believe that the credit for this victory—the credit for the strategy and tactics—was Alexander's. But Monty had led the troops and Monty had gotten the press. In Africa, Montgomery appeared to be to Alexander very much what Patton was to Bradley in Europe; he executed, and was given the credit and the press for, his superior's strategy.

The British were not at all sure that Monty would make a big-time general when they put him in command of ground forces for OVERLORD. But it was important to them that they continue to get the press. They foresaw quite clearly that they were in danger of being overshadowed by the size and weight of the

American forces and, for their purposes, they had to have a man in command who could stay in the headlines. Monty was that man. To back him up, they felt they had plenty of brainpower in London—in the Imperial General Staff—provided he could continue to keep his grip on the imagination of the world, to play the part of the dashing, invincible leader.

So we did not like Monty personally—and neither did the British.

Presently we came to the conclusion that in addition to being a boor, he was also a very bad general. So, I am quite sure, did the British. In intimate circles they were scornful. But they had put their money on Montgomery. They let it ride. Although once or twice they contemplated bringing the sounder but less colorful Alexander up from Italy, in the end they decided to bluff it out with what they had—and to use their wits in London and Paris to get for Montgomery the command of such an overwhelming force that he could not lose. Moreover, never forget, until and including the very last days of the war, the Balkan objectives were regarded as the most important in the Empire strategy. Therefore, Italy was the logical place to leave their best field commander, Alexander— who sure enough paid off by wangling enough stuff out of the Allied effort to continue his campaign all the way up the Italian boot—and in the end broke loose over the North Italian plain to get at least as far as Trieste.

So, adding it all up, we did not even have a difference with the British over Monty's ability. He was The Master to his staff, but the British Government had no illusions about him. The British simply remained loyal to him because it was in the Empire's interest to keep him out in front. The whole prestige of British arms was involved, so the position was reasonable—even though it cost a battle or two in the meantime.

It was reasonable of them, also, to have preferred the Balkans to the Channel route; it served their long-term interests, as they understood them, to get to the Balkans before the Russians. This was the secret-that-was-no-secret of their preoccupation with the Balkan route to victory.

It was just as reasonable—from their point of view—that they should conspire endlessly to get American troops under their command and to increase their share of the sinews of war that Americans were providing. If Brazil had raised a larger army than it did—one Brazilian division fought in Mark Clark's army—we would probably have thought it right, proper and natural to have seen to it that it fought under our command, regardless of how the Brazilians felt.

The figure is stronger than that of a Brazilian army fighting under an American general. The British have for generations commanded colonial armies and an important part of their attitude towards the American forces—at the beginning of the war at least—was that the Americans, in all but the name, were "just another colonial army." Moreover, on the Continent, in all the wars that have been fought since the British became a first-rate power, they have always had leadership and intelligence rather than brute force to contribute to an alliance. Other men have had to fight their battles because characteristically they engaged in wars which required more men than they had to fight them with.

The British did not feel they were doing anything wrong when they assumed they were The Boss; they were only playing a role they were long accustomed to play.

As to their spiritual title to leadership, they certainly felt their strength should count as ten because their heart was pure. In war everyone is always sure his heart is pure—but the British were doubly certain of it because they felt they had saved the world by fighting on alone after the collapse of France. Thus, in their minds, we actually *owed* them the leadership of the balance of the war.

So the British fought for what they believed in, with a courage to their convictions which excused sharp practices—and which they probably would have not felt needed any excusing, even if their moral case had been less strong—because sharp practices and looking out for one's self are still the accepted and established morality in international relations.

To repeat it: the first lesson we learned was really that the British, when you understood the whole problem, reacted very much as we—or the Russians, the French or Chinese—might have acted in the same situation. They simply reacted as a national group dealing with other national groups.

The second lesson learned was that, when we knew what we wanted, collectively we were strong enough and smart enough to get it. The British did *not* succeed in imposing their will on us, and the war was won more or less on our terms. The war was won by frontal assault on the Continent of Europe without regard to possible disturbance to the postwar balance of power in Europe.

If the British had succeeded, the war would have been won a very different way. Fought from Mediterranean bases, further from American sources, it would have been prolonged. As it was, many thousands of Americans suffered and died in Italy, primarily to secure British interests in the Mediterranean. If the main effort had been made there, many thousands more would have died simply to arrange the map of Europe the way Great Britain wanted it arranged. This much is sure. Beyond this, there is at least the speculation that we could not have won the war at all short of blasting the Continent apart with atom bombs.

If Hitler had had the summer and fall of 1944 and the winter and spring of 1945 in relative peace, no man can say that his dream of keeping us off the Continent with secret weapons might not have been fulfilled. That is simply speculation. All we *know* is that at the time we entered the continent of Europe over the Normandy beaches (a) German industrial production was still rising sharply, and (b) the head of the German State believed that he would win the war with secret weapons.

We know these things, surely—and we also know that our drive across the Channel broke up the German State and irreparably disrupted Hitler's plan. We know that the shock of the Allied landings in Normandy was so great that it precipitated an attempted assassination and coup d'état little more than a month after the landings, and that it took Hitler from then until late fall simply to reorganize his military command and to collect his forces after their defeat in France. And we know that it was Bradley's insistence on continuing the drive through the winter that denied the Germans even the benefit of a respite behind the West Wall fortification. The devil was on Hitler's heels from the minute the first doughboy landed in Normandy.

But whether or not it would have been fatal to have left Hitler in undisputed possession of Europe for another year, it is still incontrovertible—it is written in blood in the Apennine Mountains of Italy—that a main effort in the Balkans would have been infinitely more costly, and that this cost, incurred for British political objectives, would have been paid in principal part by American lives and dollars.

And now we have come to The Peace, and what is the application of the lessons we learned to the problem of The Peace? To understand what's happening, it is not necessary now to study the communiqués carefully, to sift and weigh and put together the orders and directives, to see through the veil of military censorship, to calculate and analyze. What is happening is written clear in every day's headlines. What is written clear is that our British partner is still trying to stack the cards so that when they are dealt the Empire will win. The British are stacking them persistently and skillfully so that it will seem to our interests to preserve the British Empire intact and to align ourselves with the British against the Russians where their interests conflict, not only in the Balkans but anywhere else.

Once Hitler's Third Reich was given a major role to play in the balance of power on the continent of Europe. Hitler's Third Reich is no more. We Americans are now being offered, at as favorable rates as can be devised, the exceptional privilege of taking the place of the Third Reich in the British "balance of power" policy on the Continent—and, for nothing, we have the further privilege of maintaining the British power and prestige in the Orient by force of arms. If we do not want to fire the guns in the Orient, all we need do is to give the British and the Dutch the tools and let them finish the job.

All this is according to form. The men who run the British Empire are simply looking after their own interests, and the fairness or unfairness of how they go about it, or whether this does or doesn't suit us, is beside the point. Nor does it necessarily mean that the British will succeed. It is held to be an Irish point of view that all world strategy is a British racket. This is, of course, ridiculous. The world is still a big place and the British must always temper their objectives to what is practical. But that they seek constantly to influence world strategy in such a way that the Empire benefits is not only beyond dispute but is also quite reasonable.

Nor is that fact any reason for journeying to the false conclusion that the British are either a super-race or a gang of bastards. They are simply a group of people who are looking out for themselves. They are simply continuing to act in peace as they acted in war.

When the Labor Party took over from Winston Churchill, nothing changed. Why should people have expected it to? Is Mr. Attlee supposed to be less of a British patriot than his predecessor? While the British may differ amongst themselves as to how their national income should be divided, no one wants the Empire's income as a whole cut. British foreign policy is directed to support the income and security of British subjects. Could it be otherwise? Like any other bargainer, in dealing with the rest of the world the British Empire may trade one advantage for another—or may even be forced by the market to take less than it wanted—as it was forced by the position and will of its American partner to take its victory over Germany in northwestern Europe rather than in the Balkans. But the asking price will always be what the British want—and the deal will always be described to the purchaser as a bargain. Who would expect it to be different?

14 Lessons Applied

DURING the war our objectives were not synonymous with those of the British. Neither are the things we each want in peace. This is not really a difficult thing to prove. As in war we both wanted victory but sought to win it different ways, so after victory we both want peace—but neither of us is content with just any kind of peace, and each of us wants our peace in a different form.

There is no need to go into the long inventory of traditional conflicts. We have conflicts of opinion on policy in Palestine, in India, in the Dutch East Indies, in China, all over the world—but no one difference is crucially important. Together they simply make it clear that not one but two sets of interests exist, British interests and American interests, and that these interests are not synonymous. The traditional conflicts themselves are like the small engagements that together make up a great battle or a campaign. It may not be important that any one of them is won but if too many are lost, the enemy has successfully imposed his will on us.

Today, however, there is one conflict in which the British Empire is engaged which *is* crucial, one difference of sufficient magnitude to lead to a third World War. It is a conflict not with us but between the British Empire and the Soviet Republics. Setting aside their "minor" differences—in the Middle East, say—the main issue between them is whose politics—whose social order—shall prevail in the Europe that separates the United Kingdom from the steppes of Russia. Here Great Britain and the Soviet

Union have a solid, honest and thoroughly understandable difference between them. Depending on one's personal orientation, it is possible to be entirely sympathetic with either point of view. Leaving ultimate wisdom out of the discussion—and sticking exclusively to the universally accepted principle of the right of a nation to defend itself, it is beyond dispute that whether the countries in Europe are in the British or in the Russian social order is a matter of prime concern to both.

The British have only recently had a bloody experience with long-range missiles launched from across the Channel. No defense was ever found against these long-range weapons—specifically, the high altitude V-2 rockets. The only answer to them was to see to it that the sites from which they could be launched remained in friendly hands. This was before the atom, remember. The atom, to repeat, has taken the world's eye off the destructive possibilities of even old-fashioned explosives in rockets as big as a train of box cars, rockets which fly through the stratosphere faster than the speed of sound.

The long-range rockets that blew up Antwerp and London were in their scientific infancy. They were little more than experimental models. The Normandy invasion forced the Germans to use them prematurely—before they were either perfected or produced in sufficient mass to make the cities on the British Isles totally uninhabitable. And there are no longer any secrets about how V-2's work; unused rockets were captured all over Germany.

Even before the first V-weapons were launched, knowing in London that they were being prepared, we realized the profound effect they would have on future British foreign policy. The British have always considered that they had a primary interest in the balance of power in Europe. This interest was based on the fact that if the whole continent were under the total domination of a single power—as the continent was in Napoleon's time—even the Channel was not wide enough to make them secure. Then came aircraft, piloted by man, and the Channel shrank to the size of a moat. Long-range rockets have dried it up entirely.

Even without the secret of the atom, a hostile power need never cross the Channel at all to make the British Isles uninhabitable by means of high explosives delivered in mass through the

stratosphere. The relationship of Europe to the British Isles, therefore, has already become very nearly that of the relationship of
Canada to the United States—and the British can quite logically
be as concerned with hostility in Europe as we would be with any
hostile manifestation in Canada.

Now put on top of this the fact that there are a very great
many people in Europe who, contemporary politics aside, very
definitely do not like the British. The British have mingled in
wars on the Continent for centuries. In the course of these wars,
they have made many enemies. The most effective German
propaganda posters in France when we first landed recalled the
burning of Jeanne d'Arc and showed the churches of France
aflame from British bombs. These announced the slogan "The
assassins return to the scene of their crime."

One only needs to be a little thoughtful, then, to be sympathetic to the Britons' acute concern over the politics of Europe.
There is enough potential discontent with British management
inherent in continental emotions without its being fanned by a
renunciation of Parliamentary Capitalism—or even Parliamentary
Socialist Capitalism—and an enthusiastic entrance into the Russian
Communist social order. It is very clearly an issue on which the
British might come to feel that their survival depended on their
going to war again—however little they liked the idea individually.

Now take a short flight across Europe—and it is only a flight of
a few hours now—to the capital on the other side of Germany,
and see how Europe looks from Moscow. The view from Moscow
is even grimmer. The new-born Soviet State has survived two
armed conflicts with the West—the first in the years immediately
following the Revolution that created it and the last the assault
by a Germany which most Russians believe was created by the
Western powers for the precise purpose of removing Communist
Russia from the social scheme of things. To change the management of Europe from anti- to *pro*-Soviet, to the Russians, is in-
disputably a security measure. Our own Secretary of State Byrnes,
even after his sharp falling out with the Russian Foreign Minister
Molotov, paid public tribute to the logic of the Russians' apply-
ing their own Monroe Doctrine to their neighboring states. There
is, then—without going into any of the subtleties of political

philosophy—a major conflict of security interests between the British and the Russians. Each must face the possibility of having to go to war with the other if a satisfactory adjustment of European politics cannot be worked out.

Precisely here is the real difference in British and American interests—the difference which makes the independence of American foreign policy a matter of life and death concern to us.

In this situation, which is incontrovertible, it is equally incontrovertible that the British have a primary interest in aligning us against Russia—just as even before the war the British had a recognized interest in aligning Germany against Russia. And now, in British eyes, the question of whether we will, if called upon, fight a war against Russia with them is crucial. There are not strong enough adjectives to describe its importance. The British are patently not strong enough to stand up to Russia by themselves and there is no one else but us, now, to win a war for their side. On the whole continent of Europe there are only the remnants of the beaten Fascists and Nazis, exiled Poles and starving Spaniards, for the British to recruit for war on Russia.

During the war, the British attempted to manipulate our military policy so that we would fight the war the way they wanted it fought—which was an anti-Russian way. They did not succeed. Now, with equal determination, they are attempting to manipulate American foreign policy to link our future irretrievably with theirs. If they succeed, and if there is a third world war, we will surely fight it for them—against the Russians.

The British have already made a start. They caused us to break our word to the Russians even before the war was over. We had agreed at Yalta to turn over the Russian sphere in Germany as soon as hostilities were over. Instead, on Churchill's personal persuasion, we rattled a saber at the Russians across the Elbe for months before we went back to our territory with all the grace of a grudging giver. We had solemnly sworn with our hand on the Bible that we would not allow Fascist Argentina in on our side; the Britons, who like to buy Argentine beef, persuaded us to let them in anyway—with plenty of help from some Americans in high positions. With Britain's encouragement we introduced an international double standard by proclaiming that everything the Russians did in Europe was our business but nothing we did in the Pacific was the Russians' business. I do not believe we are a dishonest people but immediately after V-E Day we were certainly made to look like one in Russian eyes. By whom? For what?

I have cast this equation in terms of our antagonizing the Russians on behalf of the British.

If you like to imagine us as in partnership with the Russians instead of the British, we would be just as vulnerable to being persuaded to fight someone else's war. I have simply not discussed this because such a partnership does not seem remotely possible. But if it *were* possible, then we would end with the same deal. The Russians' foreign policy is also adult and realistic and, like the British, the Russians use every means at their disposal to succeed. If they felt their security were threatened by the British they would, of course, do everything they knew how to make us think that the British threatened us too.

My opinion that we are actually threatened by neither the British nor the Russians must be apparent by now. This takes a word of explanation. Everyone accepts the fact that the British are only interested in holding what they have, but there still seems to be a tendency to think of the Russians as having aggressive ambitions. I think this is dangerous nonsense.

The Russians have made it very clear that they consider their own security worth fighting for—and that their safety is dependent upon whether the governments of neighboring states are friendly or unfriendly. They have also made it clear that they distrust our motives—"our" being the Anglo-American capitalist world. It is also true that there must still be at least a minority party in Soviet councils whose members feel that Russia would be better off in a wholly socialized world. And there are always the opinions of the victorious generals to be considered. But overshadowing all these things, in weighing Russia's potential for aggression, is the historic reality of Russia's isolationism, or nationalism, or group economic interests or whatever you choose to call it.

Crediting Stalin and the Russian Government with 100 per cent selfish motives, Russia today, as America in the early eighteen-hundreds, has more land and resources than it has been able to develop. It is a land in which the opportunity for the individual is at home, not abroad. This was true even before the war and was, of course, the reason why—however Marx wrote the book and Lenin preached it—Stalin's government became more interested in nationalism than in dialectics. During the course of the war, twenty years—centuries—of development in western Russia was wiped out. It is as if, during our Civil War, we had succeeded in destroying the entire productive capacity of America east of the Mississippi—and had, after the Civil War, not only the West to develop but the East to rebuild as well. A monumental job waits the Russian who survived the war—at home.

Russia has only one *primary* interest and that is to be left alone, to complete the task of educating itself, to rebuild its industries and to complete the development of its resources—and, through these giant steps, to integrate itself as a nation. Russia's whole drive is centripetal rather than centrifugal, just as in Germany and Japan the reverse was true.

As to Russia's political ideas—well, Europe once rang with similar controversy over whether to approve or disapprove of ours. At the end of the eighteenth century, our ideas on the divine right of democracy constituted the same challenge to the interests of those who believed in the divine right of kings as the Russian Communist doctrines seem to represent to our parliamentary governments today. The historical fact is that our eighteenth century ideas (which we brought, of course, from Europe) influenced the nineteenth century world and changed it, without wholly revolutionizing it. Similarly, it seems to me, many of Russia's ideas will influence and change *us*, without revolutionizing us. But whether they will or they won't, the nineteenth century fact was that America became a nation and was here to stay—and the twentieth century fact is that the Russian State, instead of flying apart under Hitler's blows, became a great nation too, and is also here to stay. Or rather we are both here to stay unless we are tricked by a third party—or our own stupidity—into a war which neither of us wants.

Unlike some commentators I have been reading, I do not think this war would extinguish the human race. I think someone would win it first. It would, however, be a war to the extinction of either the Soviet Union or the British Empire and the United States of America as we know these entities today.

And I think it would also be a wholly unnecessary war in which the millions who would die in it would have died solely because we did not have enough sense in America to perceive what was happening—and to put a stop to it—just as the hundreds of thousands who died in World War II are dead because we did not have sense enough to head off World War II when we could have—before the Axis had established itself.

15 The End of It's Sitting and Thinking

In the winter of 1946, the American intellectual and political world seems to be divided between those who think we should pool our secrets for making scientific war and those who think we should keep them to ourselves—between those who are for and those who are against the idea of a world government. This book will appear to many to have avoided this issue—perhaps, even, to be oriented away from world unity and towards nationalism. I recognize that I run that risk—and I call it risk because I consider the suppressing and secreting of scientific knowledge as sinful, and am certain that world government is both essential to civilization and inevitable. The difference I have with the Internationalist of 1946 is a difference not of principle but of timing—and of what is realistic.

The pooling of scientific knowledge so that all the world may benefit is sane, moral and sound. But I do not believe that sharing the secrets of how to make a war ever prevented one. Sharing our secrets will improve the international atmosphere, it will relieve a little tension. But it will not prevent World War III if a conflict between the British Empire and the Soviet Union is allowed to develop. And I do believe that this conflict will develop unless we in the United States use our strength and intelligence to insist on a world in which the British and the Russian social orders can co-exist and grow gradually together.

I seem, in all this, to be leaving the United Nations Organization out of my picture. This is not because I do not think that

UNO is a sound idea but simply because I regard it as no more than a tool. It will work or it won't work, depending entirely upon whether the basic policies of the three principal powers are compatible. Their compatibility is what I am discussing. If we allow British and Russian policies to become incompatible, then there is nothing that the most efficient UNO in the world can do about it. It will end another League of Nations. If, on the other hand, we do solve the problem—the UNO will function, and that's fine.

Maybe I had better state my opinion flatly that UNO can't— and can't be expected to—solve the world's problems. These are dependent upon three great national wills which cannot be held together by any organization or piece of paper. During the war, the international Combined Chiefs of Staff organization functioned efficiently solely because both British and American wills were for the destruction of Germany. Differences between the two nations were on *how* this should be done. In peace, if the national wills of Russia, Britain and America are compatible, the UNO staff organization can similarly sweat out a number of how-to-go-about-it problems. But UNO can never solve world problems on the policy-making level—because the principal powers therein will not yet relinquish their sovereignty to it.

I am also prepared to defend myself from the charge of having become an isolationist. National isolation is withdrawal from participation in world affairs. I advocate participation, not withdrawal. This advocacy is implicit in all these conclusions. I also believe that the idea of American participation in world affairs (to preserve the peace and to protect American interests) is now universally accepted by Americans. It is at least universally preached if not practiced. I am scrupulously not trying to sell the American people anything that they have not already bought.

Neither am I trying to sell them dollar diplomacy or Henry Robinson Luce's American Century. The American Century concept is a little mystic and I am not sure I understand it, but the rough idea seems to me that we in the Twentieth Century take Great Britain's place as The Master of the World. I am against the attempt. The idea seems to me simply the opposite extreme of the idea that we should be The Servant of the World. Why should we be anything but ourselves, an adult nation amongst adult nations, with a right to our own opinion and an obligation to share in the responsibility of managing the world?

Eventually, a single world government is inevitable—and has been for long before the atomic bomb. It became inevitable when transportation and communication shrunk the world so that world government became practical. The problem now is not whether there should be a world government but how to create one. I lived through a generation of futile talk about a world government when it was called a League of Nations. Talk won't make one happen. Neither will good intentions. But I believe that the logic of a single government for all the world is so great that evolution will bring one—provided that the world is permitted to evolve peacefully. This is where we come in—today.

There *is* a short cut to world government—and it is the short cut which I am against. The short cut is World War III—a world war to the annihilation of one or the other contestants. I am against this because I hate war and because professional killing seems to me an evil and unnatural thing. To those who may think of it as surgery, my reply is that it is too radical surgery for me to trust. And it seems to me unnecessary.

What I got out of World War II, in the way of intellectual convictions, was a feeling that World War III is a very lively possibility—and an equally strong belief that it can be avoided by the responsible application of the United States will to peace. But unless we Americans have an informed and unified world policy, and unless we implement this policy aggressively, the world will drift—and in a drifting world, the strong wills of the British and the Russian states could develop a conflict which could only be solved by a war to the extinction of one or the other—as the war we have just come through was to the extinction of the enemy or ourselves. I believe that it is already being falsely made to appear that this is our war.

I believe we can prevent this war if we master the lesson we should have learned in the last three years—the lesson that we are strong and able enough to impose our will to peace *if* we know what we are doing.

In this respect, at the moment, things could not look worse.

Once again, as after the last war, we are interested only in our happy present—our coming home from war, our return to peaceful ways. Economists tell us we are entering another cycle of unique prosperity: everyone who counts will be rich and we can afford—what a consolation it must be to them!—the also inevitable eight or ten million unemployed. After these few years of prosperity—during which we restock our middle-class kitchens with electric refrigerators and even build a few houses too expensive for all but a handful to live in—after we do these things, we are told by these same economists that we can expect another collapse, similar to the collapse in 1929 which followed the last postwar boom, only coming sooner this time, because the world is "speeded up."

As far as I can find out, we Americans believe our economists implicitly on both scores but, like Mark Twain's weather, no one is doing much about it. We are so pleased that the war is over that we are not even really concerned about the destructive possibility of the atom we talk so much about—at least there is no tangible evidence of it. Psychologically, the function of the atom seems to be to contribute an almost pleasant little shiver to the national spine. It has become a kind of cosmic detective story thriller—but obviously nothing more, or the political blocs which are closest to the people in this country would have more to say and do about the subject. Instead, the labor unions are wholly involved in trying to protect their memberships from the effects of the coming unemployment, the farmers are busy taking in money while food is still short and the veterans are only interested in getting home and finding a job and a place to live.

Obviously no one is really taking the editorial writers and the scientists seriously. Relatively few Americans—they say there are 130 million of us now—had any first-hand experience with the destruction and degradation wrought by even such obsolete instruments of torture and destruction as were used in World War II. To nine out of ten Americans, and nine out of ten is an impressive majority, war is still simply something that gives everyone a job—and a little inconvenience—in exchange for more money than he ever had before, whether "he" be a millionaire, a farmer, a mill hand, a servant girl, or a whore. The dead are buried now and the crosses on their graves—if their graves are lucky enough to have crosses—don't vote. The opinion of a tiny minority of soldiers who saw combat doesn't count either. The world is prepared to write off anything they say as a product of war neurosis anyway.

So from where is the leadership to come, the leadership to win the peace? I would not hazard a guess, after only six months back at home and most of these spent writing this book. Only I am buoyed by these thoughts:

Certainly, in 1937, with World War II already well begun, you could have written an even more dismal inventory of our intellectual and spiritual resources for winning it. Yet win it we did. Within the space of a few years that passed as if they were not more than a few hours we found clarity enough to go to war for our survival. Thereafter, literally within months, we laid the foundations for the mightiest armed force in the history of man. No great genius created and led this invincible force, in the sense that a Napoleon created and led the armies with which he once conquered Europe. The invincibility of American arms grew out of the whole American people—out of their brawn, their brain and, for better or for worse, their soul.

Now, no man could have foretold all this in 1937. Similarly, I do not believe any man can foretell how the American people will meet the crises that will develop during the next ten years. But we do know now that we have the capability of rising to great accomplishments. We can pull ourselves together and I suspect we will—as we begin to recover from the hangover of World War II and begin to catch on to what's being done to us and what we can do about it.

Index